CAPITALIST
MANIFESTO

ROBERT
KIYOSAKI

AUTHOR OF THE INTERNATIONAL BESTSELLER *RICH DAD POOR DAD*

PLATA®
PUBLISHING

Photo credit: back cover image of Nikita Khrushchev was provided to Wikimedia Commons by the German Federal Archive (Deutsches Bundesarchiv) as part of a cooperation project. The German Federal Archive guarantees an authentic representation only using the originals (negative and/or positive), resp. the digitalization of the originals as provided by the Digital Image Archive.

Published by Plata Publishing, LLC.
Plata Publishing, LLC
4335 N. Civic Center Plaza
Suite 100
Scottsdale, AZ 85251

Printed in the United States of America

First Edition: December 2021

ISBN: 978-1-61268-114-6

122021

This book is dedicated to
our Freedoms...
especially the Freedom of Truth

We Were Warned...

"You Americans are so gullible. No, you won't accept communism outright, but we'll keep feeding you small doses of socialism until you'll finally wake up and find you already have communism. We won't have to fight you. We'll so weaken your economy until you'll fall like overripe fruit into our hands."

— **Nikita Khrushchev**
September 29, 1959
Premier of the Soviet Union (1958 - 1964)

And Edmund Burke,
an Irish statesman, economist, and philosopher
who lived from 1729 to 1797, warned:

*"The only thing necessary for evil to triumph
is for good men to do nothing."*

My commitment to you:
I will keep this book KISS — and KISS:ES
Keep It Super Simple: Extra Simple

"Simple can be harder than complex:
You have to work hard to get your thinking clean
to make it simple. But it's worth it in the end because
once you get there, you can move mountains."
— Steve Jobs

A Message from Robert

There are three things I want to say, before you start reading this book...

First: **We learn by repetition.**
You will see several quotes and messages repeated, multiple times, throughout this book. There is method to what might be perceived as madness... and in every case that repetition is intentional and drives home key points that will help readers connect the dots between past and present and present and future.

Secondly: **The messages are more important than the messengers.**
My editors and fact-checkers are telling me that I'm driving them crazy when it comes to attribution on several of the quotes you'll find in the book. In some cases, it's not clear who actually said (or was the first to say) something and I want to be clear that the "messengers" — whether they are credible historical figures, political leaders, economists, or thought leaders — are far less important than the messages themselves. While you may feel compelled to let us know that some attributions may be in dispute, please know that we are aware of the controversy and will let the quotes — the messages — speak for themselves.

Lastly: **Games are powerful teaching tools.**
You'll see lots of references to our *CASHFLOW*® games in this book. Please know that those references are less "commercial messages" than they are testimony to the power of games — as teaching and learning tools. Rich dad taught his son and me about money and investing using the game of *Monopoly*® and the *CASHFLOW* games take those lessons to the next level through fun and engaging game play. The *CASHFLOW* game, launched in 1996, is translated into 16 languages and played in thousands of CASHFLOW Clubs around the world. *Rich Dad Poor Dad*, published in 1997 and, today, the classic in the personal finance genre and the #1 Personal Finance book of all time, was actually written as a "marketing brochure" for the *CASHFLOW* game... Rich Dad's Capitalist Tool for teaching lessons on money, investing, and capitalism in our homes.

— RTK

How to Protect Yourself
When Communists Attack

George Washington, a Founding Father of the United States of America and its first President who lived from 1732 to 1799, warned:

> *"If freedom of speech is taken away then dumb and silent, we may be led like sheep to slaughter."*

I often look back in our history, think about the massive casualties we've suffered, and ask myself: Who has killed the most people?

Q: General George Washington led America to victory over England in the Revolutionary War, How many people did our leaders have to kill to establish America's Constitutional Republic?

A: None.

Q: How many people have socialists killed?

A: After socialists took control in their countries, history reminds us that their leaders, Marx, Stalin, Lenin, Hitler, Mao, and others had to kill at least 130 million people to install a socialist form of government. In August of 2021, the murders began in Afghanistan.

Karl Marx warned:

> *"Communists everywhere support every revolutionary movement against the existing social and political order of things... They openly declare that their ends can be attained only by the forcible overthrow of all existing social conditions."*

And President George Washington declared:

> *"I'll die on my feet... before I live on my knees."*

The definition of parabellum is:

> *"If you want peace... prepare for war."*

General Washington agrees. He warned:

> *"There is nothing so likely to produce peace… as to be well prepared to meet the enemy."*

Q: How do we prepare to meet the enemy?

A: Listen to the stories of those who lived through the experiences by watching the series of Capitalist Manifesto videos

> I had these short videos prepared because I know my freedoms and my reputation will soon be under attack. You may be feeling the same way… that your freedoms are under attack. Each of the brief videos is a defensive weapon of knowledge, from real people who have fought real communists, in their country, in war, and in the United States of America.

You know we are under attack. Our freedoms are being stolen. People are forced to take vaccines, wear masks… or lose their jobs. Our President is censored. Our news is biased. Police are defunded. Elections are compromised. Our borders are invaded. Our cities are looted and burned. Our children's classrooms are indoctrination camps with parents who challenge the system labeled "domestic terrorists." America is losing wars we should never have lost. Our weapons are being turned over to our enemies, enemies who hate us, our friends and our allies.

We Have Been Warned… for Years

It is time for parabellum. If you love peace, please watch these videos and be prepared for war, a war that has already begun. Watch these videos and learn from people who are fighting back.

Another of America's greatest Presidents, Abraham Lincoln, who fought the Civil War to keep America united, said:

> *"Our fathers brought forth on this continent, a new nation, conceived in Liberty, and dedicated to the proposition that all men are created equal."*

President John F. Kennedy, in his Inaugural Address in 1961, challenged my generation:

"Ask not what your country can do for you – ask what you can do for your country."

Kennedy's words inspired my mom and dad joined the Peace Corps. I joined the Marine Corps. Our family fought for America in different ways.

Repeating President George Washington's declaration:

"I'll die on my feet... before I live on my knees."

The Capitalist Manifesto series of video lessons are from people who are fighting communism on their feet... not on their knees. In this series you will hear true stories from...

Philip Haslam... and why Robert wrote Capitalist Manifesto
Debbie D'Souza
Patrick Bet-David
Nely Galan
Barry Mitchell
Yeonmi Park
Dan Campbell
Trina White-Maduro
Brigadier General Robert Spalding
U.S. Representative Jack Bergman

To learn more about how to access the
Capitalist Manifesto Series of podcasts and videos
go to:
RichDad.com/capitalist-manifesto

**You can find The Rich Dad Brand Story
... at RichDad.com**

TABLE OF CONTENTS

INTRODUCTION

The Definition of Para Bellum

Si vis pacem, para bellum
If you want peace, prepare for war

At this stage of my life, I have very little to gain in writing this book... but a lot to lose.

I had to ask myself: **Why write a book** in a world run by Silicon Valley's liberals... those who promote censorship by today's Cancel Culture?

Why write a book in a world run by people who many label as "racists"... and who support teaching Critical Race Theory?

Why write a book, when Dr. Seuss is cancelled... accused of being hurtful and insensitive in using imagery that promotes racial stereotypes?

Why write a book in a world where elected leaders say and do virtually nothing... as protestors riot, burn, and loot the businesses of its citizens — the very people who these spineless elected leaders are supposed to protect?

Why write a book in a world where citizens demand the release of convicted criminals... and then demand to "defund the police"?

Why write a book in a world where history can be rewritten and statues of our nation's heroes are vilified and torn down... by cowards? Where the history of national landmarks like Mt. Rushmore is viewed, by some, as racist and divisive.

Why write a book in a country where the media companies can "de-platorm" people — including the President of the United States — if they don't agree with their thoughts or positions... where the unalienable right of free speech is tested again and again?

Why write a book when educators are more concerned about gender pronouns, trigger words, and union benefits... than real education — especially financial education?

As I've said, I have a lot to lose... because *Rich Dad Poor Dad* has been an international bestseller for nearly a quarter of century and has sold tens of millions of copies since it was published in 1997. For nearly 25 years, my books have been published in dozens of languages and embraced by aspiring and freedom-loving people around the world.

With so many of the freedoms and rights we hold sacred under attack... I ask myself *How can I not speak out?* Speak out in defense of free markets, capitalism, our rights under the U.S. Constitution — and how entrepreneurs can save not only capitalism, but maybe even the American Dream and the world economy.

In 1997 I wrote *Rich Dad Poor Dad* and in late 2021... *Capitalist Manifesto.* I write so we can fight the communist ideals taught in our schools by teaching capitalism... in our homes.

So, again, I had to ask myself: **Why write this book,** why write a *Capitalist Manifesto*... why take the risk when I have so little to gain? My decision was clear when I asked myself another question: ***What is more important than money?***

The answer was simple: Freedom.

In the interests of full disclosure, and although this book is not about politics or Donald Trump or the Republican Party, it's hard to keep a neutral position — on a book about capitalism — when the political party in power pushes a socialist agenda and we see our freedoms under attack. So, a word of warning: If you hate "The Donald" and conservative Republicans, you may want to think twice about reading this book.

Donald Trump and I have co-authored two books. We were starting to work on a third book, in 2015, when he announced he was running for President of the United States. This book is about something far more important than who is President or what political party is in office.

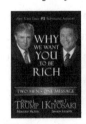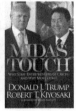

4

Listen to Your Father

George Washington is often called Father of his Country because of the key role he played as a Founding Father of the United States. He also led a rag-tag America Army to a victory over the English, at the time one of the most powerful armies in the world, in the Revolutionary War. He also led the convention that wrote the U.S. Constitution before he was elected, in 1789, as the first President of the United States.

Washington stepped down after two terms as President because he did not want to become the "King of America."

The father of our country warned:
> *"If freedom of speech is taken away then dumb and silent, we may be led, like sheep to slaughter."*

Obviously, America did not listen to our father.

In 2021, Americans are waking up to the reality our freedom of speech has been stolen. In its place we have "political correctness," gender pronouns, history being rewritten, statues being torn down, the monitoring and censorship of social media, and racists teaching racism in our schools.

The Father of our Country also warned:
> *"To contract new debts is not the way to pay old ones."*

In 2021, Americans are waking up to the reality that our leaders are borrowing money to pay our debts.

Again, Americans did not listen to our father, George Washington.

George Washington warned against The Fed, a "central bank."
> *"Paper money has had the effect in your state that it will ever have, to ruin commerce, oppress the honest, and open the door to every species of fraud and injustice."*

In 2021 America is one of the biggest debtor nations in world history, run by a corrupt central bank known as The Fed. The Fed is not federal, it is not a bank, and it has no reserves.

On September 27, 2021, the Associated Press reported:
> *"In a rare moment of ethical controversy for the Federal Reserve, two top officials resigned Monday in the wake of revelations about their financial trading that exposed potential shortcomings in the Fed's rules on investments."*

20/20 Vision
Both the Fed and the U.S. government committed to print $10.5+ trillion in 2020 through various stimulus programs to offset the global economic standstill caused by the COVID-virus quarantine. That amount — $10 trillion — works out to approximately $27 billion per day.

On May 22, 2021, *FinTech News* and TechStartups reported:
> *"40% of all U.S. dollars in existence were printed in the last 12 months: Is America repeating the same mistake of 1921 Weimar Germany?"*

In 1933, Adolf Hitler rose to power. He rose to power due the hyper-inflation in Germany. That country's hyperinflation was caused by the Weimar Republic's printing money to pay its bills and *reparations* for World War I.

On April 5, 2019, U.S. Democratic presidential contender Kamala Harris told black activists at Reverend Al Sharpton's National Action Network conference in New York that, "When I am elected president..." she would sign a bill backing a study of *reparations for descendants of slaves.*

Flashback to January 30, 1933: Hitler is appointed as chancellor of Germany by President Paul Von Hindenburg. Hindenburg made the appointment in an effort to keep Hitler and the Nazi Party "in check," however, the decision would have disastrous results for Germany and the entire European continent.

In the year and seven months that followed, Hitler was able to exploit the death of Hindenburg and combine the positions of chancellor and president into the position of Führer, the supreme leader of Germany. Then World War II began, and millions died.

In 2021, America's Debt-to-GDP is over 140% and growing. This means that for every dollar printed, our national debt grows — but our economy does not.

George Washington, one of our Founding Fathers, warned:
"The last official act of any government is to loot the treasury."

America, once the richest country in the world, is printing and spending fake money, on our way into bankruptcy.

As a wiseman once said:
"When you give a heroin addict money, the money kills the addict. Not the heroin."

Rich Dad Poor Dad

I've lost count of how many times I've asked this question — to people all over the world — over the past 25 years: What did school teach you about money?

The answer? Little to nothing. Yet a day doesn't go by without money playing a role. This is true in every part of the world, in every demographic.

The other question I've asked myself countless times: Is this failure to teach us about money just an accident... or is it an intention omission tied to an agenda?

Anyone who knows me knows my opinion on this: The omission of financial education in our schools is not an accident. It is intentional.

In 1997, I published *Rich Dad Poor Dad*. The book was self-published because every publisher in New York that we pitched it to turned the book down. A few added comments to their rejection letters, like "You don't know what you're talking about."

The editors objected to the three main points of my rich dad's lessons. They were:
1. The rich don't work for money.
2. Your house is not an asset.
3. Savers are losers.

Obviously, the editors in New York did not have fathers like my rich dad.

Obviously, most had fathers like my poor dad.

Obviously, the New York editors were following my poor dad's advice:
"Go to school, get a job, work hard, pay taxes, save money, get out of debt, buy a house, and invest for the long-term in the stock market."

I did not listen to my poor dad. I listened to my rich dad and took the road less traveled. And it wasn't without its challenges.

Kim and I were married in 1986. Ten years later, by 1996, we were financially free. We achieved financial freedom without jobs, inheritances, or government handouts; we did not win the lottery and we did not invest in the stock market. We achieved financial freedom by listening to my rich father, not my poor father.

In 1996, when we could not explain how we achieved financial freedom, Kim and I developed our *CASHFLOW* board game, a capitalist tool. Attempting to explain real financial education — real capitalism — is like attempting to teach a person to play golf, without golf clubs, golf balls, or a golf course.

The launch of the *CASHFLOW* board game, in 1996, was the start of our Capitalist Manifesto which is:

*"How to Counter Communism Taught in our Schools
by Teaching Capitalism... in our Homes."*

In 1996, a few people attempted to get the board game into schools. Kim and I offered to donate a thousand board games to the Arizona school system. Our offer was rejected.

A friend with contacts to a women's group at Harvard attempted to get the group to evaluate the game. Their reply: *"Women do not play games."*

Our problem was that we didn't know how to sell our board game. It too was complex and expensive. We did not know how to get the games into homes. So, I wrote a "brochure," a "little book" to explain the capitalist philosophy and genesis behind the game. That brochure... became *Rich Dad Poor Dad*.

In 1997, Kim and I self-published 1,000 copies of *Rich Dad Poor Dad,* not knowing if the book would sell. If the book did not sell, we knew we would not need paper for fire-starters for years.

Today, on the eve of the 25th anniversary of the release of *Rich Dad Poor Dad,* our book is still an international best-seller and ranks as the #1 Personal Finance book in history.

When *Rich Dad Poor Dad* first made *The New York Times* Bestsellers List, I was vilified for calling my poor dad "poor." After all, my poor dad was a highly educated, very smart man. He was good husband, father, and public servant... a man who, at one time, served as the Superintendent of Education for the State of Hawaii. Poor dad had graduated from the University of Hawaii in two years and went on to do post-graduate studies at Stanford University, University of Chicago, and Northwestern University.

In 1970, an honest man who had become fed up with the corruption he found as a member of the Governor of Hawaii's staff, my poor dad ran for Lt. Governor as a Republican, against his boss, the Governor of Hawaii, a Democrat.

After being crushed in the election, the Governor "blacklisted" my dad from any employment in state government in Hawaii. Unable to find a job, my poor dad found out how poor he really was, and died a poor man.

In 1991, just before his death, he was awarded an honorary PhD, by his peers, fellow schoolteachers, for his dedication to education. I remember my dad being moved to tears and saying "They did not forget me."

In 1969, after graduating from the United States Merchant Marine Academy at Kings Point, I joined the U.S. Marine Corps and went to U.S. Navy Flight School in Pensacola, Florida. After receiving my wings, I spent a year at Advanced Weapons School, flying at Camp Pendleton, California.

In 1972, I was on board an aircraft carrier, flying off the coast of Vietnam.

In January of 1973, I returned from Vietnam, to find my dad sitting alone at home, unemployed. When I asked him "What should I do when my contract with the Marines is complete in 1974," his fatherly advice was:

"Go to back to school, get your master's degree, possibly your PhD, get a job flying for the airlines, work hard, pay taxes, save money, get out of debt, buy a house, and invest for the long-term in the stock market."

As I listened to his advice, I realized that he was offering me the same advice he had followed... and that it was advice that led him into near poverty.

In January of 1973, I left my poor dad's home and went to my rich dad's office in Waikiki. I went to rich dad for *his* fatherly advice. Rich dad's advice was the opposite side of the coin from my poor dad's advice. Rich dad's fatherly advice was:

"Get a job learning to sell. Learn to invest in real estate. Learn to use debt as money. Learn to make millions and pay little in taxes, legally. Do not become an employee. Learn to be an entrepreneur so you can create jobs for hundreds of employees."

In June of 1974, at the age of 27, I returned my last salute from the Marine guard as drove through the gates and off the Marine Corps Air Station at Kaneohe Bay, Hawaii.

In June of 1974, I did not listen to my poor father but listened, instead, to the advice of my rich father.

Capitalist Manifesto

In 1997, after *Rich Dad Poor Dad* was published, I began to receive hate mail for calling my poor dad, "poor." In 2022, after *Capitalist Manifesto* is published, I know I will be attacked, vilified, and cancelled by socialist, liberal academic elite social media and the "Woke" Cancel Culture for calling my poor dad a socialist, Marxist, and communist... which he was. He just didn't know it.

As George Washington warned:

"We ought to deprecate the hazard attending ardent and susceptible minds, from being too strongly, and too early prepossessed in favor of other political systems, before they are capable of appreciating their own."

How can anyone know the differences between a capitalist, socialist, fascist, Marxist, or communist, if these socio-economic philosophies are not studied?

In 2021 millions of parents "woke" to the realization our schools are teaching Critical Race Theory, a derivative of the BLM Black Lives Matter movement, a derivative of post-modernist education... all derivatives of Marxism.

On November 2, 2021, Republicans, in an upset victory, sweep the state of Virginia's Governor, Lt Governor, and Attorney General's election. The issue was not politics. The issue was education. Parents woke up to what is being taught in schools to their children... and they pushed back, using their vote as their voice.

As George Washington warned, in 2021 parents were awakening to the fact that our schools are teaching Marxist socialism, fascism, communism, and racism, without teaching capitalism.

As I have often asked:
"What did school teach you about money?"

How can anyone know the differences between communists and capitalists if they did not study money?

The *Communist Manifesto* is about revolution. The revolution is sparked by the gap between rich and poor growing too wide.

In 2021, people were aware of the cavernous gap between rich and poor. Rather than fix the gap by "teaching people to fish," our government expands the Welfare State of America, by "giving people fish," telling them they are "entitled."

This book, *Capitalist Manifesto,* is about education... about how to teach people to fish and teaching capitalism in our homes, while communism is taught in our schools.

In 1965 I graduated from high school and left Hawaii to attend the U.S. Merchant Marine Academy. Kings Point is one of five federal academies, which are:

– U.S. Military Academy	West Point, New York
– U.S. Naval Academy	Annapolis, Maryland
– U.S. Air Force Academy	Colorado Springs, Colorado
– U.S. Coast Guard Academy	New London, Connecticut
– U..S Merchant Marine Academy	Kings Point, New York

Admission to these Federal Academies requires a Congressional appointment from a U.S. Congressman or Senator, or the Vice-president or President of the United States.

I received my nominations to U.S. Naval Academy and U.S. Merchant Marine Academy, from U.S. Senator Daniel K. Inouye, a highly decorated soldier during World War II.

Marx's Communist Manifesto

In 1965, during my freshman ("plebe") year, my English/economics teacher required our class to read Karl Marx's *Communist Manifesto* and *Das Kapital,* Hitler's *Mein Kampf,* and Mao's *Little Red Book.*

Obviously, the curriculum at a military academy is different from an academically liberal Snowflake University, where Marx's Critical Race Theory is more important than financial education.

In 1965, as I read, studied, and discussed the works of Marx, Hitler, and Mao, I began to realize my poor dad was a communist and my rich dad was a capitalist.

It wasn't until I left Hawaii to attend a military academy in New York — studying Marx, Hitler, Stalin, Lenin, and Mao — that I better understood the animosity and tension between my rich dad, a financial genius who never finished high school, and my poor dad, an academic genius who thrived in school and rose to become the Superintendent of Education of the State of Hawaii.

It wasn't until 1972, when I was flying in Vietnam as a Marine pilot, that I saw the warnings of Marx, Hitler, and Mao coming true in real life. It saddened me to see the North Vietnamese streaming into South Vietnam, and that we were unable to stop them. It saddened me to see once beautiful French chateaux on the French Indo-Chinese Riviera, bombed, blackened, and abandoned.

In 2020, as I drove past a boarded-up Polo Ralph Lauren store near my home in Phoenix, Arizona, I began to realize the lessons I learned while at the academy and while flying in Vietnam, were coming true in America.

Are George Washington's words even more true today?
> *"Let me ask you, sir, when is the time for brave men to exert themselves in the cause of liberty and their country, if this not it?"*

The Marine Corps Birthday
November 10, 1775 is the official birthday of the U.S. Marine Corps.

On June 11, 2021, I called my roommate and fellow pilot on the aircraft carrier in Vietnam. In 1972, we were both Marine lieutenants. 1/ Lt Jack Bergman went on to become Lt. General Jack Bergman and I left the Marine Corps as a first lieutenant. I was never promoted to captain.

Today Lt. General Jack Bergman is Congressman Bergman from Michigan.

I called my friend and let him know I was publishing a new book — this book, *Capitalist Manifesto*. I asked for his support by being present at the launch of *Capitalist Manifesto* on November 10, 2021, the Marine Corps Birthday.

I simply asked my friend,
> *"Is it time to fight for freedom again?"*

Jack's reply was:
> *"Semper fi."*

Semper fi means, *"Always faithful."*

As George Washington, the father of our country, asked:
> *"Let me ask you, sir, when is the time for brave men to exert themselves in the cause of liberty and their country, if this is not?"*

Once my friend Lt. General and Congressman Bergman said "yes," I had from June 11, 2021, to November 10, 2021, to write (and in some cases rewrite) this book.

The official launch of this book was on November 10, 2021, the 246th birthday of the Marines. In attendance at the 246th birthday were all rates and ranks of Marines and spouses, including a 3-star and a 4-star Marine Generals.

I chose the Marine Corps birthday because I know this book and I will be attacked. I will be criticized, vilified, and cancelled by socialist, anti-social media. The liberal left will attack me for calling highly educated people, like my poor dad, Marxists.

Again, most people have not read books written by Marx, Hitler, or Mao, so how could they know the differences between capitalism and communism?

Who Are Marxists?

In 2021, many people are woke to BLM, Black Lives Matter, and post-modern education are organizations with roots running deep into Karl Marx's *Communist Manifesto*. The leaders of BLM openly admit to being students of Marx. I give them credit for being forthright and honest.

I give them credit because America is a free country. In a free country we are free to be communist or capitalist. In a free country we are free to be Christian, Muslim, Jewish, Buddhist, or atheist. In a free country we are free to be liberal or conservative, Republican, Democrat, Libertarian, or Green.

I write this book in the name of freedom. I write this book to expose powerful organizations whose members are disciples of Marx, yet hide like rats in the shadows, nibbling at the soul our country and gnawing away at our freedoms.

In this book I will shine the light on three organizations.
- NEA: The National Education Association, the most powerful labor union in America
- IRS: The Internal Revenue Service (aka: The Taxman)
- FED: The Federal Reserve Bank

All three powerful organizations are rooted in the soul of Marxism. It is time they come out of the shadows... the shadows of the shadow banking system.

Again, this book is about freedom. This book is not about politics or parties, genders, or religions.

When we flew as Marines in Vietnam, we fought for our freedoms — our freedom to choose to be Republicans or Democrats, capitalist or communist, gay or straight, Christian, Jew, Muslim, or atheists.

George Washington had these words of warning:
"If freedom of speech is taken away then dumb and silent, we may be led, like sheep to slaughter."

And these:
"Let me ask you, sir, when is the time for brave men to exert themselves in the cause of liberty and their country, if this is not?"

Is it time to listen to our father... our father of freedom?

What Are You?

Are you a socialist, Marxist, fascist, communist, or capitalist?

A good starting point is defining our terms. So here are several that you will find used throughout this book.

Socialism:
> Noun: a political and economic theory of social organization which advocates that the means of production, distribution, and exchange should be owned or regulated by the community as a whole.

> A policy or practice based on the political and economic theory of socialism.

> **In Marxist theory:** a transitional social state between the overthrow of capitalism and the realization of Communism.

Marxism:
> Noun: the political and economic theories of Karl Marx and Friedrich Engels. Later developed by their followers to form the basis for the theory and practice of communism.

> **Philosophy:** Central to Marxist theory is an explanation of social change in terms of economic factors, according to which the means of production provide the economic base, which influences or determines the political and ideological superstructure.

> Marx and Engels predicted the revolutionary overthrow of capitalism by the proletariat and the eventual attainment of a classless communist society.

Communism:

Noun: a political theory derived from Karl Marx, advocating class war and leading to a society in which all property is publicly owned and each person works and is paid according to their abilities and needs.

The most familiar form of communism is that established by the Bolsheviks after the Russian Revolution of 1917, and it has generally been understood in terms of the system practiced by the former Soviet Union and its allies in eastern Europe, in China since 1949, and in some developing countries such as Cuba, Vietnam, and North Korea.

Communism in eastern Europe collapsed in the late 1980s and early 1990s against a background of failure to meet people's economic expectations, a shift to more democracy in political life, and increasing nationalism such as that which led to the breakup of the Soviet Union.

Communism embraced a revolutionary ideology in which the state would wither away after the overthrow of the capitalist system. In practice, however, the state grew to control all aspects of communist society.

Fascism:

Noun: an authoritarian nationalistic right-wing system of government and social organization. Extreme authoritarian, oppressive, intolerant of other views or practices.

First used in the nationalist right-wing regime of Mussolini in Italy, Hitler in Germany, and Franco in Spain.

Fascism tends to include a belief in the supremacy of one national, ethnic, or racial group, a contempt for democracy, an insistence on obedience to a powerful leader, and a strong demagogic approach.

Democracy:

Noun: a system of government by the whole population or all the eligible members of a state, typically through elected representatives.

Capitalism:

Noun: an economic and political system in which a country's trade and industry are controlled by private owners for profit, rather than by the state.

Capitalist Manifesto vs. *Communist Manifesto*

Private ownership is a key feature of capitalism. In their *Communist Manifesto* Karl Marx and Friedrich Engels warned:

"The theory of Communism may be summed up in one sentence: Abolish all private property."

Marx and Engels also warned:

"Democracy is the road to socialism."

And

"Revolutions are the locomotives of history."

"Owners of capital will stimulate working class to buy more and more of expensive goods, houses and technology, pushing them to take more and more expensive credits, until their debt becomes unbearable. The unpaid debt will lead to bankruptcy of banks which will have to be nationalized and State will have to take the road which will eventually lead to communism."

Rich dad's warning was in the form of a question:

"Why is there no financial education in our schools?"

Vladimir Lenin warned:

"Give us a child for eight years and it will be a Bolshevik forever."

Joseph Stalin warned:

"It's not the people who vote that count. It's the people who count the votes."

Adolf Hitler warned:

"Universal education is the most corroding and disintegrating poison that liberalism has ever invented for its own destruction."

Mao Tse-tung warned:

"People say that poverty is bad, but in fact poverty is good. The poorer people are, the more revolutionary they are.

A 2020 Poll
Results of a 2020 Poll by Victims of Communism Memorial Foundation give us a snapshot of the American landscape related to socialism.

That study reported that 40% of Americans had a favorable view of socialism... up from 36% in 2019. The demographic breakdown related to viewing socialism in a positive light was as follows:

47% of Millennials and 49% of Gen Z, up from 40% in 2019.

Opinions of capitalism declined slightly from 2019 to 2020 among all Americans — 58% to 55%— and 53% of Americans reported that they think a good government should favor the freedom of its citizens over the safety of its citizens.

So... where do you fit into all of this? What are you? Are you a socialist, a Marxist, fascist, communist, or capitalist?

The Purpose of
RICH DAD'S CAPITALIST MANIFESTO

The best way to counter communism taught in our schools
is to teach capitalism... in our homes.

PART ONE

The Big Picture
on
Capitalism vs. Communism

CHAPTER ONE

WE WERE WARNED

On September 29, 1959, Nikita Khrushchev, Premier of the Soviet Union, warned:

*"Your children's children will live under communism. You Americans are so gullible. No, you won't accept **communism** outright, but we will keep feeding you small doses of **socialism** until you will finally wake up and find you already have Communism. We will not have to fight you; We will so weaken your economy, until you will fall like overripe fruit into our hands."* [Emphasis added.]

On January 3, 1973, the military passenger plane I was on taxied up to the passenger terminal at Norton Air Force Base in Northern California.

There were approximately 250 Army, Navy, and Marine servicemen on board the plane, all returning from the Vietnam war.

Why do I remember the date so well? Because the date we returned home, often called our "rotation date," was a very important date for all of us. We were all conscious of the fact that many who went over to fight for our country did not return.

As the aircraft was taxing, the officer-in-charge came on over the intercom and said:

"America has changed. I suggest all of you change into civilian clothes as soon as you get your bags. Do not go off the base in your uniforms. There are thousands of protestors waiting for you. America has changed. Good luck and thank you for your service. Welcome home."

I had no one waiting for me. Many men did. Wives, children, moms, dads, families, and girlfriends were waving from the military terminal on the base.

Outside the base were thousands of protestors, most of them about the same age as us young men on the plane. As I took a deep breath, preparing to get off the plane, I could hear Khrushchev's words of warning:
"Your children's children will live under communism."

I was a Marine First Lieutenant in charge of 16 young Marines, some still teenagers. We all went over together and we were all "rotating" home together.

After gathering our bags, we thanked each other, hugging as we said our good-byes. Then we ran into the military terminal to change into civilian clothes.

Most of these young men had families waiting for them. It was heartwarming to mothers, fathers, wives, and children, all hugging and crying.

It was heartbreaking to see a few Marines crying because their wives were not there to greet them. Instead, their wives' attorneys were greeting them with divorce papers.

One of the Marines met by an attorney was a friend named John. He and I were both gunship pilots and had flown together for the entire year. I left him sobbing, as his wife's attorney broke the news. His wife Pat had moved in with another man and was filing for divorce. Welcome home.

The most dangerous part of the war was next... getting through the thousands of protestors. Immediately I was hit with a raw egg, then spit on by a young woman carrying a sign with "Baby Killers" angrily scrawled across it.

It took me nearly 20 minutes to get a cab. It was a very long 20 minutes standing alone, being verbally abused and physically assaulted, pushed and shoved by "hippies" — men and women close to my own age. Finally, a cab got through the crowd, and I was on my way to the San Francisco airport to catch a flight to Hawaii.

As the United Airlines flight crossed the Pacific, I could hear in my head the words of Nikita Khrushchev's 1959 warning:

> *"You Americans are so gullible. No, you won't accept **communism** outright, but we will keep feeding you small doses of **socialism** until you will finally wake up and find you already have Communism."*

Welcome Home

My dad, poor dad, was at the Honolulu airport to pick me up. Mom had passed away in 1970, while I was in flight school in Pensacola, Florida. There was not much conversation as dad drove us home.

The ride home was a quiet one. The Vietnam war was unpopular at home. When I was in high school, mom and dad took two years off from their careers to join the Peace Corps... so they were not thrilled when I joined the Marine Corps.

After I was at home for a few days, a local newspaper called to interview me. The reporter's angle: "Ralph Kiyosaki's son returns from Vietnam." My dad was a prominent man in Hawaii, the Superintendent of Education. He also ran for Lt. Governor of the State of Hawaii as a Republican and was crushed. The Governor black-listed my dad from government jobs in Hawaii and he was out of work.

Forbes magazine describes Hawaii as the People's Republic of Hawaii. My dad did not have a chance running as a Republican. Hawaii leans so far to the Democratic liberal left that people have joked about being amazed that the state hasn't voted to be annexed by China.

My dad was also head of the HSTA, the Hawaii State Teacher's Association, the state's teacher's union.

Anyone who has studied Marx and his *Communist Manifesto* knows labor unions are Marxists. As Marx stated:

> *"Workers of the world unite. You have nothing to lose but your chains."*

During the 2020 Presidential election, the election that unseated President Donald Trump, the largest and most powerful union in America leading the charge was The National Education Association (NEA).

In 1993 *Forbes* magazine (which has called itself the "capitalist tool") ran a series of articles, one titled: Suffer the Little Children — How the National Education Association Corrupts our Public Schools.

The 1993 *Forbes* article described the NEA this way:
> *"The "National Extortion Association"—a bare-knuckles labor union eager to use fraud and coercion to serve no interests but its own."*

The article also stated:
> *"The NEA's rise is directly linked with the 30-year decline of American education that occurred simultaneously—not just in terms of quality, but especially in terms of quantity: education's crushing, and incessantly cumulating, cost."*

On February 15, 2021: *The American Conservative* ran an article entitled: Teachers Unions Have Always Been Terrible

The article states:
> *"The behavior of teachers unions during this pandemic confirms the nickname that* Forbes *magazine gave the NEA in the 1990s: "The National Extortion Association." This latest betrayal of American students is no surprise, considering the unions' long history of sabotaging learning. Since the 1970s, the National Education Association has been the leading advocate of "no-fault" teaching: whatever happens, don't blame the teacher. Unions have launched strikes to prevent "parental interference" in public education. The Chicago Tribune concluded in 1988 that the Chicago Teachers Association has "as much control over operations of the public schools as the Chicago Board of Education" and "more control than is available to principals, parents, taxpayers, and voters."*

The NEA represents teachers and other education professionals. The NEA is the largest labor union in the United States, with nearly three million members. The NEA claims to be an advocate for education professionals and a force to unite its members to fulfill the promise of public education.

That is not my experience. When I was in high school, my dad would hold teacher's union meetings for union leaders in our home. Although I was only a teenager, I knew the teacher's union was not about improving education. All the NEA cares about, from my experience, is money and power, supporting Marx's proclamation:

"Workers of the world unite. You have nothing to lose but your chains."

In 1963, when I was in high school, rich dad's hotel and restaurant workers went on strike. The workers went on strike demanding they be allowed to join a union. My rich dad called and asked if I would come to the hotel and work the front desk, filling in to check tourists in and out. I worked the front desk for three days, taking naps in the linen closet.

When I returned home, my poor dad was extremely upset, calling me a "scab" — a traitor — for crossing the picket lines.

In 1969, the year I graduated from Kings Point, the U.S. Merchant Marine academy, I refused to join the MM&P, the labor union for merchant ship officers, Masters, Mates, and Pilots. I refused to join because I am not a Marxist.

In 1969, I joined the Marine Corps to fight Marxists in Vietnam.

In 1973, returning from Vietnam, memories of crossing the picket lines at rich dad's hotel came rushing back as I pushed my way through thousands of hippies and anti-war protestors. I rode home from the airport with poor dad in virtual silence, because we were on opposite sides of the Vietnam war and Marxist philosophy. It was a day I will never forget.

My dad, mom, and my two sisters were anti-war protestors. My younger brother joined the Air Force. We both fought in Vietnam. In 2020, my brother and I both supported Trump. My sisters hated Trump and voted for Biden.

In November of 2020, Dominion Voting Systems Corporation became a controversial topic amid allegations of voter fraud in the U.S. presidential election.

Joseph Stalin is often credited with these words:
> *"It's not the people who vote that count.*
> *It's the people who count the votes."*

And Hitler who warned:
> *"It's not truth that matters... but victory."*

In 2020, the people who voted for Biden did not care if the election was fair.

In 2020 few people cared that Hitler had warned:
> *"If you tell a big enough lie and tell it frequently enough...*
> *it will be believed."*

And that Hitler also said:
> *"How fortunate for government... that the people they administer...*
> *don't think."*

In 2021, Republicans ordered a re-count of the Presidential election ballots in Arizona and investigation into the charges of voter fraud. That investigation is still ongoing.

When I arrived home from Vietnam in 1973, I was interviewed by a local Hawaii radio station. It was the first time in my life that I had ever been asked for an interview.

When the reporter asked, "What did you learn in Vietnam?" I replied, "If I wanted to kill commies, I should have stayed home and fired a few bursts in city hall." I'm thankful that interview was never released for broadcast.

As Jack Nicholson, who played Marine Corps Colonel Frank Jessup in the movie *A Few Good Men* said:
> "You want the truth? You can't handle the truth."

That line became an instant classic, permanently etched in American culture.

> Q: Are you saying Marx's *Communist Manifesto* is infiltrating America via our educational system... via our teachers? Are you saying, "We can't handle the truth?"
>
> A: That's a question you should answer for yourself and right now the subject of what's being taught in our schools is a hot topic. Many concerned parents are asking hard questions and demanding answers, As Albert Einstein said:
>> "Whoever is careless with the truth in small matters... cannot be trusted in important affairs."

Nikita Khrushchev's 1959 warning bears repeating:
> "Your children's children will live under communism. You Americans are so gullible. No, you won't accept **communism** outright, but we will keep feeding you small doses of **socialism** until you will finally wake up and find you already have Communism. We will not have to fight you; We will so weaken your economy, until you will fall like overripe fruit into our hands." [Emphasis added.]

In 2020 COVID-19 shut down the economy. It's been like hitting 'pause'... giving us a chance to slow down, step back, and ask ourselves lots of questions. Some of the most important ones, in my opinion, are:
> *Are Americans gullible?*

> *Have we been fed small doses of socialism and are we finally waking up and finding out that communism has already taken root?*

Is America's free enterprise, capitalist system, about to fall like "overripe fruit"?

Have our schools been teaching Marxism?

Are we "woke?" Are we, to quote a published definition, "aware of and actively attentive to important facts and issues, especially issues of racial and social justice"?

And if Marx's *Communist Manifesto* is being taught in our schools, mainlined like an opioid into our children's veins by the NEA, the most powerful labor union in America, what can we do about it? That's the question: What can we do about it?

In 2021, parents are stepping up and stepping in to voice their discontent — and are being labeled as "domestic terrorists."

On October 6, 2021, *The New American* reported that:
> "Until very recently, it would have been unimaginable that the U.S. government would ever consider as domestic terrorists parents who dare to protest against the numerous destructive policies of local school boards. Yet what was until recently unimaginable has now become reality with the Biden administration, and it is not surprising that the administration's outlandish stance is drawing enormous public outrage.

> "According to a memorandum released on Monday, Attorney General Merrick Garland has instructed the Federal Bureau of Investigation (FBI) to mobilize against parents who oppose Critical Race Theory (CRT) in public schools, citing "threats" against the school board members and teachers who "participate in the vital work of running our nation's public schools."

> "Writes Garland, 'The Department takes these incidents seriously and is committed to using its authority and resources to discourage these threats, identify them when they occur, and prosecute them when appropriate.'"

On October 5, 2021 the *National Review* reported:

> "Attorney General Merrick Garland has directed the FBI and U.S. Attorneys' Offices to investigate alleged threats being made against school board officials by a growing coalition of parents who are outraged by the imposition of racialized curricula and COVID-driven shutdowns and mask mandates in their local classrooms.

> "The order, announced in a memo released Monday, comes after a group that represents school boards urged the Biden administration to review whether confrontations by outraged parents over COVID restrictions and critical race theory violate the Patriot Act."

Capitalist Tools

In 1996, Kim and I produced the *CASHFLOW* board game and, in 1997, *Rich Dad Poor Dad* was self-published because every publisher in New York turned the book down.

The *CASHFLOW* board game and *Rich Dad Poor Dad* were our original capitalist tools. They were created to combat communism taught in our schools... by teaching capitalism in our homes.

As Marx warned:
> *"The education of all children, from the moment that they can get along without a mother's care, shall be in state institutions."*

As Lenin warned:
> *"Give me your four year olds and in a generation I will build a socialist state."*

As Stalin warned:
> *"Education is a weapon whose effects depends upon who holds it in his hands and at whom it is aimed."*

And as Hitler warned:

> *"Universal education is the most corroding and disintegrating poison that liberalism has ever invented for its own destruction."*

He is also credited with saying:

> *"Let me control the textbook and I will control the state."*

This book, *Capitalist Manifesto,* is about how to take back control of our education, our economy, our country, and most importantly, our freedoms.

CHAPTER TWO

A DIFFERENT EDUCATION

"How fortunate for governments that the people they administer don't think."
— Adolf Hitler

I, too, remember July 9, 1962 as a day when all hell broke loose... just as *Discovery* magazine reported it:

> *"On July 9, 1962, the U.S. launched a Thor missile from Johnston Island, an atoll about 1,500 kilometers (900 miles) southwest of Hawaii. The missile arced up to a height of over 1,100 km (660 miles), then came back down. At the preprogrammed height of 400 km (240 miles), just seconds after 09:00 UTC, the 1.4 megaton nuclear warhead detonated.*
>
> *"And all hell broke loose.*
>
> *"1.4 megatons is the equivalent of 1.4 million tons of TNT exploding. However, nuclear weapons are fundamentally different from simple chemical explosives. TNT releases its energy in the form of heat and light. Nukes also generate heat and light, plus vast amounts of X-rays and gamma rays — high-energy forms of light — as well as subatomic particles like electrons and heavy ions."*

Blood in the Sky

On July 9, 1962, I was 15 years old. Our family was having dinner when a searing bright white flash went through the house. At first, we thought it was a flashbulb, the burst of light from an old fashioned camera. After looking around, attempting to find out what the flash was, my little sister went to the window and gasped, "Oh, my god."

For the next few hours, and what seemed like an eternity, our family watched the entire sky boil and churn, first a bright white-yellow and, in the end, a dark reddish purple. If you have ever seen an animal or human bleeding out, the sky looked exactly as the newspapers described: "Someone poured blood in the sky."

Hiding Under Our Desks

At school, all we could talk about is what we saw, what we witnessed with our own eyes. Our teachers did their best to calm us down, stay positive, and get us back to our schoolwork... but the problem was an atomic blast terrified us to the core.

During the 1960s the Cold War with Russia was red hot. That is why those words Khrushchev is said to have spoken in 1959 had such an impact on me.
"Your children's children will live under communism. You Americans are so gullible."

Witnessing the power of an atomic bomb was terrifying, a testimony to human insanity, a verification of humanity's inhumanity. It was verification that the Cold War and the threat of communism was real.

When our teachers' feeble attempts to calm down the students failed, the principal of the school decided an "atomic bomb drill" might help. I kid you not.

Hilo, Hawaii, where I grew up, is the largest most southern city in America, even farther south than Miami, Florida. We witnessed the power of "the bomb" while the rest of America slept.

Winston Churchill's March 5, 1946, warning had already come true: *"An iron curtain has descended across the continent."*

By 1962, all students knew Europe had been split by an iron curtain.

On May 7, 1954, Viet Minh troops under General Vo Nguyen Giap overran the French base at Dien Bien Phu. The victory by communist forces ended nearly a century of French colonial rule in Indochina. By 1962, we knew the war against communism was already being fought in Asia. In 1962, something told me I would be fighting in the next war.

During the Cold War the American Civil Defense Agency mandated that all schools practice "atomic bomb drills." An atomic bomb drill consisted of the principal of the school sounding an alarm and all ordering all students to hide under their wooden desks. The problem was that after witnessing a real atomic bomb blast in 1962, we the students knew too much.

We knew a wooden desk would not protect us... much like, in 2020 and 2021, when there were two schools of thought related to whether or not wearing a mask or having a vaccine shot would keep us *healthy*. And, for that matter, if going to school will make us *wealthy*.

Fallout from COVID-19

January 21, 2021: Bryan Renbaum of the *Maryland Reporter* wrote:

> *"With declining coronavirus positivity rates and vaccines becoming more readily available it is time for Maryland's students to return to their classrooms," Gov. Larry Hogan said Thursday.*

> *"There is no public health reason for school boards to be keeping students out of schools. None. This really isn't controversial. The science is clear. And nearly everyone wants to get our kids back into school," Hogan said at a news conference at St. John's College in Annapolis.*

> *"Hogan noted that state law does not permit the governor to order to schools to reopen because that decision lies with each individual jurisdiction. However, Hogan issued a stern warning to the state's teachers union,*

saying he will use what power he does have to ensure that Maryland's students return to the classroom.

"I want to make it clear to the teacher's union that we fully expect teachers to make every effort to return to the classrooms.... I want to make it perfectly clear that I will do everything I possibly ..."

Student Dropout Rate Increases
Yahoo News: May 11, 2021

"U.S. educators are doing everything they can to track down high school students who stopped showing up to classes and to help them get the credits needed to graduate, amid an anticipated surge in the country's dropout rate during the coronavirus pandemic.

"When students drop out, they typically look for an out, an opportunity to leave. And this has provided that, unfortunately," Sandy Addis, chairman of the National Dropout Prevention Center, said recently, referring to the pandemic. His group believes the dropout rate has spiked this year and will remain high for years.

"The early signs aren't encouraging. The United Nations Educational, Scientific and Cultural Organization warned that the pandemic had put 24 million children worldwide at risk of dropping out of school. And the pandemic's effects could erase gains the U.S. made in reducing its dropout rate, which fell from 9.3% in 2007 to 5.1% in 2019, according to the National Center for Education Statistics. Not finishing high school significantly hurts a person's earning potential, with dropouts bringing home an average of $150 less per week than graduates, according to U.S. Bureau of Labor Statistics data."

Bankrupt Students:
FindLaw, a Thomson Reuters business, provides online legal information and online marketing services for law firms. FindLaw.com is a free legal information website that helps consumers, small-business owners, students, and legal professionals find answers to everyday legal questions and find legal counsel when necessary.

On May 17, 2021, FindLaw had this to say about the Student Loan debt crisis:

> *"Let's take a look at some statistics to better understand the crisis:*
> - *The total outstanding federal student loan debt is $1.4 trillion.*
> - *Total private student loan debt is $124.65 billion.*
> - *On average, each U.S. household with student debt owes $47,671.*
> - *Among 2018 college grads, 65% left school with student debt.*
> - *Among 2018 college grads, average student debt ranged from $19,750 in Utah to $38,650 in Connecticut, with a U.S. average of $29,200.*
> - *About a third of Americans under 30 have student loan debt.*
> - *About one-fifth of Americans 30 to 44 have student loan debt, same with about 4% of Americans 45 and older.*
> - *About 5.2 million federal loan borrowers are in default.*

Anyone who knows anything about money knows that student loan debt is among the very worst of all types of debt. FindLaw says this about student loans:

> *"Under the current law, it is very difficult to have student loan debt discharged through bankruptcy. In order to be discharged, the borrower must show that repaying their student loans would impose an "undue hardship" on them, which is a high standard."*

Many affluent families are able to either pay for their child's education or assist their child in paying off their debt. Students from poor families do not often have that luxury.

Candace Owens is the media darling of conservatives. She is a young, ambitious, articulate, and accomplished black woman. She has the power to say what many men, especially white men, cannot say.

On the value of a college education Candance warns:

> *"I was a first-generation college student. This was supposed to be the ticket to prosperity. But it wasn't. I left college with a mountain of debt and no practical skills."*

When a student cannot pay off their student loan, that financial obligation hangs around their neck, like the proverbial albatross, forever. More damaging than not graduating from college is graduating with a student loan that affects their financial future for a very long time if not forever.

Debt Forgiveness

The 2008 real estate market crash revealed something else that I find sinister about America. After Wall Street and big-bank bankers made billions crashing the global economy, the bankers were rewarded, receiving billions in personal bonuses. While their clients took the hits, financially. What's wrong with *that* picture?

In his book *The Creature from Jekyll Island* author G. Edward Griffen writes about the creation of the Federal Reserve Bank, in 1913, and warns:
> *The name of the game is bailout.*

As Buckminster Fuller said: "They're playing games with money."

KISS: Fuller Is Correct

There are different games of money. For example, take the game of football. There are different football games. Soccer is the biggest and most popular game of football, followed by American football and rugby. All are games of football, but the game itself, the rules, and the players are very different.

The same is true with the game of money. The very rich at the top play a money game known as "bailout." If they lose the game, we the people, bail out the bankers. That is what happened in 2008.

For the average person playing the game of money, if they lose there is no bailout. They file bankruptcy.

These two different games of money drive academic elites mad. They think it's capitalists shoving their losses down on the taxpayers, and it is. That is the game of money.

The problem is that the idea of "bailing out the rich" is not a capitalist idea. It is really a Marxist idea. Later in this book you will find out how Karl Marx's *Communist Manifesto* was influential in the design of today's modern banking system, especially the Fed, aka "the Creature" from Jekyll Island.

Moral Hazard

In financial language, when bankers know they are going to be bailed out — even paid bonuses for their failures — it is known as *moral hazard*.

In economics...

> *"Moral hazard occurs when an entity has an incentive to increase its exposure to risk because it does not bear the full costs of that risk."*

As I see it, it comes down to responsibility and accountability. Who is held accountable for the consequences of these bankers' decisions and self-dealing? The richest bankers in America are bailed out, paid bonuses... even if they lose billions. Yet poor and middle class students are stuck with the worst type of debt. Does that fit the definition of *moral hazard*?

At the end of 2021 with the total outstanding federal student loan debt at approximately $1.7 trillion, it represents debt greater than all credit card debt and auto loans. What does that mean for the American economy and the future of America?

As Khrushchev warned:

> *"We will not have to fight you; We will so weaken your economy, until you will fall like overripe fruit into our hands."*

On April 16, 2015, a headline in *Investor's Business Daily* read:
> The Real Student Loan Crisis Is the one Obama Created

The article included this reporting:
> *"Irresponsibility: A new report finds that 27.3% of student loans are delinquent. Why does this matter? Because thanks to President Obama, about $1 trillion dollars of student loan debt is owed to the federal government.*

"Obama keeps trying to portray the student loan crisis as a problem suffered by students burdened by a mountain of debt when they graduate, and who are unable to make enough money to pay it back.

"But that's not the real crisis.

"First, average student loan debt is only a little over $20,000. A student who gave up his $5-a-day Starbucks habit could pay off the principal in about a decade.

"Second, despite the endless hue and cry about rising tuitions, the amount students actually pay to go to college — net of grants, aid, discounts, and what not — has barely budged, according to the College Board. The problem isn't even that, at nearly $1.2 trillion, the total amount of student loan debt now exceeds that of auto loans or credit card debt.

"The real crisis is one Obama himself manufactured since taking office.

"In 2010, Obama eliminated the federal guaranteed loan program, which let private lenders offer student loans at low interest rates. Now, the Department of Education is the only place to go for such loans.

"Obama sold this government takeover as a way to save money — why bear the costs of guaranteeing private loans, he said, when the government could cut out the middleman and lend the money itself?

"The cost savings didn't happen. In fact, the Congressional Budget Office just increased its 10-year forecast for the loan program's costs by $27 billion, or 30%.

"What did happen was an explosive growth in the amount of federal student loan debt. President Clinton phased in direct federal lending in 1993 as an option, but over the next 15 years the amount of loans was fairly stable. The result of Obama's action is striking. In each of the past six years, federal direct student loan debt has climbed by more than $100 billion.

"And since Obama keeps making it easier and easier to avoid repaying those loans, it's a problem that taxpayers will eventually have to shoulder.

"Through words and actions, Obama has encouraged irresponsibility on the part of student borrowers. He constantly talks as if student debt were an unfair burden they unknowingly had foisted upon them." [Emphasis added.]

Black on Black

There has been lots of talk over the past few years about Black Lives Matter and whether or not that organization is racist or Marxist.

The organization's three founders are still featured prominently on the group's website. They are Patrisse Cullors, Alicia Garza, and Opal Tometi. Reporting on their backgrounds paints them, primarily, as community organizers, artists, and writers. In a recently released interview that Cullors did in 2015, she said:

> *"We do have an ideological frame. Myself and Alicia in particular, are trained organizers; we are trained Marxists."*

All Life Matters

Personally, I support our freedoms of speech and assembly. Where I disagree with Black Lives Matter is that I believe *all lives — and all life —* matters. The life of every human walking this earth... as well as animals and plants and ecosystems of every kind.

I vehemently disagree with Black Lives Matter's position that America is a systemically racist country. I realize there are racists, yet as an Asian-American who has experienced racism, to blatantly say Americans are racists... is racist.

The Oxford Dictionary defines racism as: Characterized by or showing prejudice, discrimination, or antagonism against a person or people due to their membership in a particular racial or ethnic group.

According to that definition, Black Lives Matter is a racist organization. And if they were not racist, the name of their organization would be All Lives Matter. If they were environmentally conscious, the name of their organization would be All Life Matters.

The 1619 Project

It's hard not to come to the conclusion that the 1619 Project is Marxist. Karl Marx warned:

> *"Keep people from their history and they are easily controlled."*

The 1619 Project is a long-form journalism project developed by Nikole Hannah-Jones and writers from *The New York Times* and *The New York Times Magazine* which "aims to reframe the country's history by placing the consequences of slavery and the contributions of Black Americans at the very center of the United States' national narrative."

The purpose of the 1619 project is rewrite American's history, exactly as Marx suggests in his book *Communist Manifesto*.

Also, in World War II, my uncles who fought with the 442nd Infantry Battalion, an all-Japanese American battalion. The 442 was the most highly decorated in battalion World War II, were the first to open the Hitler's concentration camps.

My family did not ask for reparations for their land or that history be rewritten as Black America's history to be an economy built on slavery and the brutality of American capitalism.

As Marx taught:
   "The existence of the state is inseparable from the existence of slavery."

That is the core message of *The New York Times* 1619 Project.

It was Adolf Hitler who gloated:
   "How fortunate for governments that the people they administer don't think."

It surprises me that the writers at *The New York Times* didn't do more research or reporting on the origins of the word *slave*. If they had, it would have been reported that the word *slave* comes from *slavic,* referring to the white people of Eastern Europe. I am not saying that this justifies slavery, only that if the writers at *The New York Times* were contentious they would have included reporting on the people of Slavic countries such as Poland, Ukraine, Russia, Czechoslovakia, Bosnia, Croatia, and Macedonia... countries that have a centuries-long history of slavery.

I find it interesting that the *Times* writers don't offer more perspective on how humans have always enslaved other humans throughout history. Africans from North Africa have enslaved whites of Southern Europe. Asians have enslaved Asians and American Indians have enslaved other American Indians.

After Pearl Harbor

During World War II, members of my family had their homes, farms, and private possessions confiscated by the U.S. government and were locked in concentration camps across America.

442nd Infantry Battalion

Rather than blame and complain, the 442nd Infantry battalion was formed, almost entirely of second-generation Japanese Americans. The 442nd Infantry battalion fought from North Africa, through Italy, and into Germany. The 442nd became the most highly decorated unit for its size and length of service in the history of the U.S. military.

I had five uncles who fought in Europe. My grandmother showed me a letter from one of my uncles who describes discovering Jewish death camps, before the world knew of these Nazi camps. She thought it befitting that Japanese who were held in American concentration camps were the ones who freed Jews held in German concentration camps.

I had two other uncles fight against the Japanese in the Pacific. One was captured and held in a Japanese concentration camp. His experiences are described in book *A Spy in Their Midst,* written by another uncle of mine. The uncle that was captured was a Japanese-American spy, working for America when he was captured, tortured, and castrated by his Japanese captors. He spent the rest of his life in Japan, searching for and bringing to justice Japanese war criminals, including the officer who castrated him.

When I hear of reparations for blacks, it begs bigger questions. Not questions of whether or not slavery is an example of humanity's inhumanity. The questions I ask myself are: Why just blacks? Isn't that racist?

Candace Owen warns:

"I can't think of the last Asian that I ran into that talked about internment camps. But black people always want to talk about slavery."

Why, today, would we ask taxpayers who never owned slaves... to pay money to people who never were slaves? I can't be the only one asking: Isn't that racist?

If anyone deserves reparations, it is the American Indian. In a letter written by Dutch merchant Peter Schaghen, in 1626, to directors of the Dutch East India Company, he stated that Manhattan was purchased for "60 guilders worth of trade," or $24.

In today's dollars $24 is about $1,163, and still a bargain. If Manhattan Island cost only $1,163 in today's dollars, what is the rest of America worth?

As I've stated earlier in this book, in 2019, prior to the 2020 Presidential election, *The New York Times* reported Kamala Harris had made it clear that if she becomes President, she would support U.S. taxpayer-funded "reparations to black Americans to address the legacies of slavery and discrimination."

After Obama, the first black President, it seemed obvious that the plan was for Hillary Clinton to become the first female President. Until Trump stepped in, that is.

After Trump spoiled the academic elite's plans, it seemed apparent that the new plan was to run Joe Biden as a "white-guy temp," a cardboard cutout of a President, and have Kamala, a woman of color, step in when Biden faded into the sunset.

When President Harris, America's first female President takes over, will she pursue her campaign position related to reparations for blacks? To be fair, shouldn't President Kamala Harris include the American Indians in black reparations? How much would the American continent cost American taxpayers? The price will not be a problem because all she has to do is print more fake money, destroy the U.S. dollar, and bankrupt America.

In his book, *The Communist Manifesto*, Karl Marx warned:

"In this sense, the theory of the Communist may be summed up in the single sentence: Abolition of private property."

Are those who accuse others of being racists... racists themselves? In today's hyper-sensitive, racially charged world, it is personal and professional suicide to say anything about blacks. It is much safer for non-blacks to allow blacks to talk about blacks.

A few black Americans with the courage to publicly challenge other blacks are:

1. Candace Owens
2. Larry Elder
3. Herschel Walker
4. Diamond and Silk
5. Leo Terrell
6. Mark Robinson

My personal favorite black commentator is Thomas Sowell, who is highly educated, courageous, and eloquent... a thought leader who "floats like a butterfly" and lands punches like Mohammed Ali.

Currently Thomas Sowell is a senior fellow at Stanford University Hoover Institution. He was born in North Carolina and grew up in Harlem. He served in the Marine Corps during the Korean War. After leaving the Marine Corps he enrolled at Harvard University, graduating magna cum laude in 1958. He received a master's degree from Columbia University in 1959, and earned his doctorate in economics from the University of Chicago in 1968. Sowell has served on the faculties of several universities, including Cornell University and University of California, Los Angeles. He has also worked at think tanks such as the Urban Institute. Since 1980, he has worked at the Hoover Institution at Stanford University, where he presently serves as the Rose and Milton Friedman Senior Fellow on Public Policy. Sowell writes from a libertarian conservative perspective. Sowell has written more than 30 books and is a National Humanities Medal recipient for innovative scholarship which incorporated history, economics, and political science.

Thomas Sowell has this to say about Barack Obama and the liberal elite:

> *"Barack Obama's political genius is his ability to say things that will sound good to people who have not followed the issues in any detail — regardless of how obviously fraudulent what he says may be to those who have."*

> *"You can become President of the United States without any contact with economic reality."*

> *"It is hard to imagine a more stupid or more dangerous way of making decisions than by putting those decisions in the hands of people who pay no price for being wrong."*

> *"There is no mystery to me why Jesse Jackson says what he does or Al Sharpton and others because that benefits them, but it does not benefit the people thy lead and all the incentives of the leaders to lead people into things that do not help the people but help the leaders."*

> *"One of Barak Obama's great gifts is the ability to say things that are absolutely absurd and let them sound not only plausible, but inspiring and profound."*

> *"The old adage about giving a man a fish versus teaching him how to fish has been updated by a reader: Give a man a fish and he will ask for tartar sauce and French fries! Moreover, some politician who wants his vote will declare all these things to be among his 'basic rights.'"*

> *"Those who cry out that the government should 'do something' never even ask for data on what has actually happened when the government did something, compared to what actually happened when the government did nothing."*

> *"Over the generations, black leaders have ranged from noble souls to shameless charlatans."*

> *"The word 'racism' is like ketchup. It can be put on practically anything - and demanding evidence makes you a 'racist.'"*

On the subject of education, Thomas Sowell has said:

> *"Before so many people went to colleges and universities... common sense was much more widespread."*

"Education is not merely neglected in many of our schools today but is replaced to a great extent by ideological indoctrination."

"Apparently almost anyone can do a better job of educating children than our so-called educators in public schools. Children who are being home-schooled by their parents also score higher on tests than children educated in the public schools. Successful education shows what is possible whether in charter schools, private schools, military schools or home-schooling. The challenge is to provide more escape hatches from failing public schools, not only to help those students who escape, but also to force these institutions to get their act together before losing more students and more jobs."

The Capitalist Manifesto

In 1996 the *CASHFLOW* board game was released. In 1997, *Rich Dad Poor Dad* was published.

Both products were developed to counter what Thomas Sowell refers to as *ideological indoctrination,* aka communism taught in our schools. Rich dad's Capitalist Manifesto has been to fight communism with capitalist education, taught in homes.

Thomas Sowell mentions military schools. He fought in Korea as a U.S. Marine, and I fought in Vietnam was a U.S. Marine. Military education is different from education taught at schools.

Military schools teach students to be leaders; schools today teach students to be "snowflakes."

The Power of Words

In military schools the most important words are:
1. Mission
2. Honor
3. Discipline
4. Respect
5. Duty

In schools of "snowflake indoctrination" the most important words are:
1. Critical Race Theory
2. Triggers
3. Gender pronouns
4. Political correctness
5. Equity and Equality... and "everyone gets a trophy"

In military indoctrination, regardless of branch of service, the mindset is:
"No pain... no gain."

And:
"Suck it up, buttercup."

In snowflake indoctrination, the mindset is:
"When in pain... blame and complain."

And when snowflakes mess up, they are trained to:
"Lie, deny, coverup... and then "blame and complain."

As Thomas Sowell warned:
"One of the common failings among honorable people is a failure to appreciate how thoroughly dishonorable some other people can be, and how dangerous it is to trust them."

Repeating *Investor's Business Daily* on who caused the student loan crisis:
"In 2010, Obama eliminated the federal guaranteed loan program, which let private lenders offer student loans at low interest rates. Now, the Department of Education is the only place to go for such loans."

Repeating Thomas Sowell's warning on Obama:
"Barack Obama's political genius is his ability to say things that will sound good to people who have not followed the issues in any detail — regardless of how obviously fraudulent what he says may be to those who have. "

Repeating *Investor's Business Daily* on how Obama lies, denies, covers up, then blames and complains.

> *"Obama has encouraged irresponsibility on the part of student borrowers. He constantly talks as if student debt were an unfair burden, they unknowingly had foisted upon them."*

As Thomas Sowell warns:

> *"Facts are not liberals' strong suit. Rhetoric is."*

On July 9, 1962, after witnessing an atomic bomb blast with my own eyes, I could no longer just hide under my desk. There was too much at stake.

The Definition of Rhetoric:

"Language designed to have a persuasive or impressive effect on its audience, but often regarded as lacking in sincerity or meaningful content."

In 2020, Joe Biden won the U.S. Presidential election after hiding in his basement, while President Donald Trump flew across the nation, rallying millions of inspired voters.

As Stalin warned:

> *"Voters decide nothing. Vote counters decide everything."*

Fall-Out Shelters

Soon after the 1962 blast, families started building fallout shelters. Families would even have fallout shelter parties. When I asked my dad if we were going to build a fallout shelter, he gave me the same line he used for almost everything: *"I can't afford it."*

Every time my poor dad said, "I can't afford it," I could hear my rich dad saying:

> *"The reason poor people are poor is because they say 'I can't afford it' more than rich people. Instead of saying 'I can't afford it,' rich people ask, 'How can I afford it?'"*

Rich dad also added:

"A person who states "I can't afford it" is a person with a closed mind.

"When a person asks, "How can I afford it?" the question opens their mind, and they are open to learning."

How I Got to Military School

In 1962, I knew I was in trouble. I did not like school. I did not fit in with the "cool kids." My friends were surfers, constantly cutting classes when the surf was up.

In 1962, I failed English. The problem was the English teacher failed 80% our class... so my father fired him. When the teachers protested, my dad stood in front of the teachers and said, "Your job is to teach students... not fail them."

The next three years of high school were smooth sailing. No teacher wanted to mess with me, the Superintendent of Education's son.

Then a new English teacher came to town and threatened to fail me my senior year. I gently informed her of the fate of my previous English teacher, and I passed senior English with a D.

My dad said to me, "I would let you fail if you could not write. Your problem is, you cannot spell... and your real problem is you disagree with your teachers." That was when the First Amendment, our freedom of speech, became real to me. My dad reinforced my right to disagree with my teachers. My dad said:

"You have the right to say what you want to say, even disagree with the teacher. The problem with schoolteachers is they believe there is only one right answer... the right answer they find in the back of their test book. In the real world, real life is a multiple-choice test, filled with many right answers."

When I was 16 years old, my father lowered the boom stating he was not going to pay for my college education. As usual, he said, "I can't afford it." But the real reason was because he knew it would be a waste of his money.

He knew the only reason I wanted to go to the University of Hawaii was to become a big-wave surfer.

When I was 17 years old the University of Hawaii rejected my application for admission, stating my GPA, my grade point average, was too low. That was a shock because I had always thought that if a student could fog a mirror, the University of Hawaii would admit them.

As I've said, in 1962, by the time I was 15 years old, I knew I was in trouble. My life was not going as planned. Even if there was a real atomic bomb attack, I would still refuse to hide under my desk. I knew my dad was right. If I went to the University of Hawaii, it would be a waste of my time and his money. I knew I needed discipline.

One of my favorite poems is Robert Frost's *The Road Less Traveled.*

> *"Two roads diverged in a yellow wood,*
> *And sorry I could not travel both*
> *And be one traveler, long I stood*
> *And looked down one as far as I could*
> *To where it bent in the undergrowth;*
>
> *Then took the other, as just as fair,*
> *And having perhaps the better claim,*
> *Because it was grassy and wanted wear;*
> *Though as for that the passing there*
> *Had worn them really about the same,*
>
> *And both that morning equally lay*
> *In leaves no step had trodden black.*
> *Oh, I kept the first for another day!*
> *Yet knowing how way leads on to way,*
> *I doubted if I should ever come back.*
>
> *I shall be telling this with a sigh*
> *Somewhere ages and ages hence:*

Two roads diverged in a wood, and I -
I took the one less traveled by,
And that has made all the difference."

Having heard Khrushchev's warning in 1959, having seen an atomic bomb blast with my own eyes and being told to hide under my desk, then my father saying he would not pay for my college education, and then being rejected for admission by the University of Hawaii, I knew I had to change. And that I needed discipline.

In 1964, U.S. Senator Daniel K. Inouye offered me Congressional nominations to the U.S. Naval Academy at Annapolis, Maryland and the U.S. Merchant Marine Academy at Kings Point, New York.

Each school requires a Congressional or Presidential nomination before the admissions process can begin. It was a long and arduous admissions process, which included batteries of tests, medical and physical exams, one-on-one interviews, and written recommendations from people who knew me. Somehow, I was accepted.

I chose Kings Point because it was the Academy that I really wanted attend. When I was 14 years old, in wood shop, I built an 8-foot el Toro-class sailboat while my classmates were making salad bowls for their moms. Once my sailboat was built, I would sail it on Hilo Bay, dreaming of faraway countries such as Tahiti and meeting beautiful Tahitian women.

In 1968, my dreams came true when I sailed into Papeete, Tahiti onboard a Standard Oil tanker, as a student from Kings Point. And I did meet a beautiful Tahitian girl... just as I had hoped, proving that dreams do come true.

One advantage Kings Point had over all other academies was the starting pay for graduates. In 1965, graduates from the four other service academies were earning $200 a month. In 1965, graduates from Kings Point started at $2,000 a month. Although I was not good at math, I did know that more zeros meant more money.

In 1969, the year I graduated, many of my classmates were earning $120,000 a year, which was pretty good for a 21-year-old.

In 1969, although I had achieved my poor dad's dream of a high-paying job, again, I chose the road less traveled. In 1969 I joined the U.S. Marine Corps, earning the $200 a month pittance I had been avoiding, was assigned to U.S. Navy Flight School at Pensacola, Florida to begin pilot training.

Once again, the words at Kings Point and at Pensacola were the same:
1. Mission
2. Honor
3. Discipline
4. Respect
5. Duty

Thomas Sowell was a Marine who fought in Korea, before graduating from Harvard, magna cum laude.

Perhaps if Barack Obama had served in the Marines and fought in Desert Storm before graduating from Harvard, he might have had a different world view. If Obama had served in the U.S. military and fought in combat, the world might be a different world today. We might not be so worried about triggers, gender pronouns, critical race theory... and who is counting our ballots.

CHAPTER THREE

GREAT TEACHERS – REAL TEACHERS

ACTA NON VERBA
Deeds Not Words

Motto of the U.S. Merchant Marine Academy,
Kings Point, New York

The U.S. Merchant Marine Academy has a battle standard, a military flag. Kings Point is the only Federal Service Academy awarded a battle standard. The battle standard is carried with the colors, the American flag, always.

Kings Point's battle standard perpetuates the memory of the 142 Academy cadets/midshipmen who were casualties of World War II. The 142 died on U.S. Merchant Marine ships, carrying war supplies to Europe. They perished when German submarines, hunting in wolf packs, torpedoed their ships. Kings Point is privileged as the only academy among the nation's five federal academies authorized to carry a battle standard as part of its color guard.

Kings Point cadets/midshipmen have served in the Korean, Vietnam, and Middle East wars. I was one of approximately 30 students who served in Vietnam. And, thankfully, no student has perished since WWII.

Hell Week
I left Hawaii in August of 1965 for Kings Point via New York City. My aunt and uncle lived in Manhattan and hired a limo to take us to the academy. After the pleasantries and the pomp and circumstance of officers in dress-white uniforms greeting parents, relatives, and new students, the parents left with smiles on their faces, proud that their sons (in my case, nephew) had been accepted to such a prestigious school.

The grounds of Kings Point are breathtaking. The property on which the school is situated used to be the Walter Chrysler estate on Long Island Sound, with New York City in the distance.

Just before the parents left, the publicity officer asked if I would take a photo with another new cadet/midshipman. The other student was from Long Island and his home was less than five miles from the academy. The publicity officer wanted a picture of the student from closest to the academy and me, the student from the farthest away. As we walked out to the main gate for the photo op, I said, "This is pretty nice."

The other student shook his head and said, "Odds are you won't be here next week." He added, "Hell Week is about to begin. Twenty percent of us will be gone in a month. Sixty-five percent of our class will not graduate."

Like an idiot, I asked, "What happens to those who wash out?"

My new friend smirked and said, "You didn't read the contract, did you?"

"No," I replied feebly.

"They have the right to send us straight to Vietnam," my fellow student said, as we smiled for the camera.

As soon as all parents and family had departed and the punch and cookies were put away, the yelling and screaming started. First assignment, memorize the Mission of the U.S. Merchant Marine Academy. We would be tested after dinner that night, if we had dinner. Welcome to Hell Week.

We were now officially, *plebes*, fourth class midshipmen. A third classman, probably 19 years old, takes over and starts barking orders. About 20 of us are lined up as the third classman barks, "Section, atten-hut, dress right dress, right face, pick up your bags, forward march." Hell Week had begun.

That was Monday. A week later, on a Sunday night after dinner, our first free time, I stood on a hill and looked west over the lights of New York City toward Hawaii... and cried. I had survived Hell Week. Only four more years to go. I wondered if I had made the biggest mistake of my life.

The "wash-out rate" was as advertised. Of the approximately 400 students who started in my class, only about 165 graduated in 1969. The class of 1969 included a number of students who had washed out from the class of 1968.

Aspiring to be Anchor Man
While many of my classmates wanted to be class officers and graduate with the highest GPA, all I wanted to be was the Anchor Man spot — the graduating midshipman with the lowest GPA. Why? The Anchor Man made a lot of money because every student threw money into a pot to skew the curve for everyone. Unfortunately, my GPA was .03 points above the Anchor Man's GPA.

I believe the only reason I graduated from Kings Point was because I was interested in the subjects I was taught. I wanted to become a ship's officer and spent a year at sea traveling the world. And I had some really great teachers.

Most were real teachers who practiced what they taught. For example, I learned spherical trigonometry and celestial navigation from a real ship's navigator and spherical trigonometry teacher. The basis of celestial navigation, which is navigation by the sun, moon, and stars at sea, is spherical trigonometry.

One of my favorite teachers of all times was a U.S. Military Academy Graduate, a West Pointer, who flew B-17 bombers over Germany, was shot down twice and escaped capture twice. After leaving the Army he went to graduate school and earned a doctorate in English with a minor in Economics.

That teacher introduced our class to the teachings of Marx, Stalin, Hitler, Lenin, and Mao. It was during his classes that I realized that economic philosophies were much like religions. Just as a religious philosophy has a leader, so do economic philosophies. Our teacher emphasized the point that disciples and followers will kill for both economic and religious philosophies.

He used the IRA, the Irish Republican Army, an an example of Protestants killing Catholics, both Christian religions, in Northern Ireland.

The Tet Offensive

On January 30, 1968, the Tet Offensive began. "Tet," as it was referred to, was one of the largest escalations and military campaigns of the Vietnam War. The VC and the North Vietnamese People's Army attacked cities and military bases all around South Vietnam.

As part of my sea year from the academy, in 1966, my cargo ship had delivered bombs into Vietnam and Thailand. Having been in the war zone, the war became of special interest to me. Every night on the *CBS Evening News* I would watch and listen closely to Walter Cronkite's narration of the war's progress.

In 1968, as the Tet Offensive roared on, I began to notice a change in the news coverage. It seemed to me that the news reporting was turning against America, subtly portraying us as the "bad guys." If I hadn't been to Vietnam, I might not have noticed the subtle change.

The My Lai Massacre

This 1968 massacre was covered up for months by people in high places. Once the news broke and photos of the atrocity were released, the press focused countless hours of television, radio, and print coverage of the My Lai Massacre. The press focused on the 340 to 500 unarmed civilians killed by U.S. Army soldiers, led by Lt. William Calley.

Although Lt. Calley was the only one charged, convicted, and sentenced, many knew he was not the only officer at the massacre and that the massacre was covered up at very high levels. The truth may never come out.

I do not condone what happened at My Lai in 1968. My point in using that as an example is to show how it was used against the men and women of our armed forces. As I said, in 1968, I began to notice the corporate media turning against America.

On February 1, 1968, in a Saigon street, South Vietnam's police chief raised a gun to the head of a handcuffed Viet Cong prisoner and abruptly pulled the trigger. A few feet away, Associated Press photographer Eddie Adams pressed his shutter.

Taken during the North's surprise Tet Offensive, Adams' photo showed the war's brutality in a way Americans hadn't seen before. Protesters saw the image as graphic evidence that the United States was fighting on the side of an unjust South Vietnamese government. It won Adams a Pulitzer Prize. And it haunted him.

While at home in Hawaii, in 1969 and just before I was about to graduate from Kings Point, I met a Marine, a friend of a friend, who had just returned from Vietnam. He was at the Battle of Khe Sanh (January 21 to July 1968) in an area of northwestern Quang Tri Provence, next to Laos.

The main U.S. forces defending Khe Sanh Combat Base (KSCB) were two regiments of the United States Marine Corps supported by elements from the United States Army and the United States Air Force. The Battle of Khe Sanh was a part of the Viet Cong and North Vietnamese Tet Offensive.

Over a couple of beers, he told me he was released from the Marine Corps for what we now call PTSD, Post Traumatic Stress Disorder. Taking a sip of his beer, he said, "The truth is, I was a coward." He went on to explain that, after Khe Sanh was overrun by the VC and NVA, rather than stand and fight, he climbed into a shell crater filled with dead U.S. Marines and pulled a body of one of the Marines over him. He lay there as VC and NVA soldiers shot and bayoneted dead and dying Marines. His hand holding his beer shook as he spoke. "I can still hear and feel the bayonet of an enemy solider, piercing the body of the Marine I was hiding under," he said. Pausing to take another sip of his beer he said, "I can't forgive myself for being a coward. That's why I was released from the Marine Corps."

A Change of Career

In the Spring of 1969, I was months away from graduation. I had a job offer from Standard Oil of California, as a third mate, driving oil tankers from California to Hawaii, Tahiti, and Alaska.

I was grateful Standard Oil offered me a job because their ships officers were non-union. Although it was lower pay, I did not want to join the MM&P, the Masters, Mates and Pilot's union — on principle. I am a capitalist, not a Marxist.

Returning to Kings Point, I immediately went to see my Economics teacher. We spent long hours discussing the change in media sentiment against America, which also concerned him. He said, "While I was flying B-17s over Germany, I knew the media and the American people were supporting our troops and the war effort." He then showed me a quote from Adolf Hitler who warned:

"Demoralize the enemy from within by surprise, terror, sabotage, assassination. This is the war of the future."

I remember saying:

"It looks like Hitler is winning in Vietnam."

We spent more than an hour together as he told me about being shot down, losing many of his crew, hiding in farmhouses, risking the lives of the French farmers' families who hid him, and finally returning to England, only to be shot down once more... and escaping to fly again.

As he spoke, sharing his experiences as a pilot in WWII, I was changing. He was not attempting to sway my thinking. He was simply sharing his experiences. As I left his office, my mind was made up. I was changing careers. I was changing from a profession paying $47,000 a year, which was pretty good in 1969 for working only seven months a year with five months off, to earning $2,400 a year with two weeks a year off. It was one of the best decisions of my life.

In October of 1969, I arrived in Pensacola, Florida and another great adventure began. It was a great adventure because, once again, I had great teachers. Unlike the teachers I'd had in elementary school and high school, these guys were real teachers. They did not teach via textbooks and memorized answers. All the teachers who taught us to fly... could actually fly. They were real pilots. They were outstanding teachers who inspired me to want to be like them.

It was much like the story of rich dad and poor dad. My poor dad was a good man but, without real financial education, he did not know he was a Marxist. I wanted to be like my rich dad, a capitalist.

Rich Dad's Capitalist Manifesto means that our teachers are real teachers. Professionally, they practice what they teach. Only socialists, fascists, and Marxists use fake teachers who indoctrinate versus teach.

As Maria Montessori, educational entrepreneur and founder of the Montessori School, said,

"Growth comes from activity, not from intellectual understanding."

That is why Rich Dad's Capitalist Manifesto is built around the *CASHFLOW* board game, created in 1996.

Why Games Are Great Teachers

One reason I was inspired to become rich is because my rich dad taught his son and me financial education via the game of *Monopoly*®. He would often say:

"There are many ways to get rich. One of the best ways is found on the game of Monopoly."

And most of us know the formula:

"4 Green Houses; 1 Red Hotel. Repeat the process."

One reason games are better teachers than most schoolteachers is because games involve all four human intelligences.

AWAKEN YOUR FINANCIAL GENIUS
YOUR 4 INTELLIGENCES

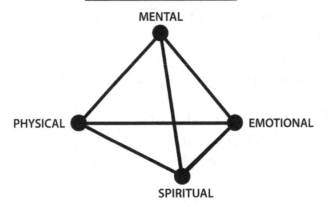

Why Schoolteachers Are Poor Teachers

Looking at the tetrahedron of the Four Intelligences, it is easy to see why most schoolteachers are poor — and poor teachers.

Teachers use mental intelligence to memorize. Memorization is not learning. Most "smart people" have memorized facts, figures, dates, and formulas. When they speak, they often sound intelligent because they can read and recite. The question is: What can they *do*?

This is why Maria Montessori's words are so profound and worth repeating:
"Growth comes from activity, not from intellectual understanding."

She also said:
"What the hand does, the mind remembers."

Two Versions of the *CASHFLOW* Game

There are two version of the *CASHFLOW* board game, one traditional and one electronic. When you play the physical *CASHFLOW* board game, you — your mind, and your hand — must fill out the numbers on the player's financial statement. That is why I recommend the board game, over the electronic version of *CASHFLOW*. The act of physically completing the financial statement is invaluable.

There are other reasons why I believe the *CASHFLOW* game is better than traditional teachers. The *CASHFLOW* game does not charge for overtime. It will work as hard as you want to work and for as long as you want to work. Even on holidays, summer vacations, and in-service days. The *CASHFLOW* game doesn't ask for days off or vacation time.

Emotionial intelligence plays a key role. The biggest reason why teachers are poor and teach others to be poor is because traditional education teaches via the emotion fear. FEAR stands for **False Evidence Appearing Real.** Traditional education teaches and keeps people poor because they teach people the fear of making mistakes and the fear of cooperation.

In my poor dad's schools, people who made mistakes were labeled "stupid"... and those who cooperated we considered "cheaters." That's not how it works in the real world.

In my rich dad's educational system, people who made mistakes and learned from their mistakes got smarter. And people who cooperate are capitalists — innovating and paving the way to the future.

Another reason why the *CASHFLOW* games are great teachers is that the game wants you to make mistakes — with play money, not real money. *CASHFLOW* games make you smarter when you make mistakes. There are lessons to be learned in every mistake and you can apply what you learn to your life and the decisions you make about money. These games, as teachers, do not want medical benefits or retirement plans. *CASHFLOW* games will serve you, your family, and friends for generations.

As Maria Montessori said:
> *"The education of a small child, therefore, does not aim at preparing him for school, but for life."*

In the real world of capitalism, we get paid for what we can do, not what we talk about. The problem with most schoolteachers is that they cannot do much. In the real world of business, people are paid for what they can do.

One reason why my poor dad was poor, after he lost his job as Superintendent of Education, was because he was of little use in the world of corporate America or in small business. He had a PhD, but no marketable skills. He was not an accountant, bookkeeper, attorney, or secretary; he could not sell, and he did not want to be a janitor.

One reason why Kings Pointers earned so much money, right after graduation, was because, included with their diploma, was a license as a ships mate or ships engineer and a commission as an ensign in the U.S. Navy or a second lieutenant in the U.S. Marine Corps.

The *CASHFLOW* game teaches financial education, financial history, and financial literacy — subjects not taught in school. Most schoolteachers do not know much about money, taxes, debt, cash flow, accounting, investing, or bookkeeping, much less financial history. Yet these subjects that are all useful and valuable in real life.

On top of that, *CASHFLOW* games do not need teachers. *The game empowers the players to be the teachers.*

As Maria Montessori said:
> *"The greatest sign of success for a teacher is to be able to say, 'The children are now working as if I did not exist.'"*

Spiritual Intelligence

The first word taught at military schools is *Mission*. Mission is spiritual. Mission is the root word of *missionary*. When I was in my MBA program, a "mission statement" was just a mental exercise, not spiritual practice. The mission statement of most corporations is often simply to "make more money." That is why many people hate corporate capitalism, yet love entrepreneurial capitalism, the spirit entrepreneurs such as Henry Ford, Thomas Edison, and Steve Jobs had when they launched their "start-ups."

Would You Give Your Life for a Mission?

That is where your spiritual intelligence begins. Would you dedicate your life to a cause, a calling bigger than yourself, and possibly give your life for the mission?

Initially, I went to Kings Point for the free education and to gain some self-discipline, which I lacked. Somewhere in the four-year process, the word *mission* became a part of me. As the Bible, John 1: 14 states:
"And the Word became flesh and dwelt among us."

Don't worry, it's not my intention to preach or try to convert you to Christianity. Just as I despise teachers who are preachers, I despise preachers who do not practice what they preach. I prefer people who keep their mouth shut and live and practice what they preach. I prefer people whose words have become their flesh, through their deeds, and their actions. Acta non verba.

In military school and in the Marines, we called people who did not walk their talk "whip jaws." The world today is filled with "whip jaws."

During the Vietnam war, I had three classmates shot down. One flew for the Navy, one for the Marine Corps, and one for the Air Force. The Marine Corps pilot and I had been friends since we were nine years old. We went to the same elementary school in Hilo, Hawaii. Robby went on to graduate from Dartmouth and flew the A-6 Intruder for the Marines.

Jim, the Navy pilot, was a friend of a friend from Hawaii who also flew the A-6 Intruder.

Neither Robby nor Jim, nor their planes, were ever found. They remain MIA, missing in action, to this day.

My high school classmate who flew the F-4 Phantom for the Air Force was shot down by a SAM, a surface-to-air missile. He spent two years in the Hanoi Hilton as a POW... before being released.

My economics teacher, a U.S. Army B-17 pilot, was shot down twice.

I was never shot down, but I did crash three times. We were flying night and day and our aircraft were more fatigued than the crews. The first time my crew and I went down was due to an engine failure, 27 miles out at sea. We swam for four hours before we were rescued. The second was a dual hydraulics failure, crashing into the back of a ship at sea. And the third crash was due to a tail rotor failure, surviving by sliding the aircraft across the deck of the aircraft carrier.

The good news is that, although we lost three aircraft, the crew of — two pilots, two gunners, and one crew chief — all returned to the United States, healthy and alive.

I give credit for our survival to the quality of the Navy and Marine flight schools and the quality of the teachers, many instructor pilots were men with real combat experience. They were great teachers because they were real teachers.

All men and women who serve in the military, in all wars, fight for one thing. We fight for our freedoms... freedoms guaranteed by the U.S. Constitution. Our freedoms are worth fighting for — and dying for.

One more important reason why the *CASHFLOW* game is better than teachers is the mission of the *CASHFLOW* game. The mission of the *CASHFLOW* game is to teach *capitalism* at home, as a counterpoint to teachers who teach *communism* and communist principles at school.

Many Marines have the Marine Corps motto tattooed on their body:
Death before Dishonor

And also the Marine Corps motto:
"*Semper Fidelis.*"
Forever Faithful.

The motto that Kings Point instills in students is:
"*ACTA NON VERBA*"
Deeds Not Words

CHAPTER FOUR

WHO KILLED THE MOST PEOPLE...
SOCIALISTS? CAPITALISTS? OR MARXISTS?

"Democracy is the road to socialism."
— Karl Marx

Late at night, on January 5, 1972, about 200 soldiers, airmen, sailors, and Marines were dropped off at Kadena Air Base on the island of Okinawa, Japan. Kadena airfield had been a Japanese airfield during World War II, and Okinawa had been the site of some of the fiercest fighting, just before the end of the war with Japan.

Groggy, without much sleep and passing through time zones, I found my way to the officer's mess hall for breakfast. The mess hall was buzzing as I searched for a seat. No one looked up. No one said "Hello." I was ignored. There was only one open seat, so I carried my tray of food to that table and sat down next to another pilot who also ignored me.

I did my best to break the ice and talk to the person next to me. Rather than respond to my questions, he just mumbled unintelligible responses. Finally, I asked the question that was on everyone's mind. Tapping him on his shoulder, I asked, "When do you rotate back to the states?"

Flashing the biggest smile I have ever seen, he turned and shouted out loud, so the entire mess hall could hear:

"I'm going home on the plane you came in on..."

The entire room broke out into roars of laughter. I had been set up. I was the FNG, the F---ing New Guy, his replacement pilot for the squadron.

Still grinning from ear to ear, the Marine picked up his bag and said, "I'll be sleeping in my own bed, with my wife, tonight. Welcome to the war." He turned and headed for the plane I had come in on.

That pilot and I have remained close friends to this day. We were both stationed in Hawaii, at Kaneohe Marine Corps Air Station when I rotated back a year later... the day our plane was met by anti-war protestors in California.

Composite Squadron

On the island of Okinawa, the Marine squadron was preparing for a "float," short for "flotilla." A flotilla is a group of seven war ships, built around an aircraft carrier. The carrier was to be our squadron's home, in the war zone.

While on Okinawa, we were integrating into a "composite" squadron. Until then, I had been assigned to a single aircraft squadron. I had come from a "gunship squadron" that had trained at Camp Pendleton, California.

The new "composite squadron," HMM-164, was made up of CH-53 Sea Stallion helicopters, often called the Jolly Green Giant.

This is the CH-46 Sea Knight, a medium troop transport helicopter.

And the UH-1 Huey gunship...

Flying as a Team

The focus of our training on Okinawa was to learn to fly together, to fly and fight as a team of different types of aircraft. This was not as easy as it might sound.

The jobs of the CH-53 and CH-46 were to insert as many troops into a LZ, a Landing Zone, as quickly as possible. The job of the Huey gunship was to fly guns and rocket support, suppressive fire, while the CH-53s and CH-46s sat on the ground, discharging or picking up Marines in battle.

Obviously, I liked the job of the gunships, far more than the transport helicopters. The thought of sitting on the ground, waiting while Marines were discharging or loading, did not appeal to me. I preferred flying and firing rockets and machine guns.

On Okinawa we practiced flying in formation, often two CH-53s and four CH-46s with two gunships as escorts. We flew in at 1,500 feet. The altitude was important because it was above the effective range of small-arms fire, such as the Viet Cong's Chinese- and Russian-made AK-47s.

The War Had Changed

Just before we were to board the ships of the battle group, we received word that we had to change our tactics. The NVA and Viet Cong now had the Russian-made SA-7, a shoulder-held rocket with infrared technology.

The intelligence officer of our new composite squadron stood up and said: "Gentlemen, the war has changed. We can no longer fly into battle at 1,500 feet. We must now fly in at tree-top level." This changed everything. It was challenging enough flying in at 1,500 feet. Our squadron now had to learn how to fly in tight formation and fight from just above the trees. This change was especially tough for gunship pilots because we had been taught to fire from 1,500 feet.

The SA-7 gave the soldier on the ground an unfair advantage. The soldier on the ground no longer needed to be a good shot. They did not need much training. All he or she had to do was point and shoot. The infrared guidance system picked up the heat from our exhaust and would fly right up our tail pipe, blowing us out of the sky. Our squadron left Okinawa and sailed to Vietnam, unprepared for what lay ahead. Technology had made our training obsolete.

The Price of Death

It cost the United States several million dollars and a few years to train an aircrew. It then cost about a million dollars for the two pilots, two gunners, and a crew chief to fly the aircraft. And it took about a billion dollars to deliver our squadron to the war zone on a flotilla of seven war ships.

Technology now gave a single person — man, woman, even a child... without any training — the power to fire a $100 shoulder-held rocket and blow our aircraft out of the sky. Inexpensive technology killed us.

Our years of education and training were now obsolete. If we wanted to survive, much less win the war, we had to relearn, retrain, and practice flying differently... as a composite squadron of different aircraft with different missions. The VC required less training. They just need to point and shoot. Technology had lowered the cost of war for the VC — and made war extremely expensive for America.

Feet Dry

Our flotilla of ships was soon "on station" off Vietnam. All we did was wait, train, and watch movies. It was boring. If we flew, our missions were just "re-supply," flying into Da Nang for whatever our commanding officers wanted.

Then, suddenly, activity began to pick up. We flew more. We were flying for different reasons. In April of 1972, I radioed back to the carrier: "feet dry." *Feet dry* meant that our flight of three aircraft, two CH-46s and one gunship, had flown about 15 miles from the carrier and had now crossed the beach. Our flight of three banked to the right and flew north over some of the most beautiful beaches in the world.

It had been six years since I was in Vietnam. In 1966, I was here as a 19-year-old midshipman, a Kings Point student for my sea year on board a rusty, bomb-carrying cargo ship. In 1966, the war was just beginning to escalate from a small rebellion into a full-blown war. In 1966, our cargo ship was "swinging on the hook," which meant we were at anchor, at Cam Ranh Bay, a large military harbor. The only action we saw or heard was from U.S. army guards stationed on our ship, dropping grenades over the side every half hour to prevent frogmen from attaching explosives to the hull of our ship. We were allowed to go ashore every day for food, cold beer, and other diversions. In 1966 all I saw were tiny fishing villages. The Vietnamese I met were warm, friendly, wonderful people. They did not seem to want to kill me, and I did not want to kill them. It did not seem like a war zone.

In 1972, as a 25-year-old, I noticed even from the air the changes caused by years of war. Flying low-level over the pristine beaches we soon came upon once-spectacular French chateaux that were now bombed out, destroyed. Vietnam was once known as the Indo-china Riviera, and I could see why. The colonial French had a great lifestyle in Vietnam. It was sad and surreal to see these once-grand chateaux and imagine what life was like, before the war, before the communists decided to take Vietnam back from the French.

Chateaux of the Rich
As I flew along the beach, passing the blackened, bombed-out, and looted French chateaux of the rich, my mind drifted back to my teacher at Kings Point, the B-17 pilot. His lessons on Marx, Lenin, Stalin, Hitler, and Mao were playing out like a movie, right in front of me, as our flight of three aircraft flew toward the city of Hue, once the capital of Vietnam.

I fixated on a beautiful yellow chateau, now bombed and blackened. Only a few years earlier, it had obviously been the home of a very rich family. I wondered what life must have been like for the family... and imagined that there were probably galas and parties and beautifully dressed people. Now it was a memory of times past. The philosophies of Marx, Lenin, Stalin, and Mao were winning. Thinking of the lessons of my economics teacher at Kings Point, I wondered if I was looking at the future of America.

America Burning
In 2020, I watched television coverage of the city of Portland, Oregon burning. It was a city where Kim and I had once lived. Then I drove past the boarded-up Neiman Marcus store, near my office in Scottsdale, Arizona... and those images brought back memories of that yellow French chateau in Vietnam. And I could hear Khrushchev's warning:

> *"You Americans are so gullible. No, you won't accept **communism** outright, but we will keep feeding you small doses of **socialism** until you will finally wake up and find you already have Communism."*

An Ancient Capital

The ancient imperial city of Hue had remained untouched through most of the war, until the French gave up and left Vietnam. As the ancient imperial capital and cradle of Vietnamese history and culture, Hue stood as a tremendous psychological prize in the struggle for control of that beleaguered country.

The Battle of Hue, from January 31 to March 2, 1968 and also called the Siege of Hue, was a major military engagement in the Tết Offensive launched by North Vietnam and the Việt Cộng during the Vietnam War. After initially losing control of most of Hue and its surroundings, the combined South Vietnamese and American forces gradually recaptured the city during one month of intense fighting.

"I'll never date a Marine again…"

As our flight of three approached the once-beautiful, now-bombed ancient city of Hue, I thought about a young woman who had turned me down for a date. I met her while I was in advanced weapons training at Camp Pendleton, California. She had been engaged to a Marine Lieutenant and they had planned on getting married when he returned from Vietnam. Tragically, he was killed at the Battle of Hue during the Tet Offensive in 1968.

She was a friend of a friend and every time I asked her out she would respond politely and with deep sadness saying, "I'll never date a Marine again." And as far as I know she never did, and she never married. The wound in her heart never healed.

America Was Winning

In 1972, my co-pilot and I played "tourist" and visited the more famous battle sites of Hue. Our guide was a South Vietnamese Marine major who fought alongside the U.S. Marines in taking back Hue. It was with the same deep sadness that I had seen in the young woman who'd lost her love that our guide said, "The battle for Hue was a turning point. The Tet Offensive of 1968 broke the back of the Viet Cong and the North Vietnamese Army. America was winning."

"What happened?" my co-pilot asked.

"The American press turned against America. After Tet, American journalists reported and photographed atrocity after atrocity, turning Americans against the war... just as America was winning. Your journalists showed the atrocities committed by your side, but not the atrocities of the VC. They reported nothing about the bravery of your young men and there were many very brave young Americans. Your doctors and nurses in field hospitals were saints. But your press made America look like the enemy. Your press won the war for the communists."

Just then, a U.S. Army jeep pulled up and two American civilians stepped out. "Are you Marines?" asked one of them.

"Yes, we are," my co-pilot replied. "Who are you?"

"We're reporters. What are you Marines doing here?"

"Fighting a war," I said sarcastically.

"Marines are not supposed to be here," the reporter stated.

"I know. We're not here," smirked my co-pilot. "We'll be back on board our carrier tonight. As long as we do not remain in Vietnam overnight, technically we're not here."

"What carrier?" asked one of the reporters.

My co-pilot and I went silent. We knew the reporters wanted to know what ship we were off of, what squadron, why we were on land, and most importantly, who was our passenger. So, we shut up. Our passenger was a one-star Marine General and the other passengers in the second aircraft were his staff. The General and his staff were in Hue planning the next offensive, an offensive that would become known as the second battle for Quang Tri.

The two reporters were insistent, intimidating. They wanted to know more than they needed to know, and more than we were willing to share. Although the four of us were all Americans, it was clear to me that we were not on the same side. We flipped the reporters our middle fingers and turned as we continued our tour of Hue with the Vietnamese major.

The Battle for Quang Tri

We flew the one-star Marine General back to our battle group and the planning for the next battle began. As we are taught:

PARABELLUM: *"If you want peace... prepare for war."*

The Battle for Quang Tri began on June 28, 1972 and lasted 81 days until September 16. During the second battle for Quang Tri, South Vietnam's Army (ARVN) defeated the North Vietnamese Army (PAVN) at the ancient citadel at Quảng Trị.

Bitter Memories

I mention the battles, victories, and the price paid at Hue and Quang Tri during the Tet Offensive in 1968 because America was winning in Vietnam. We paid the price of war — in blood, death, and broken hearts. The bitterness amongst many U.S. Vietnam vets stems from the realization that America defeated America. American media turned Americans against our troops in the field.

That realization made me take a hard look at the definition of *treason* — *"the crime of betraying one's country."*

If you have a chance to talk to a Vietnam veteran, ask him what it felt like to have his country turn against him.

Academic Elites

America's academic elite, our incompetent leaders in Washington D.C., killed more American troops than the Viet Cong and NVA. As Thomas Sowell states:

"Brainy folks were also present in Lyndon Johnson's administration, especially in the Pentagon, where Secretary of Defense Robert McNamara's brilliant 'whiz kids' tried to micro-manage the Vietnam war, with disastrous results."

At Kings Point, our economics teacher had our class study Alfred, Lord Tennyson's poem, *The Charge of the Light Brigade.* Here's how Wikipedia describes that poem:

"The Charge of the Light Brigade was a failed military action involving the British light cavalry led by Lord Cardigan against Russian forces during the Battle of Balaclava on 25 October 1854 in the Crimean War. Lord Raglan had intended to send the Light Brigade to prevent the Russians from removing captured guns from overrun Turkish positions, a task for which the light cavalry were well-suited. However, there was miscommunication in the chain of command and the Light Brigade was instead sent on a frontal assault against a different artillery battery, one well-prepared with excellent fields of defensive fire. The Light Brigade reached the battery under withering direct fire and scattered some of the gunners, but they were forced to retreat immediately, and the assault ended with very high British casualties and no decisive gains.

"The events were the subject of Alfred, Lord Tennyson's narrative poem "The Charge of the Light Brigade" (1854), published just six weeks after the event. Its lines emphasize the valour of the cavalry in bravely carrying out their orders, regardless of the nearly inevitable outcome. Responsibility for the miscommunication has remained controversial, as the order was vague and Louis Edward Nolan delivered the written orders with some verbal interpretation, then died in the first minute of the assault."

Teaching Leadership

Kings Point has been recognized as one of the top schools for teaching leadership. Our economics teacher spent many hours teaching leadership by having students discuss poems such as Tennyson's *The Charge of the Light Brigade, a* poem on the price of a leader's miscommunication to his troops.

Charge of the Light Brigade by Alfred Lord Tennyson

Half a league, half a league,
Half a league onward,
All in the valley of Death
Rode the six hundred.
'Forward, the Light Brigade!
Charge for the guns!' he said:
Into the valley of Death
Rode the six hundred.

'Forward, the Light Brigade!'
Was there a man dismay'd?
Not tho' the soldier knew
Some one had blunder'd:
Their's not to make reply,
Their's not to reason why,
Their's but to do and die:
Into the valley of Death
Rode the six hundred.

Cannon to right of them,
Cannon to left of them,
Cannon in front of them
Volley'd and thunder'd;
Storm'd at with shot and shell,
Boldly they rode and well,
Into the jaws of Death,
Into the mouth of Hell
Rode the six hundred.

Flash'd all their sabres bare,
Flash'd as they turn'd in air
Sabring the gunners there,
Charging an army, while
All the world wonder'd:
Plunged in the battery-smoke

Right thro' the line they broke;
Cossack and Russian
Reel'd from the sabre-stroke
Shatter'd and sunder'd.
Then they rode back, but not
Not the six hundred.

Cannon to right of them,
Cannon to left of them,
Cannon behind them
Volley'd and thunder'd;
Storm'd at with shot and shell,
While horse and hero fell,
They that had fought so well
Came thro' the jaws of Death,
Back from the mouth of Hell,
All that was left of them,
Left of six hundred.

When can their glory fade?
O the wild charge they made!
All the world wonder'd.
Honour the charge they made!
Honour the Light Brigade,
Noble six hundred!

U.S. corporate "fake media," the liberal elite of Silicon Valley, and the NEA should study this poem. It makes more sense than Critical Race Theory and gender pronouns. America and the world are in need of leaders who *unite with courage* rather than leaders who *divide with hate.*

Into the Valley of Death

In 1972, the Battle of Quang Tri was the first major offensive in which our squadron engaged. Due to a policy of Vietnamization, which meant teaching the Vietnamese to fight for themselves, the South Vietnamese did most of the ground fighting. The U.S. Air Force, Army, Navy, and Marines fought in support. The Air Force dropped bombs from their B-52s, the Navy fired their 16-inch cannons from their ships, and the Army Cobra helicopters flew in close ground support. Our Marine squadron provided the large helicopter troop transports to deliver the South Vietnamese Marines into the zone.

As I've stated earlier, the NVA had a new weapon, the SA-7, a shoulder-fired, heat-seeking rocket. As I've said, as pilots, we knew our training was obsolete. Our new flying tactics were untested. In theory, it all sounded good. But we would now be tested, flying and fighting from tree-top level.

At Camp Pendleton during advanced weapons training, the first time I flew an aircraft with machine guns and rockets, we had been trained to fight flying in from 1,500 feet, above enemy small arms fire. From 1,500 feet pilots have more time and can see everything. At tree-top level everything changes: aircraft are closer, response time is measured in split seconds, and communication must be more precise.

During one of the battles of Quang Tri, the U.S. Air Force, Navy, and Army pounded the LZ, the landing zone where the Marine troop transport helicopters were to land, inserting the South Vietnamese Marines.

Everything was going as planned. Air Force B-52s dropped their bombs, the Navy's cannons shelled the same LZ the Air Force was bombing, and Army Cobra helicopters were flying gun cover for the Marine heavy troop transport helicopters, filled with South Vietnamese Marines and soldiers.

As I said, we were untested. One of the CH-53s, a Jolly Green Giant flying at tree-top level, suddenly "popped up" and began climbing for altitude. The giant aircraft was filled with 62 South Vietnamese Marines and loaded with weapons. Why the pilot did what he did, no one knows. All we saw was the Jolly Green, loaded with troops, struggling to gain altitude. Suddenly a flash and puff of white smoke appeared from the tree line. A tiny rocket twisted and turned, seeking the heat trail from the exhaust of the CH-53. Once the tiny rocket crossed the heat trail, the rocket turned, tracked, flew up the 53's jet engine's exhaust, and exploded. The giant troop transport twisted, banked, and spun into the ground, killing all 62 South Vietnamese Marines and the four U.S. Marine crew chiefs and gunners on board.

U.S. Army Cobras covered the downed pilots with suppressive fire until a Marine CH-46 landed, picked up the two pilots and carried them back to the carrier.

Nobody knows why the pilot of the CH-53 "popped up." He had nothing to say. He appeared delirious. Following the incident, he was often seen walking the passageways of the ship, shaking his head, mumbling to himself. When our carrier group returned to the Philippines, this pilot was taken off rotation and a new FNG, fresh from flight school, replaced him.

Low-cost technology and low-cost training had defeated the weapons of the most powerful, most expensive, and most well-trained military in world history.

Welcome Home

Six months later, in January of 1973, my aircraft taxied up to the gate of North Air Force Base in California. As I have written earlier in this book we were greeted by thousands of American hippies, throwing eggs at us, spitting on us, calling us "baby killers."

America's news media had turned America against America. That is the power and the freedom of the press.

As Marx warned:
> *"Democracy is the road to socialism."*

In the 1960s men were burning their draft cards... and women were burning their bras. The Feminist movement had begun. According to 2020 U.S. Census Bureau, out of about 11 million single-parent families with children under the age of 18, 80 percent were headed by single mothers. Most teachers — stats put the percent at about 77 percent in traditional public schools and charter schools — are women. It's been reported that there are teachers who encourage students to 'choose their gender' at age five.

In the 1960s, a popular TV show was *Father Knows Best,* starring Robert Young. In the 1980s came *Married with Children* with Al Bundy, a hapless shoe salesman, as the central male figure. In 1988 *Roseanne,* starring Roseanne Barr, took the top spot in family sitcoms.

In 2020, young men have fewer positive male remodels. This may be why more and more women are saying, "There just aren't any men."

The Feminist Movement

In 1963, Betty Friedan's book *The Feminine Mystique* captured the frustration and the despair of a generation of college-educated housewives who felt trapped and unfulfilled.

Friedan's writing largely spoke to an audience of educated, upper-middle-class white women. Her work had such an impact that it is credited with sparking the "second wave" of the American feminist movement, women seeking equality with men.

In 2016, Hillary Clinton almost filled that dream. Unfortunately, Donald Trump spoiled the Liberal Elite's plan of having a black President, Barack Obama, followed by a female President, Hillary Clinton.

The Liberal Elite learned their lesson. The liberal academic elite are very smart. While the Republicans ran Trump and Pence — two "white-guys" — in 2020, the Democrats ran an aging white guy with a powerful black woman, a woman many expect could be the next President.

The Democrats are smart. They followed Marx's advice on how to win. As Marx taught:

> *"Everyone who knows anything of history also knows that great social revolutions are impossible without the feminine ferment. Social progress can be measured exactly by the social position of the fair sex (plain ones included)."*

A key concept of the feminist movement are the words *toxic masculinity*. Marx would probably agree, as more and more women seem to be getting behind those words.

Here's a Pop Quiz: Women say there are three types of men:
1. Nice guys
2. Bad boys
3. Wimps

Is Donald Trump a nice guy, a bad boy or a wimp? What about Joe Biden? Nice guy, or bad boy... or a wimp?

The Power of the Press

Vogue has been a leading magazine on fashion for over 100 years. Over those ten decades they have run a front cover story on every First Lady in U.S. history. The July 2021 issue of *Vogue* featured First Lady Jill Biden, an accomplished and attractive woman and wife of President Joe Biden.

Yet, *Vogue* snubbed Donald Trump's wife, Melania, who is a beautiful woman and a former model. What are we to make of that fact?

Was Marx correct when he wrote about women's upheaval? Should first lady Melania Trump have graced the cover of *Vogue*, or has woman's power and beauty gone totally political?

It makes you wonder if the first First Husband will be on *Vogue*'s cover. Will *Vogue* be that elite, that liberal and that politically... correct?

Who Has Killed the Most People?

One of the favorite quotes of my teacher at the academy was by Victor Hugo who said:

> "You have enemies? Good. That means you've stood up for something, sometime in your life."

In 1992, in the movie *A Few Good Men,* Jack Nicholson, playing Marine Colonel Nathan Jessup, delivered classic core Marine Corps truths:

Jack Nicholson: "You want answers?"

Tom Cruise: "I WANT THE TRUTH!

Jack Nicholson: "YOU CAN'T HANDLE THE TRUTH!"

(Pause)

Jack Nicholson: "Son, we live in a world that has walls, and those walls have to be guarded by men with guns. Who's gonna do it? You? You, Lt. Weinberg?

"I have a greater responsibility than you could possibly fathom. You weep for Santiago, and you curse the Marines. You have that luxury. You have the luxury of not knowing what I know; that Santiago's death, while tragic, probably saved lives. And my existence, while grotesque and incomprehensible to you, saves lives.

"You don't want the truth because deep down in places you don't talk about at parties, you want me on that wall. You need me on that wall.

"We use words like honor, code, loyalty. We use these words as the backbone of a life spent defending something.

"You use them as a punchline.

"I have neither the time nor the inclination to explain myself to a man who rises and sleeps under the blanket of the very freedom that I provide, and then questions the manner in which I provide it! I would rather you just said, "thank you" and went on your way, Otherwise, I suggest you pick up a weapon and stand a post. Either way, I don't give a damn what you think you are entitled to!"

The Southern Border Wall

President Biden and Vice President Harris should have watched this movie before they stopped construction on President Trump's southern border wall, opening the border to anyone, including sex and drug traffickers.

On the topic of Trump's wall and America's southern border, it seems the Democrats have taken a page out of Lenin's playbook on how to win elections. Lenin warned:

"One of the chief symptoms of every revolution is the sharp and sudden increase in the number of ordinary people who take an active, independent and forceful interest in politics."

Are the Democrats opening the Southern border to gain more voters?

The Truth

I'll pose the question again: Who has killed the most people? Socialists? Capitalists? Fascists? Or Marxists?

We have all heard of the 6 million Jews Hitler exterminated in his "Final Solution." While tragic, that is not what we were taught in military school. Our economics teacher went further, and deeper into the truth.

In the *Black Book of Communism: Crimes, Terror, and Repression,* authors Stephane Courtois, Andrzej Paczkowski, and Karel Bartosek opened the archives in the former Soviet Union to reveal "the truth" about socialism, communism, and fascism — truths many people already knew, but our media refused to report.

That book reports on the terror, torture, famine, mass deportations, and massacres in amazing detail. Estimates vary, but communism is responsible for the deaths of up to 100 million people. The book covers Josef Stalin's Great Purge, Mao's famines, and Pol Pot's killing fields.

The authors estimate the deaths by country or region are as follows:

- China   65 million deaths
- Soviet Union   20 million deaths
- North Korea   2 million deaths
- Cambodia   2 million deaths
- Vietnam   1 million deaths
- Africa: 1.7 million deaths
- Afghanistan   1.5 million deaths
- Eastern Europe   1 million deaths
- Latin America   150,000 deaths

Nazis… and the Japanese

Adolf Hitler's Nazis, the National Socialist German Workers' Party, put to death 6 million Jews and an estimated 12 million more minorities such as gypsies and slavs.

From the invasion of China in 1937 to the end of World War II, the Japanese military regime murdered between 3,000,000 to over 10,000,000 people, most probably almost 6,000,000 Chinese, Indonesians, Koreans, Filipinos, and Indochinese, among others, including Western prisoners of war.

Our politically correct press, teachers, and politician do not want us to know the truth. Which begs the question: Why?

Because they can't handle the truth. As Nicholson stated in *A Few Good Men*:

> *"You don't want the truth because deep down in places you don't talk about at parties, you want me on that wall. You need me on that wall.*
>
> *"We use words like honor, code, loyalty. We use these words as the backbone of a life spent defending something.*
>
> *"You use them as a punchline."*

CHAPTER FIVE

WHERE HAVE ALL OUR HEROES GONE?

"A hero is an ordinary individual who finds the strength to persevere and endure in spite of overwhelming obstacles."
— Christopher Reeve (1952-2004)
Superman

"It's a bird... It's a plane... It's Superman!" Christopher Reeve became an icon playing Superman in a number of movies. In 1995 he broke his neck, jumping horses. Paralyzed for life, he then became a real-life Superman, inspiring millions as a real human — a Man of Spiritual Steel.

In this chapter, I ask the question "Where have all our heroes gone?

President John F. Kennedy

On Friday, November 22, 1963, I was sitting in class, excited about an upcoming football game. I had finally made the varsity team and was excited about playing on Saturday. Suddenly, we heard the voice of the principal of our school over the intercom. He announced:

"President John F. Kennedy was assassinated today in Dallas, Texas."

The football game was cancelled. And the world mourned.

Remembering Where We Were

It is said we all remember where we were on certain dates. For example, most people today remember where they were on September 11, 2001. Kim and I were in Rome, Italy and learned of the 9/11 attacks from the news on a television set in our hotel room. We spent two days wandering around Rome in shock. Three days later, we were in Istanbul, addressing a group of over a thousand Muslims, teaching them about entrepreneurship and capitalism. It was a delicate three-hour talk. I began by saying, "I am afraid I do not know what a Muslim is. I believe this is the start of our problems." I believe that telling the truth is better than trying to be PC, politically correct.

Friday, November 22, 1963 left many of my generation, the Baby-Boomer generation, with a shock that has lasted a lifetime. If you ask anyone my age where they were the day President Kennedy was assassinated, odds are they will remember exactly where they were and what they were doing.

Dr. Martin Luther King, Jr.

On April 4, 1968, I was a second classman (junior) at Kings Point, with one more year until graduation. I had been out on Long Island Sound with our rowing team, practicing for an upcoming race against New York Maritime Academy, our rival from across the Sound. As we were hoisting our boats out of the water and putting the oars away, someone said, "Did you hear... Martin Luther King was killed today."

We were not allowed access to television sets and connection to the outside world was limited. Yet, Dr. King's death was one of those moments I will never forget... where I was and what I was doing.

On June 5, 1968, Robert Kennedy was assassinated. The class of 1968 had graduated early because the Vietnam war needed more merchant ships officers. The pay, double pay for sailing into the war zone, was on everyone's mind. A few were earning $120,000, tax-free, if they stayed in the war zone.

The class of 1969 also wanted to graduate early and make some war-zone pay. I remember sitting in the first-class war room, a room with a television set, when pictures of Robert Kennedy bleeding out on the floor of the Ambassador Hotel in Los Angeles made the morning news. All I could say was "Not again." What was happening in America?

Abraham, Martin and John

In 1968, a song that seemed to resonate with what so many people were feeling was *Abraham, Martin and John*, written by Dick Holler. It was first recorded by Dion, and later, in1969, by Marvin Gaye.

It is a tribute to the memory of four assassinated Americans, all icons of social change: Abraham Lincoln, Martin Luther King Jr., John F. Kennedy, and Robert F. Kennedy. It was written in response to the assassination of King and that of Robert Kennedy in April and June of1968, respectively. The lyrics reflect the sentiment of the '60s... and ask if "anybody here" has seen our old friends — Abraham, Martin, John... and Bobby.

It does seem the good die young. President John Kennedy was 46 years old; Dr. Martin Luther King, Jr. was only 39 years old. Bobby Kennedy was 42 and Abraham Lincoln was 56.

As the song asks:
> *Didn't you love the things that they stood for?*
> *Didn't they try to find some good for you and me?*
> *And we'll be free...*

I did love them. As a young man I did look up to them. They were great men. They were real leaders.

To me, Abraham Lincoln was a hero, a leader who freed the slaves and kept a nation united.

To me, the Kennedy brothers and Martin Luther King, Jr. were living American heroes.

As President Kennedy challenged us at his inauguration:
> *"Ask not what your country can do for you; ask what you can do for your country."*

Martin Luther King, Jr. proposed his dream for the future of America:

"I have a dream that my four little children will one day live in a nation where they will not be judged by the color of their skin but by the content of their character."

Robert Kennedy words of wisdom were:

"There are those that look at things the way they are, and ask why? I dream of things that never were, and ask why not?"

And Abraham Lincoln warned:

"The philosophy of the school room in one generation will be the philosophy of government in the next."

In 1967, I was sailing as a student/midshipman on cargo ships, out of San Francisco. In the streets of San Francisco, I was witnessing the Summer of Love and the hippie culture centered in Haight-Ashbury.

One of the top songs of 1967 was sung by Scott McKenzie, titled *If You're Going to San Francisco.*

In 1969, I graduated from Kings Point. I was hired by Standard Oil of California, a dream job. The problem was, the Vietnam war was still being fought and the lessons on communism vs. capitalism from my teacher at Kings Point haunted me.

In June of 1969, I was a third mate sailing on an oil tanker. Although I was making a lot of money, for a 22-year-old, I felt guilty about something. I was conflicted. Sailing across the Pacific, I kept listening to Dion singing *Abraham, Martin and John.* I was also listening to Scott McKenzie singing *If You're Going to San Francisco.* The more I listened to those songs, the more the conflict inside me grew.

In October of 1969, I resigned from Standard Oil.

In October of 1969 I drove from San Francisco to the U.S. Naval Air Station at Pensacola, Florida... my first step toward reconciling the feelings that were haunting me.

In January of 1973, nearly four years later and feeling the backlash of an unpopular war, I was spit on and hit with eggs when I arrived back in San Francisco.

As Scott McKenzie had warned:
> *"All across the nation*
> *Such a strange vibration*
> *People in motion*
> *There's a whole generation*
> *With a new explanation"*

And as Lincoln had warned:
> *"The philosophy of the school room in one generation will be the philosophy of government in the next."*

Why People Are Leaving California
In 2019, for the seventh straight year, more people left California than moved into that state, according to new census data. More than 86,000 people left California for Texas, nearly 70,000 left for Arizona, and about 55,000 left for Washington.

In 2020 California homicides surged 31%.

In 2020 California new gun sales skyrocketed.

In 2020 California renters were locked out of 7,677 homes despite the ban on evictions.

In 2020, nationwide, more than half of the people experiencing homelessness reside in California.

Pop City

In the 1970s, I was in the rock and roll business. My company produced nylon wallets, caps and bags, with rock stars' logos silk-screened on them. San Francisco was Pop City. It was the heart of rock and roll. In the 1970s, I spent a lot of time in San Francisco, working with Winterland Arena, a powerhouse in the rock and roll industry. It was through Winterland that I secured the licensing rights for the bands such as the Grateful Dead, the Police, and Duran Duran.

December 31, 1978, an extraordinary event took place at Post and Steiner streets in San Francisco as more than 5,000 Deadheads gathered with their favorite band to pay tribute and bid farewell to one of the most beloved music venues in the Bay Area, Bill Graham's historic Winterland Arena. Rock and roll was dying and Disco was on its way in.

Poop City

In the 2000s, San Francisco has become known for different things. Today it's called Poop City.

Since 2011, the San Francisco Department of Public Works started tracking the number of reports and complaints about feces on public streets and sidewalks. The data is open source and used to create graphs like this one.

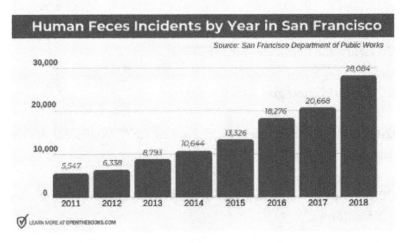

Source: San Francisco Department of Public Works

The graph depicts the year-over-year number of citizen reports of human feces in the city. It certainly seems like it's getting worse. In fact, the number of people defecating on the streets between 2001 and 2018 has increased by over 400%. This is confirmed by many news headlines reporting on this graph when it was first released.

The New Kremlin

Many of those hippies who spit on our troops when we returned to the states wound up in the NEA, the National Education Association, the California University system, and in what's been called "the new Kremlin," headquartered in Silicon Valley. Long before Silicon Valley became what some have called America's Kremlin, a beacon of socialism, fascism and communism, we were warned.

Two influential authors who warned us wrote great books such as *Atlas Shrugged, Animal Farm,* and *1984.* Unfortunately, those books are not found in the Kremlin in Moscow nor are they found in the California Kremlin, the NEA's library, the California University School system, and Silicon Valley's libraries.

Atlas Shrugged

Ayn Rand (1905-1982) was a Russian-born American writer, famous for her books *Atlas Shrugged* and *The Fountainhead.* Ayn warned:

> *"There is no difference between communism and socialism, except in the means of achieving the same ultimate end: communism proposes to enslave men by force, socialism — by vote. It is merely the difference between murder and suicide."*

She also reminded us:

> *"The smallest minority on earth is the individual. Those who deny individual rights cannot claim to be defenders of minorities."*

Animal Farm **and** *1984*

George Orwell (1903-1950) was an English novelist and critic famous for his novels *Animal Farm* (1945) and *1984* (1949).

Orwell opposed Marxist's utopian views. He was an extreme critic of the dangers of totalitarian rule, as reflected in his book *Animal Farm*. His most famous quote from *Animal Farm* is:

"All animals are equal, but some animals are more equal than others."

Orwell also said:

"Free speech is my right to say... what you don't want to hear."

"The further society drifts from the truth... the more it will hate those who speak it."

"In a time of universal deceit... telling the truth is a revolutionary act."

"But if thought corrupts language, language can also corrupt thought."

"The most effective way to destroy people... is to deny and obliterate their own understanding of their history."

"The people will believe... what the media tells them they believe."

Khrushchev's 1959 warning came true in 2020:

"Your children's children will live under communism."

In 2020 the California Kremlin censored President Trump. In July 2021 he was still censored from Facebook.

In 2020, the "Big Pharma Kremlin," aka the CDC, Centers for Disease Control, censored medical doctors who dared question the legitimacy of COVID-19. Doctors have put their jobs on the line when their views were at odds with "the powers that be."

Bobby Kennedy's Son

When Robert Kennedy, Jr., son of assassinated Senator Robert Kennedy, was asked if he would advise his mother, 92-year-old Ethel Kennedy, widow of Robert Kennedy, to take the vaccine, he said:

"The Pfizer or Moderna vaccine? No, absolutely not."

Asked if he would tell her not to take the vaccines, he said, *"Of course. Look at the clinical trials."*

Bobby Kennedy, Jr. was banned from Instagram on February 11, 2021 not just because he raised informed questions about vaccines, Bill Gates, and Big Pharma, but because he suggested that something more dangerous was afoot: The demise of democracy and the rise of a totalitarian order.

The New York Times reinforced RFK Jr's banishment with a headline that read:

> *Robert Kennedy Jr. is barred from Instagram over false coronavirus claims.*

I thought it interesting that *The New York Times* decided Bobby Kennedy Jr's claims were false.

Follow the Money

The *NYT*'s coverage and position seemed fishy to me. Whenever something seemed fishy, rich dad often said:

> *"If you want to know the truth, follow the money."*

As Ayn Rand warned in *Atlas Shrugged*:

> *"Money is the barometer of a society's virtue. When you see that trading is done, not by consent, but by compulsion—when you see that in order to produce, you need to obtain permission from men who produce nothing—when you see that money is flowing to those who deal, not in goods, but in favors—when you see that men get richer by graft and by pull... than by work, and your laws don't protect you against them, but protect them against you—when you see corruption being rewarded and honesty becoming a self-sacrifice—you may know that your society is doomed."*

As George Orwell warned:

> *"Anyone who challenges the prevailing orthodoxy finds himself silenced with surprising effectiveness. A genuinely unfashionable opinion is almost never given a fair hearing, either in the popular press or in the highbrow periodicals."*

In Stalin's words:

> *"The press must grow day in and day out – it is our Party's sharpest and most powerful weapon."*

And what gave *The New York Times* the right to decide that Robert Kennedy's claims were false?

As Hitler said:

> *"Only the continuous and steady application of the methods of suppressing a doctrine, etc., makes it possible for a plan to succeed."*

In June of 2020, a *Washington Post* columnist tried her best to make a case that I am a racist. While I take exception with her tactics and what appeared to me to be pre-determined bias that supported a self-serving agenda, I respect her right — and the rights of all of us — to free speech.

Other questions I ask myself include these...

Who gave the CDC, Centers for Disease Control, the power to "shut down" the U.S. economy while allowing selected big business to remain open and crush the real capitalists of America, small business owners and entrepreneurs?

As Lenin warned:

> *"Medicine is the keystone of the arch of socialism."*

And Marx who said:

> *"The theory of communists may be summed up in the single sentence: Abolition of private property."*

And who gave the government the right to shut down places of worship, just when spiritual support was most needed?

As Marx said:

> *"The democratic concept of man is false, because it is Christian."*

Marx also said:

> *"We know... that violent measures against religion are nonsense; but this is an opinion: as Socialism grows, religion will disappear. Its disappearance must be done by social development, in which education must play a part."*

Revisiting the Khrushchev quote that opened this book:

> *"You Americans are so gullible. No, you won't accept* **communism** *outright, but we will keep feeding you small doses of* **socialism** *until you will finally wake up and find you already have Communism.*
>
> *"We will not have to fight you; We will so weaken your economy, until you will fall like overripe fruit into our hands."*

Heroes or Victims?

On May 25, 2020, George Floyd was killed by police officer Derek Chauvin. One man was black; the other white. The aftermath has had a devastating effect on race relations in America. But did George Floyd become a hero or a martyr?

George Floyd's death, while tragic, hardly makes him a hero like John Kennedy, Bobby Kennedy, or Martin Luther King, Jr.... although many people seem to want to elevate him to the same status. The facts are that George Floyd had a long criminal past.

The Union Chief of Minneapolis Police (MPD), Bob Kroll, released a statement on June 1, 2020, shedding light on the late George Floyd's "violent criminal history." The Union Chief wrote in a letter to his acquaintances and followers on Twitter:

> *"What is not being told is the violent criminal history of George Floyd. The media will not air this."*

He also said that the ongoing protests are results of a "terrorist movement." Chief of Police Bob Kroll is a brave man.

These words, often attributed to George Orwell, heralded a warning:

> *"In a time of universal deceit... telling the truth is a revolutionary act."*

The Facts

In 2009, George Floyd was arrested for a first-degree felony charge, as per police criminal records, and for assault and armed robbery that he took part in 2007 and spent five years in prison for breaking into a woman's home. George confirmed that he wore a blue uniform to look like a government employee to gain the woman's trust, and eventually, gain access into the house.

Hennepin County medical examiners released the toxicology report on June 2, 2020, which stated that George Floyd was indeed intoxicated with Fentanyl, Methamphetamine, and traces of cannabinoids and morphine in his system at the time of his death. However, these were not termed the principal factors behind Floyd's death. Floyd has an extensive criminal past related to the drug trade and drug use and felonies. I present this information not to "make a case" or as "mitigating circumstances," but only to point to the bias — often via omissions — in how "news" today is covered and reported.

Nothing to Gain... Everything to Lose

In 2020 we entered this period of universal deceit. I have nothing to gain by writing these words of the human tragedy surrounding George Floyd and I have quite a lot to lose.

Yet I look to this wisdom of Thomas Sowell who said:
> *"If you are not prepared to use force to defend civilization, then be prepared to accept barbarism."*

Edmund Burke (1729-1797) was an Irish statesman, economist, and philosopher. Born in Dublin, Burke served as a member of parliament between 1765 and 1794 in the House of Commons of Great Britain.

And while the attribution on these words — often credited to Burke — is often disputed, the words themselves, words of courage, are a call to action:
> *"All that is required for evil to triumph is for good men to do nothing."*

The words of Dr. Martin Luther King, Jr. speak to the same point:
"Our lives begin and end the day we become silent about the things that matter."

As I've said, I have little to gain by questioning the coverage of George Floyd's death or his status as a hero. In military school and in the Marine Corps we were taught that living a life of courage is far more important — and more gut-wrenching — than living a life as a coward. It takes courage to stand on the edge of a coin, as a perspective on an issue or a belief, and look objectively at both sides, both points of view. I could not live with myself if I continued to participate in a deception or looked at this tragedy — or any issue or controversy — from only one point of view.

I know that I'm not the first to question the actions of the California Kremlin in suppressing the truth. Anyone with an open mind, in search of facts and truth, would ask: Why does the California Kremlin attack Bobby Kennedy, Jr. for criticizing vaccines, only to sanctify Bill Gates and his mass vaccination policies?

Defunding the Police
Why does Silicon Valley's California Kremlin want to defund the police? Why are they portraying our police as the bad guys... just as they did the men and women who fought in Vietnam?

The real martyr in 2020 is Derek Chauvin, the police officer convicted of murder, and three other police officers prosecuted for doing their jobs. Jobs that required that they put their lives on the line, every day.

Shore Patrol
In 1972, all pilots were required to work on Shore Patrol while in port. A patrol consisted of a lieutenant, a NCO, non-commissioned officer such as a staff sergeant, and two enlisted men. The NCO and two enlisted men carried night sticks and hand cuffs. Officers were armed with a whistle.

Olongapo, in the Philippines, is often called "Sin City." During the Vietnam war there might be 20 to 30 ships in port and tens of thousands of marines and sailors in bars, restaurants, and night clubs on a mile-long street, Olongapo. The clubs, rock bands, beer, and women were just what U.S. servicemen wanted. On any given night, "Sin City" was jumping.

I actually liked being on Shore Patrol because I saved money. I couldn't drink, and the action on the streets was more exciting than the movies on board the carrier.

Our Job One was to stop a break-out of any "insanity" as rapidly as possible. Our job was to get the situation under control as quickly as possible before it spread throughout the city. No one wanted Olongapo to be a series of drunken brawls, with chairs being thrown, people being beaten and sometimes slashed with broken San Miguel beer bottles.

If anything happened, the NCO and two enlisted Marines were to go into the brawl, break it up with night sticks to get the fight under control as quickly as possible. My job was to run into the street and blow my whistle as frantically as possible. Not a dangerous job. My whistle brought the real MPs, the military police with the paddy wagon who got the fighting sailors or marines in the back of the wagon and into the brig, back on base. The party in "Sin City" roared on... and we were on duty.

If you think the job is easy, you're delusional. It's high-speed brute force efficiency.

One night in Hong Kong, another fun city, I returned to Shore Patrol headquarters to write my report and turn in my whistle. In the cell was a Marine about the size of George Floyd. He started to act up and demanded to be released. One of my enlisted Marines walked up to the cell and rapped his night stick on the bars, telling the Marine to settle down.

The sound of the night stick on the metal bars only enraged the Marine in the cell. He grabbed the bars, screamed, and tore the cell door off its hinges.

He then charged, like the Incredible Hulk, into the cramped Shore Patrol headquarters. The enraged Marine began picking up men and tossing them around the room. Finally, it took five Marines to get one Marine on the ground. I was one of the five, holding this giant man down.

That was the first and only time I had to do what police officers do every day. It was not easy. That one Marine had more strength than five Marines. It was terrifying.

It was only later that I discovered why the Marine was able to pull the cell door off its hinges. Apparently, when the Shore Patrol headquarters was built, the cell was a fake cell. It was only a wooden room with a door of iron bars. When the Marine grabbed the door and roared, he did not turn into Superman. The door came off because the metal bars were only bolted into the wood frame. The Shore Patrol headquarters in Hong Kong were very much like a Hollywood movie set.

In 2020, when I saw photos of officer Derek Chauvin, with his knee on George Floyds neck, memories of that night in Hong Kong came rushing back. George Floyd was 46 years old, a big man, standing 6 foot-6 inches tall and weighing approximately 240 pounds. If you think you can hold him down, good luck. Only trained police officers would take on a big man like George Floyd. I wouldn't want to do it, risking my life every day, especially in rough neighborhoods where police are demonized and hated.

My economics teacher at Kings Point warned us about Hitler's defunding of the police.

> *"In 1933 Hitler appointed Hermann Göring Minister of the Interior. His first orders were to defund and eliminate the police departments so that they would not interfere with his Brown Shirts. The Brown Shirts' mission was to riot, burn, beat up and kill citizens in an effort to sway the elections to ensure their National Socialist agenda."*

In 2020, is there a 'National Socialist Party' sitting in America's academic elite strongholds known as universities, as the people behind the movement to defund the police? Is history repeating itself?

What Leaders Want to Defund the Police?

The list is longer than you might expect...

Ilhan Omar, a Democratic congresswoman from Minnesota who called for the dismantling of the Minneapolis police department, stated in a tweet that defunding the police means removing funds given from police departments and allocating it to other segments of the community.

Rashida Tlaib, a Michigan Democratic Congresswoman tweeted out her sentiments for what defunding the police means: "When we say #DefundPolice, what we mean is people are dying and we need to invest in people's livelihoods instead."

Alexandria Ocasio-Cortez, Democratic Congresswoman, of New York, criticized the New York City police budget: "It truly boggles my mind how anyone can see a $6 billion policing budget in ONE city alone – which is more than we spend on health, youth, housing, and homelessness services here *combined* – and say, 'You know what will fix police brutality? More money.'

George Soros's Open Society Foundations is one of the groups behind the "defund the police" movement taking place across America. The Soros-affiliated group has been part of the "defund the police" movement as far back as early 2016 – long before the death of George Floyd that brought that movement national attention.

Leaders Who See Police as Heroes

Not surprisingly, strong leaders who have supported "law and order" see police as heroes.

Donald Trump:

> *"Police are the most mistreated people in America."*

> *"Anybody killing policemen, policewoman, police officers... death penalty is going to happen."*

Rudy Giuliani:

> *"When they come to save your life, they don't ask if you are black or white, they just come to save you."*

We Can All Be Heroes

Personally, in these times of bitterness, acrimony, academic, racial, political, and economic divide, I prefer Christopher Reeve's definition of a hero.

> *"A hero is an ordinary individual who finds the strength to persevere and endure in spite of overwhelming obstacles."*

CHAPTER SIX

AMERICA'S POOR ARISTOCRATS

"The best way to crush the bourgeoise is to grind them between the millstones of taxation and inflation."
— Vladimir Lenin

During the Agrarian Age, there were three classes of people: aristocracy, bourgeoisie, and proletariat.

In the days of monarchies, kings and queens received their power from God. At least that's the story the peasants were told. Aristocrats were the friends and family of the king and queen.

Very few monarchies are left. England is one of them and Queen Elizabeth II has been queen of England since 1953. Her husband of 73 years, Prince Phillip, passed away, at age 99, on April 9, 2021.

Karl Marx (1818-1883) was born a Jew and became an atheist, who became a racist, like Hitler, who hated Jews. A number of people believe Karl Marx and Adolf Hitler (1889-1945) to be ideologically, economically, and politically on the same side of the same coin. They were racists, socialists, and nationalists.

Marx didn't seem too concerned about monarchies and aristocrats. Yet, Marx's disciples, Lenin, Stalin, Mao, and Khrushchev, all hated aristocrats. They murdered or starved to death millions of people. These murderous tyrants were all branches of the same tree, the Karl Marx tree.

Marxism-Leninism is the ideology that the Western academics call "communism." Marxism-Leninism holds that a two-stage communist revolution is required to replace capitalism.

Multiple sources describe the stages this way: In the first stage, a vanguard party infiltrates democracy, and begins its educational process. The ultimate goal of the vanguard party is to seize power "on behalf of the proletariat," the people of the working class, those oppressed by the bourgeoisie or the upper class. Once power was seized, on behalf of the "proletariat" a communist party "socialist state" would be established. The socialist state would control the economy and means of production and suppress the bourgeoise's counter revolution and any opposition. This would pave the way for the second stage.

The second stage would lay the foundation for a communist society that would evolve out of the socialist state. A communist society, the ideal of Marxism-Leninism, is a classless and stateless utopian world.

I write this book, *Capitalist Manifesto*, because I believe the United States and much of the Western World is approaching the last phase of the First Stage. We are at a point between the first stage and second stage. As soon as the liberals can "pack the Supreme Court" and get everyone to carry a vaccination card, the first stage will come to an end.

Just before Hitler took full control of Germany, and began his Final Solution, the extermination of the Jews, he began a series of Little Atrocities. Examples of Little Atrocities include requiring all businesses owned by Jews to place a sign on their door stating it was a Jewish business. This drove many businesses owned by Jews out of business. Another little atrocity was requiring all Jews to wear a yellow star on their clothing.

Then came concentration camps which turned into gas chambers, in support of the Final Solution, the extermination of the Jewish race.

The German people had been so desensitized with "little atrocities" that their will to resist, to fight, was weakened. Physically and emotionally devastated, the German people remained silent.

As Edmund Burke warned:

> *"The only thing necessary for evil to triumph is for good men to do nothing."*

In 2020 I began noticing little atrocities in my neighborhood. Businesses and churches put up Black Lives Matter signs. Gender pronouns altered our spoken language. Critical Race Theory was being required to be taught in schools. There are "safe spaces" in our schools, protecting students from uncensored ideas. Everyone was required to wear masks... and then double masks. There was speculation that vaccination cards might soon be required for travel. Freedom of speech is under attack and censorship prevails, organized by the "mob rules" on the web. A person is attacked viciously if their ideas are counter to the mob. The Kremlin of Silicon Valley decides which political party is allowed to express its views, what narratives are allowed, and who and what ideas are censored.

My concern is that capitalist's counter-revolution has begun, and a full-scale suppression of this counter-revolution is beginning.

Little atrocities lead to mass murder. Remember, Stage One is a "revolution of the proletariat," a revolution of the working class against the middle class.

We see that gun sales are up and it makes you wonder if people know what's coming. I ask myself: Is that why there is a yellow star in the corner of my new Arizona driver's license?

Years after Marx's death, his disciple Vladimir Lenin (1870-1924) had the Czar and his family of Russia murdered, during the Bolshevik Revolution, in 1918.

The 1917 Russian Revolution, which overthrew three centuries of tsarist rule, had its roots in Marxist beliefs. The revolution's leader, Vladimir Lenin, built his new proletarian government based on his interpretation of Marxist thought, turning Karl Marx into an internationally famous figure more than 30 years after his death.

Joseph Stalin, who followed Lenin into power, systematically murdered thousands in his own party, people on his side, just to attain absolute power via fear. In 1971, the murders had just begun.

It disturbs me that the leaders of Black Lives Matter admit to being followers of Marx.

Much like Black Lives Matter, Marx was most concerned about the struggle between the *bourgeoisie* and *proletariat*. The battle between rich and poor. According to Marx, the *bourgeoisie* hoarded the land, wealth, resources, and capital... all that, in his mind, belonged to the people. He used this socio-economic gap to incite hate and division, the fuel required for the murders to begin.

Karl Marx was an angry man. He was an intellectual, a smart man, but a poor one. He was a failure at making and managing money, and a failure in business. Apparently, he decided he would take up the cause of the *proletariat,* the working man, and vent his anger upon the *bourgeoise,* middle class capitalists.

In 2020 the Centers for Disease Control did a similar thing when they shut down small business but let select big businesses stay open during the pandemic.

Hitler hated Jews. Marx hated religions; he hated Jews, and Christians.

As Lenin said:
> *"We can and must write in a language which sows among the masses hate, revulsion, and scorn towards those who disagree with us."*

Critical Race Theory tracks with Lenin's warning.

The definition from the Critical Race Theory in Education website states, Critical Race Theory is:
> *"An outgrowth of the European Marxist school of critical theory, critical race theory is an academic movement which seeks to link racism, race, and power. Unlike the Civil Rights movement, which sought to work within*

the structures of American democracy, critical race theorists challenge *the very foundations of the liberal order, such as rationalism, constitutional law, and legal reasoning. Critical race theorists* argue *that American social life, political structures, and economic systems are founded upon race, which (in their view) is a social construct.*

"Systemic racism, in the eyes of critical race theorists, stems from the dominance of race in American life. Critical race theorists and anti-racist advocates argue that, because race is a predominant part of American life, racism itself has become internalized into the American conscious. It is because of this, they argue, *that there have been significantly different legal and economic outcomes between different racial groups."*

Critical Race Theory is supported by many institutions of higher education including: USC, UCLA, UC Santa Barbara, UC San Diego, UC Davis, UC Berkeley, Stanford University, Southwestern College, Santa Clara University, and San Jose State University.

My personal concern is that Critical Race Theory in Education fits Stage One of Marxism-Leninism: a vanguard party infiltrates democracy and begins its educational process.

Another part of Stage One is:
"The socialist state would control the economy and means of production and suppress the bourgeoise's counter revolution and any opposition."

In 2020 the CDC shut down churches at a time when millions needed spiritual support more than ever. Murder, suicide, and domestic violence escalated during the pandemic.

On May 22, 2020, The American Institute for Economic Research reported: *"California doctors say they've seen more deaths from suicide than coronavirus since lockdowns."*

A greater "little atrocity" is the number of doctors who have been fired for questioning the legitimacy of COVID-19. Like many Germans during Hitler's Final Solution, many doctors remain silent about their true thoughts on the validity of COVID-19 and the vaccines.

Blame the Capitalists!

Like many poor people, Marx blamed capitalists for his failures. Marx thought it was unfair that the *bourgeoise* came by their land and wealth from the blood, sweat, and tears of the *proletariat.*

His *Communist Manifesto* is about Stage Two: a communist society, the ideal classless and stateless, utopian world where everyone is equal. In 2020 America, Stage Two is "Everyone gets a trophy."

Marx's dream was that wealth — "the means of production" of the country — would be controlled by the state, a centrally controlled economy and government.

As Marx warned:
> *"The theory of Communism may be summed up in one sentence: Abolish all private property."*

Simply put, a communist state is a *centrally controlled* government and economy. No one owns anything. The state controls everything. Everyone is equal.

In his book *Animal Farm,* Orwell writes:
> *"All animals are equal… but some animals are more equal than others."*

I thought it was interesting to learn that Black Lives Matter co-founder and avowed Marxist, Patrisse Khan-Cullors, subscribes to Orwell's statement "… *some animals are more equal than others."* Some might call that racist.

Since coming to power in the organization's leadership and raising hundreds of millions from corporate sponsors in the name of Black Lives Matter,

Cullors purchased a luxury compound in Topanga Canyon, California for $1.4 million. She also reportedly purchased four other high-priced homes, spending in excess of $3.2 million, most located in wealthy, predominately white neighborhoods. She has also reportedly been considering property in the Bahamas at a pricy beachfront resort outside of Nassau. Condos in that development are priced between $5 million to $20 million.

As I've stated earlier in this book, Candance Owens is accomplished, articulate, and well-respected, and on the conservative side of the discussion. She is a black woman who has been forthright in saying:

"She (Cullors') has my respect because she's unapologetic in her approach. She is telling you what she is – she's a Marxist. Marxists steal money from other people and they enrich themselves... She has stolen money from other people on the pretext of a lie that is Black Lives Matter and she has enriched herself and she has bought four homes. You have to appreciate the honesty. She is not hiding by any means. She is a Communist through and through and she has been unbelievably unapologetic in her approach."

I support the freedom for BLM to say what they want to say. Personally, I am in the All Lives Matter camp. And, once again, putting a finer point on it: *All Life Matters.*

Have you wondered, as I have, why Black Lives Matter has had so much corporate support? One answer is that, much like Hitler had Jews place the word *Jew* on their places of business to keep Germans from doing business with them, corporations need to comply with BLM to ensure blacks continued to support their businesses. Another thought on this parallels the "protection money" organized crime is said to charge businesses... aka *virtue signaling* and *extortion.*

As Candace Owens states, Patrisse Khan-Cullors is "unapologetic in her approach."

As Orwell said about communism:
"Some animals are more equal than others."

Thomas Sowell warned:
> *"The welfare state is not really about the welfare of the masses. It is about the egos of the elites."*

Martin Luther King, Jr. said:
> *"Freedom is never voluntarily given by the oppressor; it must be demanded by the oppressed."*

Voltaire (1694-1778), a French historian and writer said:
> *"I do not agree with what you have to say, but I'll defend to the death your right to say it."*

Frederick Douglass (1818-1895), a man who escaped slavery and became an American social reformer, abolitionist, writer, and statesman, said:
> *"To suppress free speech is a double wrong. It violates the rights of the hearer as well as those of the speaker."*

Winston Churchill (1874-1965), Prime Minister of the United Kingdom, said:
> *"Everyone is in favour of free speech. Hardly a day passes without its being extolled, but some people's idea of it is that they are free to say what they like, but if anyone says anything back, that is an outrage."*

How Does Marxism Begin?

The First Stage of Marxism-Leninism began in America in 1913. As Marx said:
> *"The establishment of a central bank is 90% of communizing a nation."*

In 1913, The Federal Reserve Bank of America was founded. The Fed is a Central Bank. The Fed has the power to print money, which causes inflation. Also in 1913, the 16th Amendment was passed. The 16th Amendment gave the U.S. government the power to tax the people. Until that time America was fundamentally a tax-free nation, founded in 1773 during the Boston Tea Party, a tax revolt.

With the creation of the Federal Reserve Bank and the passing of the 16th Amendment, in 1913, the seeds of Marxism were sown.

As Lenin warned:
> *"The best way to crush the bourgeoise is to grind them between the millstones of taxation and inflation."*

The facts are America was founded in 1776 as an anti-central government, anti-central bank, anti-centrally controlled economy, and an anti-tax economy.

America is a Republic, not a monarchy; a Republic is decentralized, a monarchy is centralized.

George Washington was not seated as a king for life. He was America's first President, who stepped down from power after eight years in office.

Fast forward to August 15, 1971, when President Richard Nixon took the U.S. dollar off the gold standard. From that point on the U.S. dollar became fake money and the U.S. government could just print the money it needed to pay its bills.

Fast forward again to March of 2020... when the Federal Reserve Bank began printing $60 million every minute.

And repeating Lenin's warning:
> *"The best way to destroy the capitalist system is to debauch the currency."*

America was not founded in 1619 as a slave nation, as today's academic elites, Black Lives Matter, *New York Times*, and devotees of Critical Race Theory would like us to believe.

As Marx warned:
> *"Keep people from their history and they are easily controlled."*

In Hitler's words:

> *"All propaganda has to be popular and has to accommodate itself to the comprehension of the least intelligent of those whom it seeks to reach."*

And Orwell warned:

> *"The most effective way to destroy people is to deny and obliterate their own understanding of history."*

That is why tearing down statues that memorialized our history during the 2020 riots disturbed me so deeply.

Bye, Bye... American Pie

Consider these words from Don McLean's classic 1971 song:

> *"Oh, and while the King was looking down*
> *The jester stole his thorny crown"*

> *"The courtroom was adjourned*
> *No verdict was returned"*

In the 2020 presidential election, the voting rules were changed in the eleventh hour. The "verdict," like in the song, is still in dispute and the source of much frustration and distrust of the election process. Allegations still abound related to ballots from dead people, the lack of signature verifications, and numbers — of voters and absentee ballots and margins of error — as the United States prepares for 2022 mid-term elections.

As Stalin warned:

> *"It's not the people who vote that count. It's the people who count the votes."*

"And while Lenin read a book on Marx..."

As Candace Owens states when discussing Black Lives Matter's founder:

> *"She (Cullors') has my respect because she's unapologetic in her approach. She is telling you what she is – she's a Marxist. Marxists steal money from other people and they enrich themselves."*

Critical Race Theory in Education acknowledges being Marxist. Its website boasts that they studied the book of Marx stating:

> *"An outgrowth of the European Marxist school of critical theory, critical race theory is an academic movement which seeks to link racism, race, and power."*

The song *American Pie* ends with these words...

> *"The quartet practiced in the park*
> *And we sang dirges in the dark*
> *The day the music died."*

The Day America Died

In July of 2021, President Biden denied Independence Day fireworks displays over Mt. Rushmore.

And...

> *"We were singing Bye, Bye, Miss American Pie..."*

Repeating Marx's warning:

> *"Keep people from their history and they are easily controlled."*

And as Orwell — prophetically — warned:

> *"Who controls the past controls the future.*
> *Who controls the present controls the past."*

Our past is being changed by the academic elite, such as the *New York Times* that promotes changing America's founding to 1619 and that America is a systemically racist country.

All of this begs the question: Is Stage One of Marxism-Leninism nearly complete? And is the suppression of the bourgeoise's counter revolution about to begin?

More questions to consider:

> Is this why defunding the police is gaining in popularity?

Why do the academic elite want to attack the Second Amendment, banning gun sales? Is that why, in 2020, gun sales are soaring?

Do people know the Stage One is ending and the suppression is about to begin?

As Lenin warned:

"One man with a gun can control 100 without one."

Bitcoin to the Rescue

One reason why Bitcoin supporters are fanatical is because they too are against the words *central control*. Central control are the core words of Marxist philosophy.

Bitcoin fanatics are committed to saving capitalism from the central control of Marxism. Bitcoin-fanatics are "DeFi"... or Decentralized Finance.

As I've pointed out: the Federal Reserve Bank, U.S. Treasury, and Wall Street are Centralized Finance. The term *globalism*, popular with the liberal elite, is centralized world government.

Again, pay close attention to the words *central control*. They are far more a part of the Communist lexicon than Capitalist's vocabulary.

Rise of the Bourgeoisie

Bourgeoisie is a socio-economically defined class of modern society. Generally speaking, being bourgeoisie means belonging to the middle or upper middle class. The Agrarian Age of monarchies and aristocrats came to an end at the start of the Industrial Age. The golden age for aristocrats ended when the castle walls they hid behind were blown apart.

The Bitcoin Revolution Is On

The "gunpowder revolution" brought down the monarchs and aristocrats It began in Europe in the mid-1400s and was a development that would permanently transform the nature of warfare worldwide. Gunpowder, invented in China by the 9ᵗʰ century and brought to Europe in the 1200s, soon became the key ingredient in a revolution in ballistic (projectile-firing) weapons.

Entrepreneurs, industrialists armed with cannons and gunpowder, aimed their cannon at castle walls... and, as they say, "the rest is history." As monarchies, castles, and aristocratic families fell to canons and firepower, the bourgeoise — entrepreneurs who made the canon and gunpowder— rose to power. The gunpowder revolution, aka the Industrial Age, spread across the world.

The Bitcoin revolution will be bigger than the gunpower revolution.

The Last Samurai

The movie *The Last Samurai* starring Tom Cruise is a movie about this revolution. The samurai class, members of the aristocratic class of Japan, went to war using swords, while their opponents used guns, canons, and gunpowder. That is where the title of the movie *The Last Samurai* comes from. It was the end of the aristocrats, the friends and family of the Emperor of Japan.

My family is from the samurai class. Pictured below is my great, great, great, great uncle, with our family sword.

He was one of the *first* samurai photographed when Commodore Matthew Perry opened the door for trade with Japan in the 1850s. He may have been one of the first samurai photographed, but he was one of the last samurai. The industrialists, the bourgeoise, were the new rulers of Japan.

After Japan's defeat in World War II, the country rose to be an extremely

119

rich global powerhouse. Today, Japan has one of the worst economies in the world.

In 2021, Japan is on the verge of bankruptcy. Today, many Japanese continue to believe the Emperor of Japan is descendent of God.

Marx Hated the Bourgeoisie

The bourgeoisie is the social class that came to own the means of production, the factories, and the land. Marx believed all the bourgeoisie cared about was their economic supremacy in society.

Simply said: Marx thought the bourgeoisie were greedy, arrogant, and uncaring... and, even today, many are. Many would say that some of the worse live in Silicon Valley, Washington, DC, and on Wall Street. Many believe they are the new aristocracy and that they have the right to censor us, tell us what to do, what to think, and what to believe.

The aristocrats of Silicon Valley have achieved wealth and power, far beyond any king or queen of old. They are the cause of the growing economic gap between the middle class and poor.

The Politics of Marx

As the gap between rich and poor gets wider, many politicians run on Marxist philosophies. These politicians claim to hate *the bourgeoisie*, yet they themselves *are* the bourgeoisie. Two such politicians are U.S. Senator from Vermont and former Presidential candidate Bernie Sanders and U.S. Senator Elizabeth Warren from Massachusetts.

In Sanders' words:

> *"A nation will not survive morally or economically when, so few have so much and so many have so little."*

Senator Sanders' net worth is reported at nearly $3 million. He's made millions on his book deals.

Senator Elizabeth Warren from Massachusetts has said:

> *"If you don't have a seat at the table, you're probably on the menu."*

Senator Warren's net worth is reported to be $8.75 million.

Many politicians claim to be part of the "proletariat" and claim to speak for the proletariat, only because they want their vote. The facts are most of these fake-proletariat politicians receive their campaign funds from the aristocrats, America's monarchs with castles — today called *campuses* — in Silicon Valley, the towers in New York City, and Deep State of Washington, DC... financed by China.

Ayn Rand warned:

> *"When you see that trading is done, not by consent, but by compulsion... when you see that in order to produce, you need to obtain permission from men who produce nothing – when you see that money is flowing to those who deal, not in goods, but in favors – when you see that men get richer and pull – than by hard work, and laws don't protect you against them, but protect them against you – when your see corruption being rewarded – and honesty becoming self-sacrifice – you may know that your society is doomed."*

Thomas Sowell best describes politicians like Bernie and "Pocahontas" (Trump's jab at Warren for claiming to be American Indian) best, stating:

> *"In liberal logic, if life is unfair then the answer is to turn more tax money over to politicians... to spend in ways that will increase their chances of getting reelected."*

Thomas Sowell also warned:

> *"Helping those who have been struck by unforeseeable misfortunes... is fundamentally different from making dependency a way of life."*

And as Marx and members of the British Communist Party have warned:

> *"Democracy is the road to socialism."*

Help for the Proletariat

It's likely that we've all heard this adage:

> *"Give a man a fish, feed him for a day. Teach a man to fish, feed him for a lifetime."*

Karl Marx is said to have said:

> *"Catch a man a fish, and you can sell it to him. Teach a man to fish, and you ruin a wonderful business opportunity."*

Thomas Sowell's take:

> *"The more people who are dependent on government handouts, the more votes the left can depend on for an ever-expanding welfare state."*

Rich Dad's Capitalist Manifesto

The COVID-19 pandemic has triggered a wide variety of changes, with an important one being a new awareness of the part of parents all that "educating" their children in today's world entails. Many parents have home-schooled their children over the past year or two and have learned a lot — about their children, themselves, traditional education, the school system... and the power and responsibility they have as their child's most important teachers.

It is Rich Dad's position that the best way to beat communism taught in our schools is to teach capitalism in our homes. We at Rich Dad believe it is best to teach people to fish, at home.

Why at home? Because the environment in which children are raised, what they are exposed to, and the values a parent places on learning will shape their lives. Making a decision and a commitment to learrn about money at home is action any parent can take to counter a warning often attributed to Lenin: *"Give us the child for eight years and it will be a Bolshevik forever"*

And the risk of the ideological indoctrination that Thomas Sowell speaks about:

> *"Education is not merely neglected in many of our schools today but is replaced to a great extent by ideological indoctrination."*

How to Teach Capitalism at Home

In 1996 Kim and I created the *CASHFLOW* board game to teach people about money, a subject not taught in our schools. We wanted people to teach people, using the game as a tool — and we intentionally stayed out of the educational system.

In 1997 *Rich Dad Poor Dad* was self-published when attempts to find a publisher failed. As I've said, the academic elite criticized the book saying, "You do not know what you're talking about."

By self-publishing we were able to control 100 percent of the content — we could go directly to the people and bypassing, in large part, the academic elite.

The people who caused the crash in the Repo Market in 2008 were the academic elite, PhDs like my poor dad. The academic elite in America today are the modern aristocracy. The best book I have read on America's aristocracy is *Tailspin* by Steven Brill, a graduate of Yale and Yale Law.

Steven's book begins with:

> *"Lately, most Americans, regardless of their political leanings, have been asking themselves some version of the same question: How did we get here? How did the world's greatest democracy and economy become a land of crumbling roads, galloping income inequality, bitter polarization and dysfunctional government?"*

Steven Brill is a brilliant lawyer and investigative journalist. He pinpoints where the descent, decline, and corruption of America began. America's demise originated in our finest schools, the most prestigious institutions of higher education, including his alma mater, Yale.

Brill describes how a poor kid from Far Rockaway, Queens, New York, became a member of America's aristocracy. While in junior high school, Brill heard about President Kennedy going to a "prep school." The problem was, Brill was from such a poor school in a poor neighborhood, even his teachers had never heard of a "prep school."

Wanting to follow in Kennedy's footsteps, in 1964, Brill was admitted to an exclusive prep school, Deerfield Academy in Western Massachusetts. The headmaster told his poor, worried parents, who ran a perpetually struggling liquor store, not to worry about the cost of the prep school. Deerfield's financial-aid policy was that parents should send a check to the school every year for whatever they could afford.

Brill writes:

"Three years later, in 1967, I found myself sitting in the headmaster's office one day in the fall of my senior year with a man named R. Inslee Clark Jr., the dean of admissions at Yale. Clark looked over my record and asked me a bunch of questions, most of which were about where I had grown up and how I had ended up at Deerfield. Then he paused, looked me in the eye and asked if I really wanted to go to Yale – if it was my first choice. When I said yes, Clark's reply was instant: "Then I can promise you that you are in. I will tell Mr. Boyden that you don't have to apply anywhere else. Just kind of keep it to yourself.

"What I didn't know then was that I was part of a revolution being led by Clark, whose nickname was Inky. I was about to become one of what would come to be known as Inky's boys and, later, girls. We were part of a meritocracy infusion that flourished at Yale and other elite education institutions, law firms and investment banks in the mid-1960s and '70s. It produced great progress in equalizing opportunity. But it had the unintended consequence of entrenching a new aristocracy of rich knowledge workers who were much smarter and more driven than the old-boy network of heirs born on third base—and much more able to enrich and protect the clients who could afford them."

What does Steven Brill mean by this? He's telling us that poor kids were being admitted to the schools of the rich. Poor kids were studying with the children of America's aristocracy. The aristocracy of America, families like the Kennedys, were admitting very smart kids from poor families into Ivy League schools such as Harvard, Princeton, and Yale.

In the 1960s, smart poor kids were mingling with America's elite and, According to Brill, the financial problems that America faces today began when smart poor kids were hungrier for financial success than the rich kids from America's aristocracy. That is why the subtitle of *Tailspin* referred to in a *TIME* magazine article is How My Generation Broke America.

Earlier in this book I mentioned that Kings Point, the U.S. Merchant Marine Academy, was located in the heart land of America's Industrial Age wealth and aristocracy. The academy was on the grounds of the Walter Chrysler estate, overlooking Long Island Sound with New York City in the distance. One of Kings Point's events, the Sailing Dance, was on the list of the New York Social Registry. Parents among the ranks of the socially elite would call the school to ask if a midshipman would invite their daughter to the Sailing Dance. We met some very rich young women.

I was much like Steven Brill, a kid from a poor family, being exposed to the lifestyle of America's social, economic, and political aristocrats. In 1969, I invited one of those "rich girls" to the Sailing Dance. I was shocked when I went to pick her up. It took minutes to drive up the winding, tree-lined driveway in the small rental car I could barely afford. Her home looked like a smaller version of Buckingham Palace.

Needless to say, that was our one and only date. As the often-quoted line from *The Great Gatsby* goes:
"*Rich girls don't marry poor boys.*"

Q: So is Brill saying the poorer smart kids destroyed America because they did not have the wealth of America's aristocracy?
A: I believe he is.

Q: And that very smart poor kids became America's new aristocracy — America's meritocracy, hungrier for money than their classmates from America's aristocracy.

A: Yes. Brill writes:

> *"The Meritocracy's ascent was about more than personal profit. As my generation of achievers graduated from elite universities and moved into the professional world, their personal successes often had serious societal consequences. They upended corporate America and Wall Street with inventions in law and finance that created an economy built on deals that moved assets around instead of building new ones. They created exotic, and risky, financial instruments, including derivatives and credit default swaps, that produced sugar highs of immediate profits but separated those taking the risk from those who would bear the consequences. They organized hedge funds that turned owning stock into a minute-by-minute bet rather than a long-term investment. They invented proxy fights, leveraged buyouts and stock buybacks that gave lawyers and bankers a bonanza of new fees and maximized short-term profits for increasingly unsentimental shareholders, but deadened incentives for the long-term growth of the rest of the economy."*

Q: Is that culture still taught in our finest schools today?

A: According to Steven Brill, the answer is yes. That is why he wrote *Tailspin* in 2018 and why I wrote *Rich Dad Poor Dad* in 1997. This book, *Capitalist Manifesto,* is written to give the reader a basic understanding of real financial education, an education that includes the history of money, why the rich are getting richer, why communism is taking control of America, and, most importantly, how our freedoms are being stolen, via smart poor kids, educated in America's finest schools.

In the 1960s, America's meritocracy, the academic-financial elite, graduates of our most prestigious schools such as Stanford, University of Chicago, and Wharton, began seeping into the economy. Many young Baby Boomers, some with PhDs, began running Silicon Valley, the Central Bank, also known as the Fed, and today they run Wall

Street, commercial banks, the U.S. government, our universities, government financial institutions such as Fannie Mae and Freddy Mac, and the private financial engineering firms such as today's hedge funds, mutual funds, and private equity firms, most running on money from China and Europe.

As Steven Brill describes, these very smart students from the ranks of the proletariat, working class families, are the people who caused the 2008 crash in the Repo market. The same crash that the financial media called the "subprime market crash." They blamed the working-class *proletariat* for a Repo Market crash. The facts are that the crash was caused by the *academic-financial elite* from *proletariat* working class families, America's new aristocracy.

After the 2008 Repo market crash, followed by the subprime market crash, America's new academic-financial elites from poor families were paid bonuses while their peers, America's working-class proletariat, lost their homes... and the taxpayer footed the bill.

Repeating Thomas Sowell warning:

> *"One of the common failings among honorable people is a failure to appreciate how thoroughly dishonorable some other people can be, and how dangerous it is to trust them."*

Repeating Steven Brill's words:

> *"As my generation of achievers graduated from elite universities and moved into the professional world, their personal successes often had serious societal consequences.*

> *"They upended corporate America and Wall Street with inventions in law and finance that created an economy built on deals that moved assets around instead of building new ones. They created exotic, and risky, financial instruments, including derivatives and credit default swaps, that produced sugar highs of immediate profits but separated those taking the risk from those who would bear the consequences*

> *"They organized hedge funds that turned owning stock into a minute-by-minute bet rather than a long-term investment. They invented proxy*

127

fights, leveraged buyouts and stock buybacks that gave lawyers and bankers a bonanza of new fees and maximized short-term profits for increasingly unsentimental shareholders, but deadened incentives for the long-term growth of the rest of the economy."

Steven Brill is saying that America's new aristocracy, made up of poor kids attending our greatest schools, started a whole new financial services industry. Being politically correct, this new financial services industry is called "financial engineering." In reality, these "financial engineers" build financial Frankenstein monsters. And the Repo Market is the bank for these new American aristocrats who build the Frankenstein monsters.

The Giant Financial Crash that No One Heard About
On September 17, 2019, a crash occurred in the Repo Market of the Shadow Banking System. Interest rates spiked up to 10%. That was very big news, but few people knew about it. And fewer still reported it. Although the crash was very big news, the news never made it to the masses thanks to decisions by the mainstream media, aka fake news outlets.

For Ken McElroy, who is our investment partner in nearly a billion dollars of real estate, the crash in the Repo Market was BIN — Big Important News... that no one heard about.

How Crashes Make the Rich Richer
Crashes in the Repo Market are great times to get rich, if you know what you are doing. The last time Ken and I were aware of a Repo Market crash was in 2008. Again, no one noticed. Ken, Kim, and I went on full "red alert." It was not long before the real estate market began to crumble.

Rather than tell their audiences the truth, fake news outlets such as CNBC and CNN began re-naming the crash. Rather tell the truth, the fake news reporting in 2008 was calling this crash a "subprime real estate market crash." Fake news outlets were blaming the crash on "subprime borrowers," aka poor people, the proletariat, buying homes they could not afford.

What IS the Repo Market?

I will do my best to KISS, Keep It Super Simple. Which is no easy task because the Repo Market is one of those subjects about which the more you find out the more you realize how much you don't know.

Repo Market simply mean "repurchase" — not repossess, as in having a car repossessed. The repurchase agreement, or "repo" market, is an obscure but important part of the financial system. I think of the Repo Market as a pawn shop for the biggest financial institutions in the world.

THE SHADOW BANKING SYSTEM

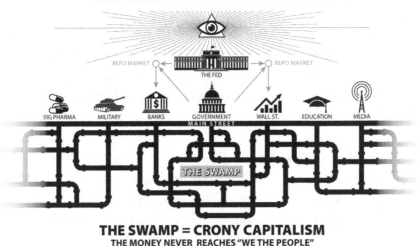

THE SWAMP = CRONY CAPITALISM
THE MONEY NEVER REACHES "WE THE PEOPLE"

The Repo Market is a key component of the Shadow Banking System.

Why the Repo Market Is Important

There are two types of financial institutions in the Repo Market. They are:

FI-1: Financial Institution #1, securities and no cash

FI-2: Financial Institutions #2, cash, but their cash is not earning interest

When Financial Institution #1 needs money, because they are building Frankenstein monsters, they go to the Repo Market for short-term, often overnight, money.

Much like a pawn shop, Financial Institution #2, has cash. FI-2s are often Money Market Mutual Funds, sold by banks and financial planners.

When FI-1 needs cash, they go to the Repo Market FI-2 in search of it. FI-2 wants "collateral" or security from FI-1, much like a pawn shop would ask you to turn over your wedding ring, for a short-term loan. In a pawn-shop scenario, if you don't pay back the pawn shop, it sells your wedding ring.

In the Repo Market the number one security are U.S. Treasury Bills, offered by the U.S. government. As long as FI-1 puts up their U.S. Treasury Bills as security, the FI-2 is happy to give the Frankenstein monster-builder the cash.

And everything works out fine... as long as FI-1 repays the loan to FI-2. And the U.S. Treasury Biills s are returned to FI-1. If you think of the Repo Market as a giant pawn shop, supervised by the U.S. government and the Federal Reserve Bank, you understand more about the Repo Market than 99% of the people in the world.

In very simplest of explanations, that's all the Repo Market is. And, on average, $2 trillion to $4 trillion in repurchase agreements — collateralized short-term loans — are traded each day. In reality, the Repo Market is an essential component of an extremely complex financial system known as the Shadow Banking System.

If you would like to learn more about the Shadow Banking System, Jim Rickards, fellow author and friend, simplifies these rabbit warrens.

Jim Rickards is a *New York Times* best-selling author of the *Road to Ruin, Currency Wars, The Death of Money* and *The New Case for Gold*, which has been translated into 16 languages He has spent over 35 years in investment banking, international economics, political and national intelligence advisory roles on international economics and financial threats to the Department of Defense and the U.S. intelligence community, aka the CIA. Jim also served as a facilitator of the first-ever financial war games conducted by the Pentagon.

Jim warns:

> *"University biologists working with infectious viruses have airtight facilities to ensure that the objects of their study do not escape from the laboratory and damage the population at large. Unfortunately, no such safeguards are imposed on economics departments."*

The Crash No One Heard

As I mentioned just a few pages ago, on September 17, 2019 interest rates in the Repo Market shot up to 10%. This was a giant crash. It meant something was wrong with the collateral. Everyone wanted cash. Mom and pop on Main Street never heard about this crash. The vast majority, probably 99%, of the people in the world did not hear about the crash. If I did not have friends like Jim Rickards, I would probably not have been aware of the crash either.

KISS: Keeping it Super Simple:

> *"If the repo market freezes, the world economy fails."*

Crashes Make the Rich Richer

Ken McElroy and I were excited because when the Repo Market crash occurred in 2008, because it was an opportunity to make money. Crashes are great times to get rich, if you have a solid financial education and understand what you're doing.

In 2008, people with homes and 401(k)s and IRAs took a bath. Many real estate "flippers" were wiped out. And yet, in 2008, some of the best real estate in the world "went on sale" as interest rates fell.

One reason why the rich get richer is because they shop for the best investments when investments and cash, the price of money, are "on sale." On the flip side: One reason why the poor get poorer, is because they shop for investments at the top of markets, when prices are at their highest. It's often called FOMO, Fear of Missing Out. Just before the Repo crash and the subprime real estate crash in 2008, mortgage brokers were offering NINJA loans, "No Income No Job" loans. Suddenly every wannabe real estate investor in town was "flipping real estate."

Then, suddenly, the Repo Market crashed and millions lost their homes, jobs, savings, and retirements. The world has not completely recovered since 2008. Since 2008, the problem in the Repo Market and the Shadow Banking system has only grown into an even bigger, King-Kong of a Frankenstein monster.

After September 17, 2019, Ken McElroy and I waited for more news, but nothing happened. Enter the Coronavirus.

COVID-19 and a Global Pandemic

In late October of 2019, a friend called from Singapore and warned me of a strange virus coming out of China. Today, the world knows it was COVID-19.

At first, I didn't put two and two together. At first, I didn't think the crash in the Repo Market and COVID-19 were related. I have no proof, but after my experience with fake news in Vietnam, I have very little faith in the legitimacy of corporate news organizations. I offer no proof of the relationship between the Repo Market crash and COVID-19, yet something is fishy. People were lying.

On June 30, 2021, CBS News reported:
> *"Covid-19 Wuhan lab-leak hypotheses are "absolutely legitimate and plausible. The U.S. intelligence community is nearly halfway through a 90-day review of the origins of Covid-19 Investigators are looking at whether the virus emerged naturally from human contact with an infected animal or if it accidentally escaped from a lab in Wuhan, China."*

Repeating Jim Rickards' words, as someone who has worked with both the CIA and the Pentagon:
> *"University biologists working with infectious viruses have airtight facilities to ensure that the objects of their study do not escape from the laboratory and damage the population at large. Unfortunately, no such safeguards are imposed on economics departments."*

I am not saying they are related, just that I am suspicious. At Kings Point, our instructor spoke at length about the relationship between medicine and socialism.

As Lenin said:

"Medicine is the keystone in the arch of socialism."

Obamacare

The Affordable Care Act (ACA), formally known as the Patient Protection and Affordable Care Act and, colloquially, as Obamacare, is a United States federal statute enacted by the 111th United States Congress and signed into law by President Barack Obama on March 23, 2010.

Many viewed it as a step toward socialism. My concern with Obama is he is in the same category as Steven Brill, a brilliant person from a bourgeoise family. Obama was not from a poor family, as many would like us to think. I have friends who went to school with him and his sister and know his family. He went to a private and very prestigious high school in Hawaii — Punahou School. A prep school very much like the one Brill attended... for free.

Then, like Brill who went on to Yale, Obama went on to Harvard.

Before Obama became President, he was probably already a millionaire, but not by a lot. When Barack joined the U.S. Senate in 2005, he was making $85,000 a year, according to *Forbes*.

In 2018, his net worth was estimated to be $140 million. Not bad for a President earning $400,000 a year. To me, this is an example of a poor person going to school with kids of America's aristocrats, like the Kennedy and Bush families.

Repo Reverse

In June of 2021, the Repo Market went in reverse. In a normal Repo Market, the Federal Reserve Bank flows money to the biggest commercial banks such as JP Morgan, Wells Fargo, and Goldman Sachs.

In a Reverse Repo the biggest banks flow their cash back to the Fed. This is not a good sign. It could mean a number of things. On the surface, it means the banks want to get closer to the best securities. Again, those being U.S. Treasuries. It could mean the Frankenstein monsters are growing... Who knows? Don't forget: crashes make the rich richer.

George Gammon does a great job explaining Repo and Reverse Repo on his *Rebel Capitalist* podcast on YouTube. On July 6, 2021, George does an outstanding job simplifying an extremely complex subject — the Repo Market — and explaining why the shift to the reverse Repo market is signaling the arrival of what could be the greatest crash in world history.

Bailout Is the Name of the Game
In his book *The Creature from Jekyll Island* author G. Edward Griffin describes the secretive formation of U.S. Federal Bank, aka The Creature.

In his book, Edward Griffin states:
   "Bailout is the name of the game."

In 2021, the Fed and the Treasury estimate that the next bailout will be $150 triillion.

The Repo and Reverse Repo markets are essential to the bailouts of the rich. These Repo Market bails out the poor kids, graduates of our finest schools, who build Frankenstein monsters that destroy the economy and steal the wealth of the working class. America's poor Aristocrats rip off the bourgeoise and proletariat via their money and investments via taxes, savings, inflation, and investments in the stock, bond, and real estate markets.

As Warren Buffett said:
   "The arithmetic makes it plain that inflation is a far more devastating tax than anything that has been enacted by our legislatures."

It seems to me that much of our homelessness and social problems, like hate and racial division, are caused by America's poor aristocrats following the tenets of Marxism-Leninism taught in our finest schools.

Repeating the warning:
> *"The socialist state would control the economy and means of production and suppress the bourgeoise's counter revolution and any opposition."*

In closing this chapter, the questions I'll pose are these: Is Stage One of Marxism-Leninism almost complete? And is the suppression of capitalist and capitalism about to begin?

I ask myself... Is this why gun sales are soaring? And why the tensions of social unrest and discontent are reverberating?

The Future
The following chapters are about the future... about what lies ahead. And, specifically, thoughts on these questions:
What can I do?
How can I be an architect of the future... and not its victim?

How can I fight communism taught in our schools by teaching capitalism at home?

CHAPTER SEVEN

WHAT CAN I DO?
"I'M JUST A LITTLE GUY."

"If you want to teach people a new way of thinking, don't bother trying to teach them. Instead, give them a tool, the use of which will lead to new ways of thinking."
— Dr. R Buckminster Fuller (1895-1983)

In 1967, a classmate and I hitchhiked from Kings Point, New York to Montreal, Canada. We were going to see Expo 67, the World's Fair on the Future. My primary reason for wanting to see Expo 67 was because Dr. R. Buckminster Fuller's geodesic dome was the U.S. Pavilion at the World's Fair. It was a life-changing weekend.

In 1981, I flew from Hawaii to a ski resort located at Kirkwood, California, near Lake Tahoe. I was one of approximately 100 participants in a week-long event with the futurist Buckminster Fuller.

My dad, poor dad, was fascinated with Bucky Fuller. He and I would sit for hours building models out of thin wooden dowels and glue. Fuller called these models the "building blocks of the universe." Pictured below are the "building blocks of universe."

GOD'S BUILDING BLOCKS OF THE UNIVERSE

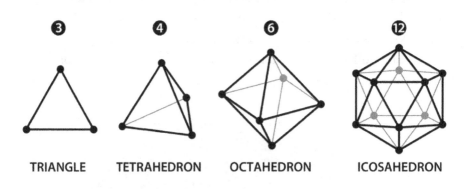

❸	❹	❻	⑫
TRIANGLE	TETRAHEDRON	OCTAHEDRON	ICOSAHEDRON

My dad, a schoolteacher, was intrigued with Fuller because he claimed we were lying to our children. According to Fuller, schools were teaching students the mathematics of humans, not the mathematical coordinates of God.

*Bucky Fuller did not follow any religious doctrine. When he used the word **god** he was referring to "the mysterious integrity governing the universe."*

Squares Do Not Exist

One especially hot button of Fuller's was the use of the words *square*. Fuller told us that "Squares do not exist in the Universe."

Why was he so adamant about this? It was because squares have no integrity — they do not hold their shape. Fuller said, "When you draw a square on a chalk board, the only thing giving the square integrity is the chalk board. Without the chalk board the square could not hold its shape."

Why is this important? In this chapter you will find out why our educational system is out of integrity. Much of what is taught in schools is opinions, not facts... and definitely not science.

In words often attributed to Plato (428/427-348/347 BC), the philosopher believed that *"Neither perception nor true opinion, nor reason or explanation combined with true opinion could be knowledge."* Put another way, by those who have studied Plato: *"Opinion is really the lowest form of human knowledge. It requires no accountability, no understanding."*

The reason my dad, poor dad, had me built models out of thin wooden dowels and glue was to test the model — to see if it held its shape. If it held its shape, the model had integrity.

When I glued four wooden dowels together as shown in the drawing below it was easy to get the four dowels to move. Adding more glue did not help. It still shifted and didn't hold its shape.

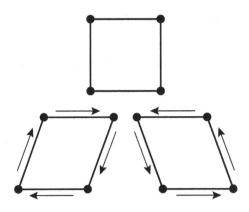

When I built a triangle, as pictured below, the triangle was stronger. It held its shape.

Fuller was proving that the mathematics taught in our schools was "out of integrity." Here are two definitions for integrity:

1 – Quality of being honest. Strong moral principles, moral uprightness.

2 – The state of being whole and undivided.

My poor dad, a schoolteacher and scholar, agreed. He said, "Our math is built on 'squares' when it should be built on 'triangles.' Our math is out of integrity."

What my poor dad could *not* see was that failing to teach the subject of money in school was also out of integrity.

My dad and most teachers are more like Karl Marx. Marx, an intellectual who was a failure at business and managing money, was not a capitalist. I believe that is why Marxism-Leninism principles and ideals have been so easily absorbed into our schools, via our teachers.

My poor dad did not like my rich dad. Rich dad was a capitalist. Like Marx, my poor dad saw capitalists as "oppressors," and workers as "oppressed victims." Like Marx, my dad never realized that it was his lack of financial education and real business experience that caused him to see a world in which he was a victim of the rich.

Maria Montessori, an educational entrepreneur, says this about the importance of education:

> "*An education capable of saving humanity is no small undertaking: it involves the spiritual development of man, the enhancement of his value as an individual, and the preparation of young people to understand the times in which they live.*"

Building Blocks of the Universe

Pictured again below are the shapes Fuller called the "building blocks of the universe." They are building blocks and structurally sound because they have integrity. They hold their shape.

GOD'S BUILDING BLOCKS OF THE UNIVERSE

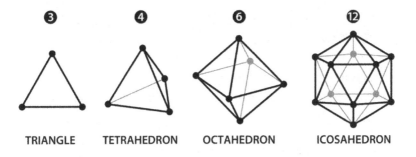

TRIANGLE   TETRAHEDRON   OCTAHEDRON   ICOSAHEDRON

The geodesic dome that was the U.S. Pavilion at Expo 67, pictured on page 137, was a model of mathematics and architecture with integrity.

BUCKY FULLER

Fuller was considered one of America's greatest architects... yet, interestingly, he was not an architect.

In spite of that fact, a bust of Fuller was on display at the American Institute of Architects in Washington D.C. for many years. Simply put, Fuller used the mathematics of God — the building blocks of God, not humans — in his architecture. If God was commissioned to build the U.S. Pavilion at Expo 67... it might have looked like Fuller's geodesic dome.

Opinions Not Facts
Bucky Fuller often said,
> *"Our educational system is built on opinions... not facts."*

When Thomas Sowell was asked in an interview about his shift from Marxism he attributed it to one thing: Facts.

Gad Saad, a Lebanese-born Jew who barely escaped Lebanon. Gad shares Fuller's view on the hypocrisy in education. Today Gad is a professor of Evolutionary Behavioral Science at Concordia University in Montreal, Canada and the author of *The Parasitic Mind*.

In his book, Gad warns:
> *"'Science is based on evidence, not politics. In science knowing is always preferable to not knowing.' But today in academia, progressive ideology trumps scientific facts."*

Gad makes fun of progressive ideology in education, saying:
> *"Oh, you are a non-binary bisexual chemist? Well, this completely changes the atomic numbers of Carbon, Palladium, and Uranium."*

He writes:
> *"Progressives seem to believe that if they say the words 'diversity, inclusion, and equity' often enough, all problems will be solved."*

And, on how to fix the educational system, Gad writes:
> *"If you want to know what's wrong with higher education, this reversal of traditional university priorities–with social justice now at the top and scholarship lower on the totem pole–is a good place to start."*

Lying to Our Children
Fuller's hot button was mathematics. He was critical of math based on fake assumptions, fake math. To compute the area of a circle, modern math uses "pi r squared."

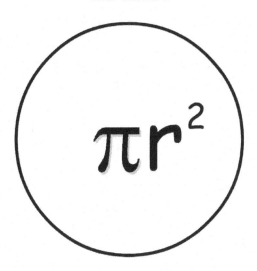

Pi is equal to approximately 3.14159265358979323846...

The digits go on and on with no pattern and no end.

Fuller asked:
> *"Do you think god would leave the area of circle to be unresolved?"*

And why he said repeatedly:
> *"How dare we lie to our students."*

The Planet's Friendly Genius
Later in his life, Fuller came to be known as the The Planet's Friendly Genius. John Denver wrote a song for Bucky calling him The Grandfather of the Future. The song is titled *What One Man Can Do*.

Fuller was born on July 12, 1895, in Milton, Massachusetts. He attended Milton Academy in Massachusetts. Immediately he began disagreeing with the way geometry was taught in school. He could not accept that a chalk dot on the chalkboard represented an "empty" point or that a line could stretch to infinity. To him this was illogical and led him to develop his own mathematics called Synergetics.

After graduating from Milton Academy, he headed off to Harvard University. His family handed him a diary of four generations of Fullers, all who had graduated from Harvard before him. They also gave him enough money, which he was expected to budget, and get him through four years at Harvard.

He was expelled from Harvard twice, the first time for spending all his money partying with a troupe of Radio City Rockette dancers. The second time he was expelled, his family collected more money for his four-year education and he was readmitted to Harvard. Once again, he returned to New York City and spent the money and engaged in what Harvard called "excessive socialization." Harvard did not readmit Fuller again.

Interestingly, and although Fuller is not a graduate of that institution, Harvard does claim him as one of its most notable graduates.

Although Fuller did not graduate from Harvard, he did receive an appointment to — and graduated from — the U.S. Naval Academy, one of the five federal academies and a sister school to the U.S. Merchant Marine Academy.

Fuller often said to our class:
"Men of the sea... are different from men of the land."

He expanded on that saying, "When you are on the ocean, you are subject to the forces of nature, the breath of God. When you are on the ocean, God does not care if you are rich or poor, black of white, smart or stupid. When you live on the sea, you learn to tune into the forces of God."

Again, when Fuller used the word *God* it was not in a religious context. God, to Fuller, was "the mysterious integrity governing universe."

Men of the Land
Most despots, tyrants, entrepreneurs, and CEOs are men of the land. Most think they are smarter than God. When men of the sea think they are more powerful than God, they become captains of the Titanic, the transatlantic passenger ship, advertised as "unsinkable."

I've been the captain of my own Titanic... many times.

In 2020, the global economy was sinking, officially entering a recession in February of that year, because men and women who graduated from our finest land-based schools, thought they are smarter than God.

Would the outcome, the economic picture, have been different if men (and women) of the sea were at the country's helm and running the Fed and the U.S. Treasury? We'll never know.

Depression and Epiphany

In 1981, Fuller told our class that when he was living in Chicago, married with a daughter, he had started a small construction business and was struggling financially. Fuller told us that, on a weekend in 1922, there was the Harvard/Yale game that he wanted to go to. At the time, his daughter Alexandra was about four years old and struggling with complications from polio and spinal meningitis.

His wife, Anne, asked Bucky to tell his daughter where he was going before he left. When he said goodbye to Alexandra she asked him: "Will you bring me back a Harvard pennant?"

Fuller promised Alexandra he would and caught the train from Chicago to Boston. As usual, Fuller partied on for days, during and after the game. He finally received word from his wife that Alexandra had taken a turn for the worse and that he needed to hurry home.

Back in Chicago, he rushed up the stairs to their one-bedroom apartment and picked up his daughter who was burning up with fever. In 1981, Fuller told our class how he held his daughter in his arms and how she opened her eyes when she realized he was home. She smiled, and asked, "Daddy, did you bring me my pennant?"

Fuller slowly shook his head and replied, "No darling... I forgot." Alexandra closed her eyes and died in his arms, just days before her fourth birthday.

That was in 1922.

In 1927, Fuller contemplated suicide by drowning, so his wife and new daughter, Allegra, could benefit from his life insurance. His plan was to swim out from the shore of Lake Michigan, and slowly disappear below the waves from exhaustion.

In 1981, Fuller stood on stage and slowly told our class that as he stood on the shore of Lake Michigan he experienced a profound moment which would provide direction and purpose for the rest of his life. Fuller said he felt as though he was suspended several feet above the ground, enclosed in a white sphere of light. A voice spoke to him saying:

> *"You do not belong to you. You belong to the Universe. Your significance will remain forever obscure to you, but you may assume that you are fulfilling your role if you apply yourself to converting your experiences to the highest advantage of others."*

Never Work for Money Again
In 1927, Fuller was 32 years old. He told us that his out-of-body experience led to a profound re-examination of his life. He said he ultimately chose to embark on "an experiment to find what a single individual could contribute to changing the world and benefiting all humanity."

He said to our class:

> *"I set out, about 50 years ago to see what a penniless, unknown human individual with a dependent wife and newborn child might be able to do effectively on behalf of all humanity."*

In 1927... He returned home from Lake Michigan to his one-bedroom apartment and vowed never to work for money again.

Fuller told our class that he would get up each morning and, after breakfast, clear off the kitchen table, only to work on things his intuition inspired him to work on. He spent a lot of time using toothpicks and dried peas, creating the building blocks of the universe. From those toothpicks and dried peas, he discovered God's real mathematics, a math he named Synergetics.

GOD'S BUILDING BLOCKS OF THE UNIVERSE

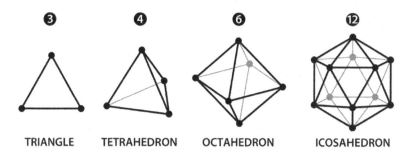

❸	❹	❻	⑫
TRIANGLE	TETRAHEDRON	OCTAHEDRON	ICOSAHEDRON

Fuller derived his math, Synergetics, from the definition of synergy:
> *"Synergy means behavior of whole systems unpredicted by the behavior of their parts, taken separately."*

KISS... Keeping It Super Simple...

Synergy means:
> 1+1+1=6 or 11 or 60

Margaret Mead, an American cultural anthropologist who lived from 1901 to 1978, said:
> *"Never doubt that a small group of thoughtful, committed citizens can change the world; indeed, it's the only thing that ever has."*

This was Margaret Mead's way of explaining synergy when a small group of humans band together to change the world.

In 1981, I remember sitting in disbelief as Fuller explained to our class that if he was "doing what God wanted done" then life support would show up. If he was not "doing what God wanted done" his family went hungry.

In 1981, I was pretty defeated. I was pretty beat-up. And I felt powerless. I had returned from Vietnam, being a witness to lessons on Marxism and Fascism taught at the academy, being aware of our media turning against U.S. soldiers in the field, and realizing Marxism-Leninism was seeping into America via educators, good people like my dad. I felt totally powerless, like a victim.

Here are three definitions of victim:

    1 – A person harmed, injured, or killed as a result of a crime, accident, event, or action

    2 – A person who is tricked or duped

    3 – A living creature killed as a religious sacrifice

In 1981, I could not get out the pictures — images of the North Vietnamese tanks rolling through the gates of the U.S. Embassy in Saigon, in 1975, signaling America's loss of the war — out of my head. Replaying, over and over in my head, was the newsreel of helicopters on rooftops, transporting as many Vietnamese soldiers, men who would surely be murdered for siding with America, to safety. I could not forget the faces of friends and fellow pilots, men whose planes never returned to the carrier and would never return home. Nor could I forget the American hippies spitting on my men and me when we returned home to America.

In 1981, I was still angry. I felt betrayed. I saw myself as a victim.

After five days with Bucky Fuller, I was transformed. Rather than remain a victim, trying to figure out how to get rich, I sat in the five-day seminar with Fuller contemplating my future. I thought about Fuller's words as he asked himself, at the lowest point in his life, "What does God want done?"

In August of 1981, I returned home to Hawaii and my rock and roll business. I had secured two more licenses for the bands Van Halen and Judas Priest, which were monster bands at the time. But as much fun as the rock and roll business was... that week with Fuller had changed me. I kept asking myself, "What does God want done?"

I did not know what God wanted done. I just knew selling hats, wallets, and T-shirts with rock bands' logos on them at rock concerts and in retail stores was not what I wanted to do anymore.

There is a popular saying that goes:
   "Do what you love... and the money will follow."

In 1981, I had been doing what I loved... until I met Fuller in person. And I remembered the feeling I'd had, riding the monorail through Fuller's dome in 1967.

In 1981, I realized that the inspiration for that dome came from Fuller's kitchen table, in 1927, after vowing to never work for money again. It was a result of asking himself "What does God want done?"

As Fuller said:
   "You either make money... or you make sense. They are mutually exclusive."

In 1981, I was just starting to make a lot of money in rock and roll. Unfortunately, making money manufacturing rock and roll products was making less and less sense.

Rather than do what I loved I began asking myself: *"What does God want done?"*

I asked myself that question again and again. And soon I began seeing a lot that needed to be done.

Fuller's exact words were:
   "The things to do are the things that need doing, that you see need to be done, that no one else seems to see need to be done."

I stopped asking myself, *"How much money will I make?"* and focused, instead, on finding a need that I could address... a problem I could solve.

I replaced my words with Fuller's words:

> *"Observation of my life to date shows that the larger the number for whom I work, the more positively effective I become. Thus, it is obvious that if I work always and only for all humanity, I will be optimally effective."*

As time went on, I simplified Fuller's words to:

> *"The more people I serve, the more effective I become."*

I had the good fortune to study with Fuller again, in the summers of 1982 and 1983. Each event was transformational.

Fuller's Death

In 1983, two weeks after spending another week with him, I was driving down the H-1, the highway running thorough Honolulu, when the newscaster announced Buckminster Fuller had passed away in Los Angeles.

The date was July 1, 1983. I pulled my car over to the side of the road and cried. I found out later that Fuller had been delivering another of his talks, in Los Angeles, when he stopped, looked up, and paused for a long while.

A friend of mine who was in the audience said, "Fuller turned to the audience and said, 'my wife has taken a turn for the worse. Is it time for us to pass on together?'"

Bucky had made a pact with his wife that they would not see the other pass away. Fuller left the conference and rushed to be at her side. Anne was in a coma and did not know Bucky was there. Fuller lay his head down at her side and passed away a few hours later. A few days later, Anne passed away, never coming out of her coma. They kept their agreement, never to see each other pass from this life.

Critics of Fuller claim his story of his life is not true, yet I know from firsthand experience that being around him was always a transformational experience. I will always remember, riding the monorail through his geodesic dome, the U.S. Pavilion at Expo 67, as a magical and inspirational experience.

Fuller was very critical of education and educators. Obviously, many of his critics are from academia.

Fuller said:

> *"Our school systems are all non-synergetic. We take the whole child and fractionate the scope of his or her comprehending coordination by putting the children in elementary schools—to become preoccupied with elements or isolated facts only."*

Here, again, is the definition of synergy:

> *"Synergy means behavior of whole systems unpredicted by the behavior of their parts, taken separately."*

Why Elementary School Is Boring

In describing the existing school system, Fuller was saying that elementary schools made school boring. Rather than study a subject, like a puppy, the synergetic whole puppy is broken into elements, such as math, science, reading, writing, history, and other boring, unrelated elements. That causes education to be boring... and not real and relatable.

I think that's a part of why kids in school often feel stupid. I know that was true to me. I wanted to learn about money. But rather than study money as a whole subject, we studied math. Boredom set in — and I checked out.

Thank goodness my poor dad, the head of education, suggested I begin studying with rich dad when I was nine. I discovered that — while I didn't like school — I loved learning.

Schools Force Specialization

Fuller had more to say on the topic as he continued to explain what happens after schools break a subject into elements:

> *"Thereafter we force them to choose some specialization, forcing them to forget the whole. ... We may well ask how it happened that the entire scheme of advanced education is devoted exclusively to ever narrower specialization."*

Q: So, the smart students go on to law school, med school, or nursing school?

A: The more highly educated a student the more highly specialized they become. Or as Fuller said: *"The entire scheme of advanced education... is devoted exclusively to ever narrower specialization."*

Q: What's wrong with being a specialist?

A: Well, Fuller certainly had an opinion on that when he warned:
   "Specialization breeds bias that ultimately aggregate as international and ideological discord, which, in turn leads to war."

Q: Your rich dad agreed, didn't he? Is that why he created the Cashflow Quadrant?

A: Yes. The Cashflow Quadrant is book #2 in the Rich Dad Series, an integral book in the Capitalist Manifesto.

Pictured below is the Cashflow Quadrant:

   E stands for employee

   S stands for specialist or small business owner

   B stands for big business or brand

   I stands for insider or investor

Es and Ss to invest from the outside, in assets such as stocks, bonds, mutual funds, and ETFs. Bs and Is invest from the inside.

The school system programs students to: *"Go to school, get a job, pay taxes, buy a house because a house is an asset, get out of debt, invest for the long term in stocks, bonds, mutual funds, and ETFs, and save money."*

Thomas Sowell's words of warning:
> *"Education is not merely neglected in many of our schools today but is replaced to a great extent by ideological indoctrination."*

Q: So students are programmed to work for money?
A: Yes. The majority become slaves to money, job security, a steady paycheck, Wall Street's stock and bond market, and reliant upon government welfare programs such as Social Security and Medicare.

As Fuller said:
> *"Everything we see is inside our own heads."*

Q: And what people in the E and S quadrants see inside their heads are steady paychecks, job security, and financial security?
A: Exactly.

Q: Is that why there is no financial education in our schools?
A: That's a question you should probably answer for yourself. I have voiced my opinions, but what you think is what really matters.

Fuller warned:
> *"Specialization is in fact only a fancy form of slavery wherein the 'expert' is fooled into accepting his slavery by making him feel that in return he is in a socially and culturally preferred, ergo, highly secure, lifelong position."*

Q: Is that why, when you were 10 years old, rich dad refused to pay you to work for him? Because that would be programing you to think like an employee? To see the world through the eyes of an employee, to see the world as a specialist?
A: Exactly.

Brain Slaves

The history of education begins with illiterate and ambitious war lords, financing schools to take advantage of "brain slaves."

Fuller had this to say about the history of education:

"We find that the historical beginnings of schools and tutoring were established, and economically supported by illiterate and vastly ambitious warlords who required a wide variety of brain slaves with which to logistically and ballistically overwhelm those who opposed their expansion of physical conquest."

Fuller's warlords were those on the right side of rich dad's Cashflow Quadrant — the Bs and Is.

And he takes the distinctions even further. To keep the smarter "brain slaves" under control, the illiterate warlord divided and conquered the smart brain slaves by making them even more specialized.

Fuller writes:

"They also simultaneously DIVIDED and CONQUERED any and all "bright ones" who might otherwise rise within their realms to threaten their supremacy."

"The warlord vitiated their threat by making them all specialists and reserving to himself exclusively the right to think about and act comprehensively."

Q: What does this mean: "...*vitiated* their threat by making them all specialists"?

A: Vitiate means the warlord intentionally spoiled or impaired the power of the smarter brain slaves, by making them even more specialized. For example, a smart attorney is encouraged and compensated for being, let's say, a patent attorney or an economist may be encouraged to be an economist specializing in labor economics.

Q: And the specialist brain slave loses power by becoming more specialized?

A: Yes.

Q: And the war lord increases his power by becoming more of a generalist, while his brain slaves become more specialized?

A: Correct.

Q: And what did Fuller mean when he wrote: *"And reserving to himself exclusively the right to think and act comprehensively?"*

A: The war lord reserved the exclusive right to think "big picture." Fuller said that God designed humans to be generalists. That means humans can do many things. They can plant crops, hunt animals, build a shelter, cook, clean, play a musical instrument, drive a car, fly, and be a caretaker.

That is why schools today continue to teach the "smart students" to be highly specialized specialists.

As a futurist, Fuller predicted:
"Man is going to be displaced altogether as a specialist by the computer."

In 2020, many medical doctors are being replaced by the computer, which can do so much more for so much less. Soon truck drivers will be replaced.

Q: And as computers replace specialists, our schools continue to teach students to become more specialized? It doesn't make sense.

A: That is why Fuller said:
"The warlord vitiated their threat by making them all specialists and reserving to himself exclusively the right to think about and act comprehensively."

The "brain slave" specialists are *differentiators,* focused on the smaller and smaller picture, while the warlord is the only *integrator.* The only to see or understand the big picture.

Let's look at a real-life example. As a real estate investor and entrepreneur, I own thousands of properties. I operate out of the B and I quadrants. The more properties I acquire, the more my cash flow increases.

I deal with a number of real estate brokers. They operate out of the S quadrant.

As my holding grow, I work less and less, creating more and more cashflow without working and with a plan in place to minimize my taxes. The real estate broker, on the other hand, needs to keep working harder and harder, to find new clients to generate new commission money, which is taxed at the highest tax rate.

That is why, according to Bucky Fuller, the history of education begins with illiterate and ambitious warlords, financing schools to take advantage of "brain slaves."

In real estate terms, the S-quadrant real estate broker works for one or two clients at a time. The B- and I-quadrant investors and business owners serve more and more people, with each property they acquire. Those in the B and I quadrants make more money and pay less, legally, in taxes.

What Can a Little Guy Do?
A question that Fuller asked himself was "What can I do, I'm just a little guy?" I found myself asking the same question. He summarized the answer in these words:

> *"The things to do are: the things that need doing, that you see need to be done, and that no one else seems to seed need to be done."*

Q: But people need money. Isn't that why people go to school, get a job, and go to work? Without money most people can't survive.

A: That's what we are taught to be in school... to be slaves to money. Most people leave school and begin living paycheck to paycheck. Many live paycheck to paycheck their entire lives.

Another Fuller insight:

"Everything you've learned in school as "obvious" becomes less and less obvious as you begin to study the universe."

The Hot Subject

Over the three summers I spent studying with Fuller, in 1981, 1982, and 1983, the subject of how a person could survive financially doing "only what God wants done" was a hot topic. The fear of not having money was an emotional hot button. For most students, it was a primal fear. That primal fear keeps people living life as "wage slaves."

Fuller did his best to change the pictures in our head. He told stories to open our eyes.

For example, one story that Fuller told our class held a lesson:

"Children will draw pictures with everything in them... houses and trees and people and animals... and the sun AND the moon.

"Grown-ups say, 'That's a nice picture, honey, but you put the sun in the sky at the same time as the moon ... and that isn't right.' But it is right, the child is right. The sun and the moon are in the sky at the same time."

One of Fuller's favorite nuggets of genius is one that struck a chord with me the first time I hear it... and still does today. He told us:

"We are called to be architects of the future, not its victims."

Today many of our leaders want us to be victims. They want us to see ourselves as victims, dependent on the mercy and largess of our leaders and our government.

By 2020, Nancy Pelosi, the first woman Speaker of the House, had been a professional politician for three decades, since 1987. As Speaker of the House, she is one of the most powerful women in America. Her net worth is estimated to be $120 million. Her ability to inspire victims is astounding.

Some of her more memorable statements are:

> *"Elect us, hold us accountable, and make a judgement and then go from there. But I tell you that if the Democrats win and have substantial majorities, the Congress of the United States will be more bipartisan."*

Are you kidding me?

Pelosi also said:

> *"Unemployment benefits are creating jobs faster than practically any other program."*

Are you *kidding* me?

And this:

> *"I believe in natural gas as a clean cheap alternative to fossil fuels."*

I cannot help but ask: Is she *that* misinformed?

More Pelosi...

> *"If I had my way, sporting guns would be strictly regulated, the rest would be confiscated."*

That is what Hitler did.

And finally, vintage Pelosi:

> *"Pass the bill to find out what is in it."*

The full quote is actually *"We have to pass the bill so that you can find out what is in it, away from the fog of the controversy."* And these politicians should inspire our trust?

As Marx warned:

> *"For the bureaucrat, the world is a mere object to be manipulated by him (her)."*

And Hitler said:

"What luck for governments, that the people are stupid."

In an interview with Patrick Bet-David for his Valuetainment podcast in July 2021, Professor Gad Saad states:

"I argue that contrary to the current pandemic that we're facing with Covid, we've faced another pandemic for the past forty, fifty years. And in this case the virus is not a biological virus, it's a mind virus. That's why I call these ideas pathogens, or parasitic ideas. And so, where do these ideas come from? So, if we are trying to find out where the Covid virus came from, we're not allowed to say because to say where it comes from would be racist of course. So where do these idea pathogens come from? They all come from the university eco-system. In other words, as I always remind people, it takes intellectuals and professors to come up with some of the dumbest ideas."

Gad goes on stating:

"How we can vaccinate ourselves against these bad ideas."

Rich dad often said:

"Be very careful who you hire as employees, especially your executives. One highly educated Marxist can infect your entire company."

That is why rich dad fought so hard to keep his businesses non-union... and he won.

Repeating Ayn Rand's words from her book *Atlas Shrugged*:

"When you see that in order to produce, you need to obtain permission from men who produce nothing—when you see that money is flowing to those who deal not in goods, but in favors—when you see that men get rich more easily by graft than by work, and your laws no longer protect you against them, but protect them against you... you may know that your society is doomed."

But Wait... It Gets Worse

On May 11, 2021... Under Commentary in the *Babylon Bee*:

> *"Some smart expert analysts are seeing a connection between incentivizing people to stay home... and them staying home."*

The article continues with these comments:

> *"It's really bizarre..." said one government official.*

> *"It seems that when you just send people check... they don't really see a point to going to work."*

> *"We could not possibly have foreseen this."*

Rich dad said:

> *"You always get what you pay for. If you pay people not to work, they stop working."*

As the First Stage of Marxism-Leninism comes to end, and the suppression of opposition begins, the academic elite are pushing for MMT, Modern Monetary Theory, and UBI, Universal Basis Income.

MMT: Modern Monetary Theory

The central idea of Modern Monetary Theory or MMT is that governments with a fiat currency system under their control can and should print (or create with a few keystrokes in today's digital age) as much money as they need to spend because they cannot go broke or be insolvent unless a political decision to do so is made.

Are they nuts? That is exactly what Germany did after World War I's Treaty of Versailles, which led to the Weimar Republic, to the rise of Adolf Hitler, and the death of 42 million people. I like to call MMT: Marxist Monetary Theory.

UBI: Universal Basic Income

Universal Basic Income, UBI, is a government program in which every adult citizen receives a set amount of money regularly. The goals of a basic income system are to alleviate poverty and replace other need-based social programs that potentially require greater bureaucratic involvement. The idea of universal basic income has gained momentum in the United States as automation increasingly replaces workers in manufacturing and other sectors of the economy.

Are they nuts? Rather than teach students to "go to school to get a job," why not teach them to "go to school and become an entrepreneur, who creates jobs"?

Q: What's wrong with printing money and paying people not to work?
A: Where do I start? How about with inflation. The definition of inflation is: *"A general increase in prices... and decline in the purchasing value of money."*

Repeating Warren Buffett's warning on inflation:
> *"The arithmetic makes it plain that inflation is a far more devastating tax than anything that has been enacted by our legislature. The inflation tax has a fantastic ability to simply consume capital."*

Thomas Sowell warns:
> *"Hyperinflation can take virtually your entire life's savings, without the government having to bother raising the official tax rate at all."*

And repeating Hitler's words, yet again, because it drives home the point:
> *"What luck for governments, that the people are stupid."*

Remember when we could poke fun, via self-deprecating humor, at ourselves? When we could use humor as a tool, a mechanism to shine a light on issues and ideas. America's comedians say it best:

George Carlin says:
> *"Never underestimate the power of stupid people in large groups."*

Will Rogers advises:
> *"Always drink upstream from the herd."*

Gad Saad warns:

"The West is currently suffering from such a devastating pandemic, a collective malady that destroys people's capacity to think rationally. Unlike other pandemics where biological pathogens are to blame, the current culprit is composed of a collection of bad ideas, spawned on university campuses, that chip away at our edifices of reason, freedom, and individual dignity."

Gad goes a step farther in stating:

"The granddaddy of all idea pathogens... is what's called post-modernism."

Q: What is post-modernism?

A: Here's the way it's positioned on the National Association of Scholars website:

"The two contending ideologies within Postmodernism are Marxism and Historicism, with all their current spin-offs—social justice, diversity, multiculturalism, sustainability, and global citizenship."

"After World War II and the revelations about Stalin's crimes, academic Marxists began migrating from traditional, economic Marxism to a culture-based version, even dropping the Marxist name. The first group, the Frankfurt School—which led to the rise of Western Marxism and Cultural Marxism—originated in Germany. Some of the School's members migrated to the United States."

Q: So post-modernism has its roots in Marxism?

A: Yes. In the interview with Patrick Bet-David, Gad Saad describes "post-modernism" as having "no universal truths."

That is why I posted the quote that's often credited to Plato:
"Opinion is really the lowest form of human knowledge. It requires no accountability, no understanding."

Q: What did Fuller think of post-modernism?

A: Fuller would have totally disagreed with post-modernism's philosophy that "There are no universal truths." And that we are shackled by our personal bias and subjectivity.

Fuller would have agreed with Plato position that *"Opinion is really the lowest form of human knowledge. It requires no accountability, no understanding."* Post-modernism is based on opinions, bias, diversity, critical subjectivity, and oppression. Post-modernism supports the ideas of society's creation of victims. Post modernists fail to realize they are the problem.

Again, I think of Fuller's words, words of defiance and hope:
"*We are called to be architects of the future, not its victims.*"

That is why so many people subscribe to MMT and UBI, as solutions to income inequality.

Historically, MMT and UBI have led to rising poverty, greater income inequality, financial chaos, revolution, and the death of millions.

So, are we at the end of the First Stage of Marxism-Leninism?

I have presented different points of views. I have my ideas on what the start of Second Stage of Marxism-Leninism will look like. I believe I saw the future, the Second Stage, while flying over the burned-out chateaux along the beaches of the French Indo-Chinese Riviera in Vietnam so many years ago.

A more important question is: "What is your vision of the future?

Are you like the Jews in Germany, in 1933, who allowed Hitler to make them wear yellow stars? Today we wear masks and are forced — many at the risk of losing their jobs — to be vaccinated.

When Fuller's book *Grunch of Giants* was released, posthumously about a month after his death in July of 1983, I found my answer to the question "What does God want done?"

In his book, GRUNCH stands for **Gr**oss **Un**iversal **C**ash **H**eist.

In 1983, I met a most beautiful and amazing woman named Kim.

In 1984, Kim, our friend Blair Singer, and I sold everything and left Hawaii for California to find out if we could do what God wanted done. It was the beginning of the worst years of our lives. Kim and I were homeless for a period of time, but we kept going. These words from Fuller kept us going:

> *"If you want to teach people a new way of thinking, don't bother trying to teach them. Instead, give them a tool, the use of which will lead to new ways of thinking."*

From 1984 to 1994 we struggled, moving from failure to failure. But we didn't give up.

In 1994, we were financially free. Kim was 37 and I was 47. It took us 10 years to achieve financial freedom and we saw that we need to share how we did it. And to create tools and a path so that others could do the same. Our mission — to elevate the financial well-being of humanity —became the Mission of The Rich Dad Company.

In 1996, Kim and I produced the *CASHFLOW* board game. We followed Bucky's words and *"created a tool, the use of which will lead to a new way of thinking."*

Fuller also said:

> *"In order for a world-around democracy to prosper, world society must learn how to prosper."*

Kim and I created the *CASHFLOW* game in 1996, following Maria Montessori's words of wisdom:

> *"What the hand does, the mind remembers."*

On the heels of creating the *CASHFLOW* game, I wrote *Rich Dad Poor Dad* in 1997. Again I followed Bucky Fuller's guidance:

> *"I would say then that you are faced with a future in which education is going to be number one amongst the great world industries."*

In 1997, Kim and I formed The Rich Dad Company... with the *CASHFLOW* game as our capitalist tool.

We were inspired by Fuller's words:

> *"I set about fifty-five years ago [1927] to see what a penniless, unknown human individual with a dependent wife and newborn child might be able to do effectively on behalf of all humanity."*

In 1996, our Capitalist Manifesto began...

All we did was create products that counter communism taught in schools, by creating products that teach capitalism in our homes. At first Kim and I were ridiculed and criticized.

So, in 1997, we self-published *Rich Dad Poor Dad*. Again, we were guided by Fuller's wisdom:

> *"My ideas have undergone a process of emergence by emergency. When they are needed badly enough, they are accepted."*

In 2021, *Rich Dad Poor Dad* remains the number one book in personal finance throughout the world. The pandemic was that emergency. The pandemic revealed the Marxist idea pathogens that come from inside the university ecosystem. It focused a light, a beacon, on the perils of post-modernism thought and gave parents of schoolchildren a new and powerful voice for change.

Post Modernism education lacks integrity. It can't hold its shape because it is based on opinions, not principles. Worst of all, it fails to prepare students for the real world.

In the next chapter, I will explain how Fuller and rich dad countered the Marxist ideas found in post-modern education... with Generalized Principles.

CHAPTER EIGHT

SELF-DEFENSE

*"Only two things are infinite, the universe and human stupidity...
and I'm not sure about the former."*
— Albert Einstein

Human stupidity is infinite? It's enough to make you stop and think about it, that's for sure. And then I look at the world around me and maybe it's not so far off the mark. And they *are* words often attributed to Albert Einstein...

One thing I do know is that *my* stupidity is infinite. And it's from my infinite pool of stupidity that I find knowledge, information, and occasionally some wisdom.

As Nelson Mandela said:
> *"The greatest glory in living lies not in never falling... but in rising every time we fall."*

Schools teach stupidity when they punish students for making mistakes. How does a person learn if they never make a mistake? How does a child learn to walk if they never fall, or are punished for falling?

If, as Nelson Mandela said, the "glory lies not in never failing" then why is making mistakes so stigmatized? Making mistakes does not mean you're stupid. Mistakes are how we learn, opportunities to learn how to do something differently or better. Yet in my experience teachers focus on mistakes, versus moving through them to find the lessons there. I think that's one of the reasons why most teachers are poor.

Bucky Fuller addresses this when he writes about how God designed humans:
> *"Human beings were given a left foot and a right foot to make a mistake first to the left, then to the right, left again and repeat.*

I heard Fuller on stage once when he put it this way:
> *"God did not give us a right foot and a wrong foot."*

One definition of intelligence is:
> *"The ability to acquire and apply knowledge and skills."*

An intelligent person is someone who makes mistakes and learns from their mistakes. Schools focus so much on memorizing the "right answers" and so little on what we can learn from our mistakes. Fuller once told our class:
> *"God designed humans to learn by making mistakes."*

I think about babies learning to walk, kids learning to ride bikes... and drive cars. What if we were punished every time you fell or made a mistake? We might all still be crawling.

I believe we were designed to learn from our mistakes. Then schools punish us for making them.

One of my favorite quotes from Einstein is:
> *"Imagination is more important than knowledge. Knowledge is limited. Imagination encircles the world."*

Elon Musk says:
> *"As much as possible, avoid hiring MBAs. MBA programs don't teach people how to create companies."*

Kim and I made this mistake once. We paid an executive headhunter to find a CEO with an MBA. Not only did we have to pay the headhunter a percentage of the new CEO's salary, but we paid the new CEO a $250,000 signing bonus. Kim and I agree with Elon Musk. Entrepreneurs do not need MBAs.

Steve Jobs said:
> *"Innovation distinguishes between a leader and a follower."*

Repeating Einstein's words:
> *"Imagination is more important than knowledge."*

And rich dad, who said:
> *"Entrepreneurs require imagination, courage, and especially the humility to learn from their mistakes."*

The biggest killer of imagination is school. School teaches students that there are right answers and wrong answers and only schoolteachers know the right answers. There are cases, I'm sure, where if a teacher admitted to making a mistake he or she would be fired. Or at least they *think* they would be. That is a terrible way to live. And I do think that is why most teachers are poor. Oftentimes they see only one "answer," one path. Many live in fear of not finding that "right answer," of making mistakes that could lead them to discovering and living the life they deserve.

I Love Rock 'n' Roll

I loved rock 'n' roll. That's why I was in the rock and roll business... until I met Bucky Fuller. One of my favorite rock stars was Jimi Hendrix, a rock legend. He was not a college professor... but he was a very smart man.

A quote widely attributed to Hendrix is this:
> *"Knowledge speaks but wisdom listens."*

Red Hot Real Estate

In 2008, the real estate market was red hot. Everyone was talking about real estate. People were quitting their jobs to become professional real estate flippers.

I remember standing at the checkout counter at Safeway when the clerk handed me her real estate card. Smiling, she started telling me about how much money people were making in real estate by flipping houses.

As she packed my groceries into bags, I asked her, "What happen if the real estate market crashes?"She replied, "The price of real estate always goes up." She then tried to get me to invest with her. I listened to her pitch, but said nothing.

Joseph P. Kennedy, father of President John Kennedy, said:
   "If shoe shine boys are giving you stock tips, it's time to get out of the market."

In 2008, Ken McElroy and I were waiting for the real estate market to crash. In 2008, we already knew there was a crash in the Repo Market. In 2008, Ken and I were owners of about 2,500 apartment units.

We were losing tenants that year because banks had loosened their qualifying requirements and our tenants were buying homes, rather than renting. In many cases they were homes they couldn't afford. We knew that because most of those tenants could barely afford the security deposit on their rental.
So, in 2008, Kenny and I waited and listened.

In 2008, one of the biggest crashes in history occurred. Ken and I knew the crash took place in the derivatives market.

Warren Buffett warned about derivatives saying:
   "Derivatives are financial weapons of mass destruction."

Rather than blame the giant commercial banks, the financial press blamed the crash on 'subprime real estate investors.' "Banksters" — aka "gangsters with MBAs" — were paid billions in bonuses while mom and pop lost everything.

Crashes Make the Rich Richer
In 2010, Kim, Ken, and I borrowed over $300 million and bought great apartment complexes at rock-bottom prices, and at extremely low interest rates.

As rich dad taught his son and me:

> *"You make your money when buy... not when you sell."*

And as Warren Buffett has said:

> *"The rich invest in time. The poor invest in money."*

In 2021 Ken, Kim, and I control over 8,000 rental units. We are over a billion dollars in debt and know first-hand that — if you understand markets and debt and how to use it wisely — crashes can make you rich. In 2021, we are waiting for the next crash.

Repo Market Crash

As I've stated in a previous chapter, on September 17, 2019 there was giant crash in the Repo Market with interest rates spiking to 10%.

In April 2021, the Reverse Repo kicked in. Again, no one seems to have noticed.

In 2021 the stock market and real estate market are at all-time highs as government stimulus checks flood the economy. In the summer of 2021, as I write this book, my phone is running hot. It seems everyone has a "deal of a lifetime" that they want me to invest in.

FOMO + Greed = Insanity

To invest at the top of a market is insanity... yet that is when so many people invest. FOMO — the Fear Of Missing Out — takes over. Greed is not good at market tops.

This quote bears repeating:

> *"Only two things are infinite, the universe and human stupidity... and I'm not sure about the former."*

If I've learned one thing about human nature it's that greed can make people do stupid things.

For many years I have asked people I meet: *"What did school teach you about money."* I estimate that 90 percent of the time all I get is a blank stare. It's almost as if they are embarrassed to say "Nothing." Most of the time, the person is an educated, hardworking individual. I suspect that the person is too embarrassed to ask a question. The fear of looking stupid, taught by our schools, is an epidemic.

As Gad Saad, an evolutionary psychologist and professor, said:

> *"And in this case the virus is not a biological virus, it's a mind virus. That's why I call them idea pathogens, or parasitic ideas.*
>
> *"So where do these idea pathogens come from? They all come from the university eco-system. In other words, as I always remind people, it takes intellectuals and professors to come up with some of the dumbest ideas."*

I grew up in a family of highly educated educators. In the culture of academcs, it is a sign of weakness to say, *"I don't know."*

The **definition** of a **pathogen** is: A bacterium, virus, or other microorganism that can cause disease.

So, many academics think they have — or pretend they have — all the answers. Even worse, I've observed them saying: *"Yeah, I know that."* It seems to be more of a defensive move than an outright lie. But regardless of what it actually is, to me it's a sign of a closed mind.

I like the words of Confucius (551-479 BC):

> *"The man who asks a question is a fool for a minute.*
> *The man who does not ask is a fool for life."*

If you take a minute to think about it, how many times have you been afraid of looking stupid? I lost count a long ago. Once you realize how much you can learn by asking questions, you lose your feel of looking stupid.

The fear of being stupid is an idea pathogen.

I remember when I was in high school, I never had any dates. One day my rich dad asked me, "Why don't you date anyone?" When I said, "I'm afraid she'll say 'No,'" he just laughed and said, "So you decided to say "'No,' for her."

It took me awhile to clear that idea pathogen.

In 1983, a few months after Fuller passed away, I saw the most beautiful woman I have ever seen. Her name was Kim. Immediately, I asked her if she would go out with me. Kim said "No," for six months. I kept asking, kept looking foolish, until one day she said "Yes." If not for Kim, there would be no Rich Dad Company. I would not be a rich man today if I had let myself say "No" for Kim.

Let me ask you a question: How many times do you reject yourself?

Repeating words of wisdom from Confucius:
"The man who asks a question is a fool for a minute. The man who does not ask is a fool for life."

My concern about modern education is that it's built on a foundation of fear. Most people leave school with the fear of making mistakes, the fear of looking stupid... and the fear of failing.

Pathogen of Fear
As Gad Saad says: "It's a mind virus." I call education a pathogen of fear. That is why stupidity is infinite. This pathogen of fear is the primary reason most people will never be rich. People leave school so afraid of making mistakes that they remain stupid and, in many cases, poor. Just because it's easier to pretend you know it all than to ask questions that will open your mind and teach you things you may not know. Fear, in my opinion, is the primary reason why the gap between rich and poor, the haves and the have nots, grows wider.

Fear vs. Freedom
Making matters worse, the pathogen of fear causes many to spend their lives clinging to security rather than taking a shot at freedom — true freedom.

My rich dad did not finish school. He dropped out of school at age 13 because his father died and he had to take over the family business. My rich dad did what few people do. He admitted to himself that he didn't know everything and surrounded himself with what Fuller called "brain slaves."

The history of education begins with "illiterate and ambitious war lords" who were financing schools to take advantage of "brain slaves." In Fuller's words:

> *"We find that the historical beginnings of schools and tutoring were established, and economically supported by illiterate and vastly ambitious warlords... who required a wide variety of brain slaves... with which to logistically and ballistically overwhelm those who opposed their expansion of physical conquest."*

Rich dad did not finish high school, much less college, so he used "brain slaves" — like lawyers and accountants — to fight his battles in areas where he just didn't have the knowledge or experience.

As I have written about in previous books, some of favorite times were the Saturdays when rich dad held his monthly meetings. He bought breakfast, and "brain slaves" came to share their knowledge. Rich dad would ask questions, sharing his business problems, and then rich dad listened.

Rich dad's son Mike and I would sit, enjoy the breakfast, and learn more in two hours about the real world than we were learning in high school. All rich dad did was present his business problems and ask questions from a table filled with very smart people — "brain slaves" who were accountants, attorneys, construction workers, human resource specialists, real estate agents, insurance agents, and so on. He could not afford to pay them by the hour, so he bought them breakfast and they had fun showing off how smart they were... solving rich dad's problems. On top of that, many in the group became great friends and started doing business with each other.

As Jimi Hendrix said:

> *"Knowledge speaks... but wisdom listens."*

Rich dad asked questions and listened. That is how he became rich.

And exactly as Fuller has said:

"The warlord vitiated their threat by making them all specialists... and reserving to himself exclusively the right to think about and act comprehensively."

When he taught our class, Fuller said:

"Schools teach students to be specialists. I teach you to be generalists."

Specialists focus on the small picture. A generalist focuses on the big picture The specialist "brain slaves" stayed small and rich dad got richer. His business empire kept growing all across Hawaii. If you look at Waikiki Beach today, the Hyatt Regency hotel sits in the most prominent position in Waikiki. With the help of his Saturday breakfasts, rich dad acquired the land under that magnificent hotel in 1969. He sold it just before the 2008 crash and made yet another fortune.

Again, as Jimi Hendrix said:

"Knowledge speaks... but wisdom listens."

Rich dad became rich because he listened to smart people.

Q: How did rich dad vitiate the threat from the brain slaves?

A: If anyone of the brain slaves had an idea rich dad was interested in, rich dad often hired him or her on the spot, promising to pay them what they asked.

Q: So, only rich dad gained from the knowledge he was now paying the brain slave for?

A: You got it. "Vitiate" means rich dad intentionally spoiled or impaired the power of the smarter brain slaves by paying them to become even more specialized, solving rich dad's problems. And everyone enjoyed a free, tax-deductible breakfast on rich dad.

Q: When you were 10 years old... did you knew you were going to be a war lord?

A: Yes. I knew I was not smart enough to be a brain slave. I knew I was not smart enough to be a lawyer, accountant, or medical doctor. But I knew I was smart enough to be a capitalist.

Rich dad used the Cashflow Quadrant to guide his son and me to becoming capitalists, on the B- and I-side of the quadrant.

War lords are capitalists on the right side of the Quadrant. Most brain slaves are specialists, prisoners of their education, on the E and S side of the quadrant.

The Rich Dad Company produces products for people from any quadrant who value their freedom more than job security.

Henry Ford (1863-1947) one of America's greatest capitalists, says this about financial security:

> *"If money is your hope for independence you will never find it. The only real security that man will have in this world is a reserve of knowledge, experience and ability."*

Becoming a capitalist is financial self-defense against communism. For example, over the past 25 years The Rich Dad Company has grown into a decentralized global brand, a network. Networks are priceless. Global, decentralized networks are a defense against centralized communism. McDonald's is a decentralized fast-food franchise network. Bitcoin is a decentralized cryptocurrency network. Rich Dad is a global financial education network built with book sellers and volunteer leaders running CASHFLOW Clubs.

True capitalists build and belong to decentralized global networks. Schools produce brain slaves without networks.

Free Lessons — Cartoon Animations Teach Capitalism

In support of Rich Dad's Capitalist Manifesto, we are producing a series of animated cartoons. These animations will make financial education simpler and more enjoyable for people of all ages. It is one way of fighting communism taught in our schools by teaching capitalism in our homes.

The first animated cartoon is about a King, a war lord, wanting to maintain power over his kingdom. Merlin, his wise and trusted advisor, proposes that the war lord start his own school system. The king is shocked at first. "Educate our people?" he asks Merlin. And Merlin replies that the purpose of the king's educational system is to create "specialists," brain slaves.

By developing his own school system, the king gains more power and more wealth by a teaching the smart students to be specialists:

As Bucky Fuller warned:

"Specialization is in fact only a fancy form of slavery wherein the "expert" is fooled into accepting slavery by making him feel that he in turn is a socially and culturally preferred-ergo highly secure-life long position."

How Schools Teach People to Be Poor

The list of the number of different ways the educational system teaches people to be poor is a long one. One way is to indoctrinate students to work for job security. The mantra goes:

"Go to school, get a good job, work hard, pay taxes, save money, buy a house because a house is an asset and your largest investment, and save for your retirement by investing in stocks, bonds, mutual funds, and ETFs."

In many ways, security — including job security — is the opposite of freedom. With freedom comes choices, which is why I put such a high value on freedom... all types of freedom.

Q: So when schools punish us for mistakes we gain less knowledge, experience, and ability?

A: Yes.

Q: And if we work at a job and are afraid of being fired for making a mistake, we gain less knowledge, experience, and ability?

A: Yes. That is why the pathogenic mind virus of the educational system is that mistakes make you stupid.

Q: And people who "memorize right answers" and "make no mistakes" are not smart?

A: Yes. It's really the opposite. Mistakes make you smart — if you learn from them. When you make a mistake and learn, you gain knowledge, experience, and the ability to apply that knowledge. If you don't make mistakes, out of fear, your stupidity remains infinite.

That is why these words are so profound:

"Information is not knowledge. The only source of knowledge is experience."

Q: Does that mean we have to find a place where we can make mistakes and learn without fear of being labeled stupid or getting fired?

A: Yes. Think of it this way: Tiger Woods, arguably the greatest golfer in the world, has hit more bad drives and missed more putts than I ever will. That is why he is the greatest.

Or Thomas Edison... who failed 1,014 times before inventing the electric light bulb. In school, the teachers labeled Edison, one of America's greatest inventors "addled."

Q: What does *addled* mean?

A: It means unable to think clearly, or confused.

Fuller said:

"I am convinced all of humanity is born with more gifts than we know. Most are born geniuses and just get de-geniused rapidly."

And Elon Musk is credited with saying:

"Don't confuse schooling with education. I didn't go to Harvard but the people that work for me did."

Elon Musk is a genius. He is an entrepreneur, a capitalist, a war lord. His staff who went to Harvard are his "brain slaves." Becoming a war lord, an entrepreneur, a capitalist is self-defense against communist brain slaves running our schools.

If we are to defeat communism taught by *brain slaves* in our schools, we need to teach more people to be *war lords*... in our homes.

Think about these words: stupidity is infinite.

The infinite is the home of entrepreneurs, capitalists, and war lords. The infinite is not the home of brain slaves.

In the next chapter I'll get into how war lords attain infinite returns.

CHAPTER NINE

INFINITE RETURNS

"Some say knowledge is power, but it is not true.
Character is power."
— Sathya Sai Baba (1926-2011)

Sai Baba was an Indian guru and philanthropist. The organization he founded has more than 2,000 centers in 120 countries. Through this organization, Sai Baba established a network of free specialty and general hospitals, medical clinics, drinking water projects, a university, ashrams, and schools.

This chapter is on Infinite Returns. Infinite returns are how you can acquire the power to create money without money. All you need is *education... on what is infinite.*

Allocation of Scarce Resources
Before you can access *education of the infinite,* it is important to understand that modern education is education based on scarcity.

For example, a thought leader in the school of economics is Thomas Malthus (1766-1834). Malthusian Economics is economic theory based on population growth and scarcity of life support on planet Earth. Simply said, Malthusian economics is about the *allocation of scarce resources.* His ideas continue to affect and infect all discussions on economics. So often the discussion is about scarcity versus abundance. The *infinite* is far beyond *abundance.*

Interestingly, Thomas Malthus was not trained as an economist. He was trained to be preacher who gained his reputation speaking on political economy and demographics. His works had a profound impact, positively and negatively, on other economists such as John Maynard Keynes and Karl Marx.

KISS: Keeping It Super Simple
Modern economics is the economics of **scarcity**.

To achieve infinite returns, one must understand the economics of **infinite** and the economics of **scarcity**.

You Become What You Study

In 1974, I was leaving the Marine Corps. Both dads, rich dad and poor dad, agreed on one thing. They both agreed that I needed to continue my education, continue to study, and evolve into a lifelong learner.

My rich dad said:
"A person's life ends... when they stop learning."

My poor dad said:
"You become what you study."

For example, I went to flight school to become a pilot. I studied with rich dad to become a capitalist and an entrepreneur.

If I wanted to be a specialist, such as a medical doctor or lawyer, I would go to medical school or law school. Fuller called the products of these narrow specialties "brain slaves."

In Marx's words from *Communist Manifesto*:
"The bourgeoisie has stripped of its halo every occupation hitherto honored and looked up to with reverent awe. It has converted the physician, the lawyer, the priest, the poet, the man of science into its paid wage-laborers."

While both of my dads agreed upon the importance of education and lifelong learning, they did not agree on what to study, or where to study. Rich dad was constantly flying to Honolulu to take business courses and attend seminars. Poor dad never left the university system. In his mind, if it was not taught in a university, it was not real education.

My poor dad thought my rich dad was foolish for attending seminars. My rich dad thought my poor dad was foolish for studying at universities.

At least they agreed on the importance of lifelong learning.

The Problem with Modern Education

I know I'm repeating myself here, from a previous chapter, but it's important, I think, to look again at Gad Saad's comments on the flaws of the Marxist-based, postmodern education that is running our schools:

> *"The West is currently suffering from such a devastating pandemic, a collective malady that destroys people's capacity to think rationally. Unlike other pandemics where biological pathogens are to blame, the current culprit is composed of a collection of bad ideas, spawned on university campuses, that chip away at people's ability to think rationally."*

My good fortune was having two father figures in my life — two men with almost opposite points of view on what type of education was valuable, war lord or brain slave.

For example, my poor dad wanted me to return to school, get my Master's degree and then my PhD. He did not care what subjects I studied, just as long as I had advanced degrees, a Master's and a PhD.

In 1973, while still flying for the Marine Corps in Hawaii, I attended night school at the University of Hawaii. I enrolled in their MBA program. It was not easy attending class, surrounded by college kids, while I was still in my Marine Corps flight suit.

In 1973, we were still fighting the Vietnam War. And the anti-war protests were still raging. In 1973, attending anti-war protests on campus was the "cool" thing to do. So I would sit in class, avoiding any contact with other students.

Six months into the MBA program, I dropped out. Not because of the anti-war protests, but because of boredom. I had been an apprentice to rich dad since I was 10 years old and what I learned from him about business did not jive with what my professors were teaching. Simply put, my professors taught from textbooks. My rich dad taught from real life.

Starting at the age of 10, about twice a week, I would study with rich dad by playing *Monopoly,* then applying what I learned from that game to working in his office and assisting him in managing his investments.

As Maria Montessori said:
    "What the hand does, the mind remembers."

And in Albert Einstein's words:
    "The only source of knowledge is experience."

The Best Education
The best education I received was collecting rent from rich dad's tenants. Not far from his office, rich dad was building rental properties. One of my first assignments was to collect rent from tenants who were late in paying. Obviously, many tenants felt embarrassed by having a 10-year-old knocking on their door, asking them for the rent money.

Donald Trump once told me his father had him do the same when he was a boy. It is a great financial education.

Listening to their stories of woe, sorrow, and loss — their excuses about why they had no money as their TV set blared in the background — was by far the best real-life financial education I could have ever asked for. Hearing their stories of woe... was a graduate-level education in human psychosis. It's not that I did not feel sorry for or have compassion for them. I did. No one likes witnessing human suffering. The lesson I learned was that feeling sorry for them, or having compassion, would not solve their underlying problems.

In other words, money was not their problem. And I realized giving them money would not solve their problems. Giving people money only made their real problems worse.

As Jimi Hendrix said:
> *"Knowledge speaks but wisdom listens."*

In 2021, America sunk to a new level of poverty, as millions were trained to wait for their government stimulus checks, with the message: *"The government will solve your problems."*

Socialism in America
The greatest threat to America today, from my point of view, is the growing welfare state and the entitlement mentality.

The end of American independence began with The Social Security Act, drafted by President Franklin D. Roosevelt in 1935.

Social Security will be bankrupt in 2034.

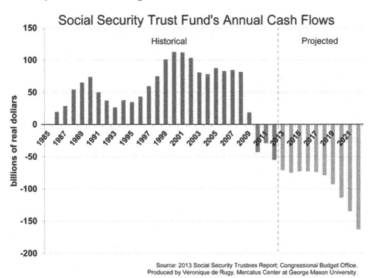

SOURCE: Congressional Budget Office

In 1965, President Lyndon B. Johnson signed Medicare into law.

Medicare will be bankrupt by 2026.

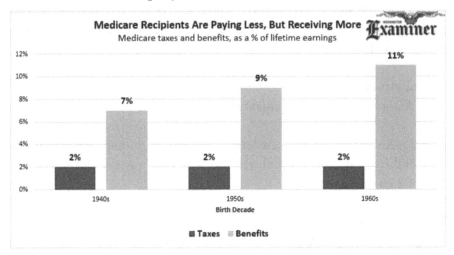

SOURCE: Congressional Budget Office

Ronald Reagan warned:

> *"One of the traditional methods of imposing statism or socialism has been by way of medicine."*

And Lenin warned:

> *"Medicine is the keystone of the arch of socialism."*

Repeating Henry Ford's warning:

> *"If money is your hope for independence, you will never have it. The only real security that a man will have in this word is a reserve of knowledge, experience, and ability."*

Most of the people I was collecting rent from were good hard-working people. They had jobs. Most had graduated from high school. A few had college degrees. Their problem was that they had stopped learning. I suspect most of them were counting on Social Security and Medicare to take care of them in old age.

In 2020 and 2021, homelessness is exploding just as Social Security and Medicare go broke.

So rather than get my Master's degree (and possibly a PhD) rich dad suggested I learn to invest in real estate and learn to be an entrepreneur. He often said:
"The purpose of a business is to acquire real estate."

If you read *Rich Dad Poor Dad* you may recall me writing about Ray Kroc of McDonald's saying:
"McDonald's is not in the hamburger business. McDonalds is in the real estate business."

McDonald's now owns more real estate than the Catholic Church.

Rich dad was also in the real estate business. He did not buy his real estate. His businesses bought his real estate.

I knew real estate was a path to wealth. And in 1973, I was watching television when an infomercial came on saying, "You, too, can buy real estate without money." Since Marine pilots were not paid much, I called the number on the TV screen and showed up for the free seminar. The free seminar explained what the 3-day seminar covered and how much it cost, which was $385 — a fortune for a Marine earning $500 a month. I signed up anyway, putting the course on my credit card, and a few weeks later was sitting in a seminar. It was like the seminars my rich dad would attend... the ones that my poor dad thought were a waste of money, and a scam, because it was not education taught by a university.

I loved the 3-day seminar. The instructor was a real, real estate investor. He came with photos and real contracts of deals he'd put together for "nothing down." I found out I loved learning... from real teachers.

At the end of the seminar, the instructor said:
"Now the seminar begins."

My mind race for a moment. I thought the seminar was over. Then I thought, again, about what Jimi Hendrix said:

"Knowledge speaks but wisdom listens."

I then listened to a real, real estate investor giving our class some real, real-life homework. His homework was for us to look at 100 properties in 90 days. After physically inspecting each property, we were to write a one-page report on the pros and cons, based upon the guidelines he used for evaluating a property.

To our class of approximately 30 newbies, the assignment sounded simple enough. We did not have to buy anything in 90 days, so most of us were relieved. All 30 students promised to do this simple homework assignment. At the end of the 90 days, I estimate that fewer than five completed the homework. Like the tenants who were late in paying their rent on rich dad's properties, most of those who did not evaluate the 100 properties always had "something come up."

I did complete the homework. I looked at 100 properties in 90 days and purchased a 1-bedroom, 1-bath condo, near the beach on the island of Maui — for nothing down.

The price of the property, in foreclosure, was $18,000, with 10% down. I pulled out my credit card, charged the $1,800 down payment on the card and in a few weeks I owned my first investment property.

My net income, after mortgage and expenses, was $25.00 a month. It was an infinite return because I had none of my own money in the investment.

Granted, $25.00 was not a lot of money, but it was infinite. Infinite returns are how you can acquire the power to create money without money. All you need is *education on what is infinite.*

Homework Becomes a Habit

A few months later, the real estate instructor came to town and we had lunch together. I was excited to tell him about what I learned doing my homework.

As our lunch came to an end the instructor said:

> *"Turn my homework assignment into your habit. The assignment I gave your class to do is what I do every day. My assignment to the class is my habit. That is why I make so much money."*

Today, as a man old enough to collect Social Security and Medicare, I go to the gym and look at new investment opportunities on a weekly basis. They are habits.

As my instructor spoke, memories of collecting rent, as a 10-year-old-boy, and listening to excuses and tales of woe came rushing back. Not only had these people stopped learning, but they had also developed a habit of making excuses, telling tales of woe, and watching television. They had developed the habits of the poor.

The Scarcity Mindset

Although most of rich dad's tenants were educated, had jobs, and were honest people, most of them were infected with education on scarcity.

That is why people like my poor dad, a highly educated man, repeatedly said:

> *"I can't afford it."*

My poor dad had a PhD in *"I can't afford it."*

How'd You Do It?

When people ask, "How did Kim, Kenny and you come up with $300 million in properties following the subprime real estate crash in 2008?" I respond by saying:

> *"We do our homework. We do our homework every day. It's a habit."*

Repeating Henry Ford's words:

> *"If money is your hope of independence, you will never have it. The only real security that a man will have in this world is a reserve of knowledge, experience, and ability."*

Stimulus Checks

In 2021, the government began handing out free mony in the form of "stimulus checks." Socialist and Marxists call this MMT, Modern Monetary Theory, and UBI, Universal Basic Income. I call MMT and UBI "communism."

These words have been attributed to Marx:

> *"Owners of capital will stimulate working class to buy more and more of expensive goods, houses and technology, pushing them to take more and more expensive credits, until their debt becomes unbearable. The unpaid debt will lead to bankruptcy of banks which will have to be nationalized and State will have to take the road which will eventually lead to communism."*

Communism... in Two Easy Steps

Again, in the words of the British Communist Party and Karl Marx:

> *"Democracy is the road to socialism."*

The first step is Democracy... the second is Socialism. And the third step is Communism.

As we were taught at military school, Marxism-Leninism, is the ideology that the Western academics call "communism." Marxism-Leninism will come in Two Stages.

The definition of socialism:
A political and economic theory of social organization which advocates that the means of production, distribution, and exchange should be owned or regulated by the state.

The First Step

In the first stage, a vanguard party infiltrates democracy and begins its educational process. Critical Race Theory and postmodern education is now taught in schools, businesses, and even the military.

The goal, of the vanguard party is to seize power "on behalf of the proletariat," "the working class of people" — those oppressed by the bourgeoisie, "the upper class of people." That is where Black Lives Matters fits into the infiltration process.

The facts that support the position that Stage One of Marxism-Leninism is complete are:

1: President Trump censored
2: Origin of COVID-19 questionable
3: Wuhan Lab funded by the United States
4: Medical doctors fired for questioning COVID-19
5: Businesses are shut down... and America becomes a police state
6: Schools are closed... and students study from home
7: Churches are closed
8: Masks are mandated... like Hitler forced Jews to wear yellow stars
9: Key Trump people, like General Flynn and Roger Stone, are arrested
10: Biden and Harris take office in a questionable election
11: The January 6 storming of the Capital is blamed on Trump
12: Burning and looting of our cities
13: Defunding our police
14: Stopping the construction of Trump's wall at the Southern border
15: Opening the Southern border to anyone
16: Paying people not to work
17: Printing trillions of dollars in fake dollars.
18: Blowing a bigger asset bubble than 2008
19: Rising homelessness, despair, violence
20: More and more Americans dependent upon the government

Possible Future Events:

   1: Biggest market crash in world history

   2: Hyperinflation

   3: Greatest Depression in world history

   4: Civil unrest that could lead to revolution

   5: Stage Two of Marxism-Leninism... communism begins

Suppression has begun. Stage One is nearly complete. We see its earmarks all around us: the suppression of the opposition, censorship, defunding the police, the arrest of critics, and civil unrest about to begin.

Americans Living in Fear

In 2020, America was divided and gripped in a pandemic of fear. America fears a small group of Cancel Culture bullies, modern day Hitler youth. Americans are living in fear of Americans.

On the subject of intellectual terrorists, Gad Saad warned:

> *"Social justice warriors and their ilk are intellectual terrorists, and they can wreak havoc on reason and our public life, limiting people's willingness to speak and think freely, without ever constituting a majority."*

On the subject of free expression, Dennis Prager, founder of Prager University, warns:

> *"There are two ways to choke off free expression... Clamp down on free speech and declare some topics off-limits. That strategy is straightforward enough. The other, more insidious way to limit free expression is to try to change the very language people use."*

Changing Our Language

Gad Saad said this about being politically correct:

> *"These politically correct language initiatives are misguided and harmful. They create highly entitled professional "victims" who expect to be free from any offense, and they engender a stifling atmosphere where all individuals walk on eggshells lest they might commit a linguistic capital crime."*

The Not-So-Cold War

In the 1960s America was in a Cold War with Russia. In 1962 I saw an atomic bomb explode from our kitchen window.

Between 1965 to 1969 my economics instructor, a former B-17 pilot in WWII, had us study Marx, Lenin, Stalin, Hitler, and Mao. He was preparing us for the next war.

In 1966, I sailed into Vietnam as a student on board a bomb carrying cargo ship. In 1973, as a Marine, flying along the beaches of the French-Indo Chinese Riviera, I could see my instructor's warnings on Marxism-Leninism coming to life.

In 2006, Donald Trump and I published our first book. That book, titled *Why We Want You to Be Rich,* carried our message about the future: prepare for turbulent times.

In 2008, the subprime market crashed. In 2020, the global economy shut down as riots break out. In 2020, seeing the boarded-up Neiman Marcus store near my office in Scottsdale, Arizona, I knew I had to write this book.

In 2020, I was afraid the Second Stage of Marxism-Leninism is about to begin.

Socialism by Another Name

It was President Ronald Reagan who warned:

> *"Now back in 1927 an America socialist Norman Thomas, six times candidate for president on the Socialist Party Ticket, said the American people would never vote for socialism. But he said under the name of liberalism the American people, will adopt every fragment of the socialist program."*

And as Khrushchev said:

> *"You Americans are so gullible."*

So how does a person fight back? Where do you even begin?

A great first step in investing in education. Education of the infinite.

In 1973, I dropped out of my MBA program. It was not infinite education. That same year I enrolled in investing in real estate without money. It was infinite education. I was learning how to make money without money.

In 1973, I was also being courts-martialed for the second time. The first time I was brought up on charges was in Vietnam. The second time was in Hawaii. Like Bucky Fuller, who was thrown out of Harvard twice for having too much fun with women and alcohol, I too as having too much fun. Twice,

Many people returned from Vietnam with PTSD, Post Traumatic Stress Disorder. I did not have PTSD. I returned from Vietnam with a severe case of IABPD, I-Am-Bulletproof Disorder. After crashing and losing three aircraft in Vietnam, I thought I was bulletproof. My self-confidence was sky-high. I was not cocky. I was not arrogant. I was simply extremely confident... convinced that I was bulletproof.

The first courts-martial was for having far too much fun drinking and partying in Hong Kong. The prosecutor dropped the charges when he realized I was not a criminal. Just a kid guilty of too much alcohol-fueled carousing.

I was up on charges for my second courts-martial for drinking and flying female companions to deserted islands in Hawaii. I remember like it was yesterday, taxiing my helicopter to the hangar and shutting the engine down. Immediately after the engine stopped, Military Police cars surrounded my aircraft so I could not run. Opening my door, empty beer cars fell out of the helicopter; then I fell out. I was not in my official fire-retardant flight suit or flight boots. I was in purple swim trunks, shirtless, and wearing rubber slippers. When they opened the back compartment, they found women's clothes, which added to my problems.

The next day I was officially placed under house arrest, which was not so bad. My "house" was my condo at the Ilikai, a luxury hotel on Waikiki Beach. Relieved of my duties, I was on paid vacation at the pool, having even more fun under house arrest. I even got a part-time job, as assistant manager of the hotel's night club. I was enjoying life, a life of wine, women, and song, making extra money while under house arrest.

While sitting at the hotel pool, I met a young woman who invited me to a guest preview seminar. I was not interested in the seminar, but I was interested in her. The guest seminar was for EST, which stood for Erhard Seminars Training. The guest seminar was held in the Hilton Hawaiian Village Dome, a dome built by Bucky Fuller. Since I had never been in Bucky's dome, which was next door to the Ilikai Hotel, I became even more excited about attending the guest seminar with the young woman. I was not breaking the rules of my house arrest because I was within the five-mile radius of my condo at the Ilikai Hotel.

The two-weekend seminar blew my mind. It was just what I needed. It opened my mind to a world I was not aware existed. The seminar opened my mind to a different type of education — education of personal responsibility.

In 1973, my first seminar on infinite education was on real estate. In that same year EST was my second seminar on personal responsibility and the importance of telling the truth.

There is a reason that I started this chapter with the quote from Sai Baba:
"Some say knowledge is power, but it is not true.
Character is power."

Sai Baba was not a part of the seminar. I mention him because the seminar opened my mind to people I hated: the hippies who spit on my men and me when we returned from Vietnam. Sitting next people I thought I hated, over the course of two weekends, was a transformational experience for me. While I did not agree with them, I began to see the world from their point of view.

In 1968, the Beatles, one of my favorite bands, had traveled to India to study with Maharishi Mahesh Yogi. The Maharishi had first met the Beatles in 1967. They were fascinated with his techniques of Transcendental Meditation, which is why they traveled to his spiritual training camp in Rishikesh India, in 1968.

In 1973, I realized many of the participants in the EST seminar were much like the Beatles. They were people in search of infinite education, known as spiritual enlightenment. I had entered the "New Age" educational movement, an education on the powers of infinite spirituality.

When I returned to the Marine Corps Air Station, after the EST seminar and my exposure to a very different type of infinite spiritual education, I was different. I returned after calling the prosecutor and informing him I was coming in to tell the truth... the whole truth, and nothing but the truth. While technically still under house arrest, I walked into the court room and took the stand. The prosecutor, a Marine captain, asked me if I wanted to be represented by my own attorney. I declined. Once sworn in, I began telling the court the truth.

At the end of nearly four hours of testimony I was exhausted. I held nothing back. I even told the court about of things I did that no one could ever have found out.

In the movie *A Few Good Men*, military lawyer Daniel Kaffee (Tom Cruise) is interrogating Col. Nathan Jessup (Jack Nicholson) and demands, "I want the truth!" Jessup's reply: "You can't handle the truth."

After EST, I needed to tell the Marine Corps the truth. Once I told them everything, I looked up and said, "How long will I be in jail?"

The prosecutor nodded and said, "Thank you. You're not going to jail. You did the honorable thing. You will be a free man, with an honorable discharge, just as soon as I finish the paperwork."

About a two months later, I drove off the Marine Airbase, a free man, honorably discharged. The prosecutor had kept his word. As I drove toward the main gate, I recalled the lesson I learned in Sunday school, from the Bible, John 8: 32:

"And you will know the truth, and the truth will set you free."

Approaching the main gate, the Marine guard saluted and I returned his salute, my last act as a Marine Officer. In 1974, driving away from a life that began the day I entered the academy in 1965, I realized I had finally become a Marine. I now embodied the words that carried so much meaning — *mission, duty, honor, code, discipline, sacrifice,* and *service.*

Also, I embodied the words of Said Baba that I had learned at EST:
"Some say knowledge is power, but it is not true. Character is power."

Until that point, I had been man of weak character.

As I watched the Marine Airbase fade into the distance, I better understood why Marines tattoo these words on their bodies: death before dishonor. And why, when they greet another Marine, they say, "Semper fi," short for "Semper fidelis." I finally became a Marine the day I left the Marine Corps.

The meaning of Semper Fidelis
*Semper fidelis is Latin for **always faithful**. Semper Fidelis is the motto of every Marine — an eternal and collective commitment to the success of our battles, the progress of our Nation, and the steadfast loyalty to the fellow Marines who fight beside us. Established in 1883, this motto distinguishes the bond developed and shared between Marines. It goes beyond any words that are spoken... as it is a warriorhood that is lived.*

Culture... and Cults

The media has stigmatized the word cult. Just the mention of the word brings to mind images of Waco and David Koresh, of Jim Jones and the Jonestown Massacre. And the Salem witch hunts, the Red Scare and the Moonies. The media loves cults because they can be big news. Stories on cults sell newspapers and magazines, drive spikes in viewership, and can set social media on fire. The public has always been fascinated with cults, especially anything outside organized religions.

It's easy to forget that *cult* is also short for *culture.* It also means a devotion to study. Yet many people, it seems, have come to associate the word *cult* with fringe cult leaders and indoctrination rather than its root in culture and study.

Since 1996, The Rich Dad Company has stood for the study of capitalism. We are a capitalist cult, a culture for capitalists.

As Stage One of Marxism-Leninism comes to an end, will the Rich Dad Company be targeted when the oppression begins? I see it already happening and remain vigilant... ever conscious of our freedoms.

Unfortunately, since the 1930s, cults became the object of sociological study in the context of the study of religious behavior. Since the 1940s the Christian counter cult movement has opposed some sects and new religious movements, labeling them "cults" because of their unorthodox beliefs.

The Marine Corps is a culture of warriors. So is the Army, Navy, Air Force, and Coast Guard. So are our police, fire fighters, and first responders. They all belong to a culture of warriors.

America is also a culture of freedom. And a culture of free market capitalism. That is why people from all over the world dream of living here and why many are willing to risk their lives to get to the United States.

And more and more so, it seems to me, it is becoming a culture of entitlement. In 2020 America's culture is under attacked by cultures of greed, laziness, ignorance, paranoia, and 'snowflake' sensitivities. Members of these cults want equality without earning it. That was Karl Marx's ideal for communism. Today, Marx's cult is the "everyone gets a trophy" cult.

In 2020 the words *Semper Fidelis* are inclusive of anyone who fights for freedom, regardless of race, gender, country, religion, education, or financial status.

Abraham Lincoln warned:
> *"At what point then is the approach of danger to be expected? I answer, if it ever reach us, it must spring up amongst us. It cannot come from abroad. If destruction be our lot, we must ourselves be its author and finisher."*

In 1984, Kim, Blair Singer, and I began teaching for an organization that taught entrepreneurship based upon Fuller's Generalized Principles and rich dad's principles of money. Entrepreneurs from all over Australia were signing up for our programs. Even the government, military, and firefighters were sending their leaders to our programs on transformational entrepreneurship and leadership. What made our programs powerful was that we taught via games, not lectures.

Ten years later, in 1994, we were closed. We were accused of being a cult by the ABC, the Australian Broadcasting Commission, and the Christian Cult Awareness Network. They had asked to do a piece on on the organization "to showcase the success of our work." It turned out to be a hatchet job. We were accused of being a cult because participants had such powerful breakthrough experiences, both personally and professionally.

They actually did us a favor. Being entrepreneurs, we took what we taught and packaged it into products.

In 1996, Kim and I repackaged our seminar into our board game *CASHFLOW.* When the media and cult hunters, again, tried to accuse us of teaching the occult, we told them to play the game. We asked that they let the public decide if we were in into the occult, voodoo magic, or Satanic worship. The media and cult hunters never bothered us again.

After playing the game, the public knew the truth. We were teaching financial education for entrepreneurs and those who sought financial freedom.

In 1997 *Rich Dad Poor Dad* was published. In 1997, The Rich Dad Company rose from the ashes. Sometimes we must die... to be reborn. Our Capitalist Manifesto carries on the Education of the Infinite, in both money and spirit.

Racist Cults
Today the latest cults are racists cults. And I find it interesting that "racists" are accusing others of being "racists."

We all know the names of these racist cults. They have spread their hate all over the world via the education system. These racist cults have infected America, with their toxic poisons. How dare we allow these racist cults to spread their toxic ideology that proports "America is systemically racist."

Nelson Mandela, the leader credited with spearheading the resistance to South Africa's policy of apartheid, said:

"No one is born hating another person because of the color of their skin, or his background, or his religion. People must learn to hate, and if they can learn to hate, they can be taught to love, for love comes more naturally to the human heart than its opposite."

Why do we allow this viral pathogen of hate to be taught in our schools?

As Thomas Sowell warned:

"Over the generations, black leaders have ranged from noble souls to shameless charlatans."

Why do our corporations endorse and disseminate their toxic poison via corporate policy?

These racist cults are the worst and most vile of all because their poison is pushed through the veins of corporate and social media, and through academia, poisoning the minds of our youth.

As Gad Saad warns:

"Social justice warriors and their ilk are intellectual terrorists, and they can wreak havoc on reason and our public life, limiting people's willingness to speak and think freely, without ever constituting a majority."

Gad also asked:

"How far do you go back unfolding history until you find the villain of your choice?"

Is this why *The New York Times* is rewriting history, claiming America was founded in 1619 as a racist country? A narrative that debunks the 1776 American Revolution and that fight for freedom...

Gad also points out:

> *"An analysis of political campaign donations across a broad range of industries uncovered that the four most liberal professions, in decreasing order, were the entertainment industry, academia, online computer services, and newspapers and print media."*

And:

> *"A 2013 study from Indiana University's School of Journalism revealed that American journalists were nearly four times more likely to be Democrats than Republicans."*

EST transformed into Landmark and although I have not participated in a Landmark Forum, I have many friends who have. I am thankful Landmark carries on with Education on Infinite.

The Difference Between Infinite and Abundant

There are differences between abundant and infinite. A real-life example of the difference between abundance and infinite is how Sai Baba's organization has grown to 2,000 centers in more than 100 countries, powered mainly by volunteers. Sai Baba's work grows via the spirit of the Infinite. Infinite takes us beyond abundance.

Today Rich Dad has thousands of CASHFLOW Clubs, all over the world, many teaching for free, powered by the spirit of Infinite. And the culture of the Marines, the spirit of Semper Fidelis, is carried on in CASHFLOW Clubs throughout the world.

I have been on this earth for more than seven decades and I have never seen America so divided. I have lost friends... just because Donald Trump is my friend. I have lost friends because I've dared to question and challenge so many things in our world today — the status quo, what I see as fake news, and how the powers that be are playing games with our money. We have lost our sense of humor. Laughing today is risky. Comedians are no longer funny. When sharing ideas is cause for conflict and the drawing of battle lines, I fear for our future.

I take heart in Gad Saad's words:
> *"Anyone who is willing to end a relationship because of a reasoned difference of opinion is not worthy of your friendship."*

A Culture of Capitalists

Later in this book you will hear from my team. We meet via Zoom once a week. We are a cult, a culture of professional friends, all spiritual capitalists. And we study together.

Staying connected with like-minded individuals is essential, especially in these trying times. I hope you do whatever it takes to stay connected and stay strong. Pray, meditate, fast, exercise, join a church, religion, or spiritual study group and meet or talk regularly.

Your body is your outer strength. Your spirit is your inner strength.

And it's your spirit that gives you the power to be anti-fragile. Being anti-fragile gives you the power to bounce back stronger, better, of stronger character, no matter what life throws at you.

As Sai Baba said:
> *"Some say knowledge is power, but it is not true.*
> *Character is power."*

Your spirit is your true character.

Your spirit is your ticket into the world of the infinite.

CHAPTER TEN

ARCHITECTS OF THE FUTURE

"We are called to be architects of the future, not its victims."
— R. Buckminster Fuller

I have lost count of the number of people who, when I meet them, say to me: "I have $10,000. What should I do with my money?"

On one hand, I'm happy that they're thinking about their financial future. On the other hand I just want to scream. And there are three reasons for that. One: if you don't know what to do with you money, don't advertise that fact and invite unscrupulous advice or investment options. Two: it speaks to me of a fear and desperation... that people who don't even know me (and whose financial picture *I don't know*) would ask me to give them advice. And third — this one's the kicker — if we were taught about money in school we'd know at least a little about money, investing, markets and risk. We'd have a starting point for learning more, life-long learning on the road to financial freedom... because we can always get smarter with our money and how we invest it. [OK... I'm off the soapbox... and on to the guts of this chapter...]

If someone doesn't know what to do with their money... there are probably better questions to ask than "What should I do with my money?" A few of them are:

1 – "Why is there no financial education in our schools?

2 – "Is the lack of financial education in schools just a mistake?

3 – "Why is the gap between rich and poor increasing?

4 – "Why is the government handing out free money?

5 – "What is money? And how can I make my money work for me?"

6 – "How can I achieve infinite returns?

7 – "How can I make money without money?"

8 – "Why do the rich pay less in taxes?"

9 – "What happens to my tax dollars?"

10 – "How do I protect myself from Marxism-Leninism?

The answers to these questions require real financial education... the kind that's not taught in schools.

A Very Brief History of Money
When I was a kid in the 1950s, the only people who invested in the stock market were gamblers. Rich dad laughed at them. He stayed away from them. Rich dad was an entrepreneur. He did not like doing business with gamblers. He called them "get-rich-quick dreamers." Rich dad did not buy stocks. As an entrepreneur, created his own assets and investments.

My poor dad never invested. He saved money and was counting on his teacher's pension and Social Security to keep him alive after he retired.

In the 1950s, investors bought bonds and saved money. In the 1950s it was the "smart thing to do." In the 1950s, bonds and savings were not risky. They were safe, steady, and secure. Rich dad owned a few bonds. He did save money. He stayed out of stocks. In the 1950s, "passbook savings accounts" paid 5% or more in interest... and it was called "the magic" of compounding interest...

In 1971 President Richard Nixon took the dollar off the gold standard. Nixon broke the promise America made at the Bretton Woods Conference in New Hampshire in 1944. America's promise: the U.S. dollar would be the "Reserve Currency" of the world. In 1944, in exchange for the Reserve Currency status, America promised to back each dollar with gold and not print money. Being the Reserve Currency of the world, meant the U.S. dollar was "as good as gold."

In 1971, President Nixon broke that promise. Remember his nickname... "Tricky Dick?"

In 1971, the U.S. dollar became debt and savers became losers as the biggest money printing operation in world history began. In 1971, the way the U.S. dollar was created was via a system of debt and taxes. The U.S. government paid its bills with *fiat money*. Fiat money is government money, or fake money.

Fiat money is money created by creating debt, and the taxpayer pays the debt via taxes.

A 50-Year Milestone

As I am finishing this book in August of 2021, we've hit a milestone — the 50th anniversary — of the biggest cash heist in history... August 15, 1971. The day Nixon took the U.S. dollar off the gold standard.

Podcast: 50th Anniversary of Nixon's 1971 Decision

You may want to go to Rich Dad's archives of podcasts, accessible via RichDad.com and listen to this 50th Anniversary radio program on Nixon taking the U.S. dollar off the gold standard. The guests for that segment marking this world-changing event — the greatest of all bank robberies in history — are Ken McElroy and Tom Wheelwright. They are my "go-to" guys — Kenny for debt and Tom for taxes.

Today's Bank Robbers

The difference between a bank heist in the 1970s and one today is that the bankers are the robbers. Today's bank robberies are inside jobs. Today's bank robbers wear suits, not masks. They are not uneducated. As Steven Brill describes, in his book *Tailspin*, today's bank robbers have been educated at the world's finest prep schools and universities. They are armed with college degrees, not guns.

In 1974, ERISA, Employee Retirement Income Security Act was passed and Americans were forced into the stock market. Workers without financial education became the gamblers my rich dad avoided. Rich dad smirked at ERISA's name, saying "Anything the government proposes, in this case Employee Income Security, means employee's income is in trouble." Rich dad was correct. ERISA morphed into the 401(k)s that many employees in the E quadrant have today. The 401(k) and IRAs for the self-employed, sent the S-quadrant workers without financial education into the stock market, a den of thieves, vipers, and financial planners. The stock market took off. Bankers got richer. The gap between rich and poor became as big as the Grand Canyon. In 1974, Marxist-Leninists began licking their chops.

Shift from DB to DC
The 401(k)s and IRAs are DC retirement plans — Defined Contribution plans. Simply put, "What you put in, you get back." If a person hasn't funded his or her DC retirement plan... then there is no retire plan — and no retirement benefits.

For example, an employee can contribute to their 401(k) for years but if there is a giant stock market crash, all that they've accumulated could be wiped out in a day. If they are retired, they do not have the time to recover.

The saying is:
The bull walks up the stairs, the bear goes out the window."

If the worker is 65 years old, they do not have luxury of "investing for the long-term." If you have a 401(k) or IRA, I am not suggesting that you get out of the market. All I am saying is... be aware.

Rich dad warned:
"Everyone is happy when the Bull is going up the ladder.
People are depressed when the Bear goes out the window.
That is why it is called a Depression."

Rich dad and poor dad were both children during the Great Depression. That depression lasted from 1929 to 1954. The Dow Jones Industrial Average hit an all-time high of 381 in 1929 and crashed. The world entered the Great Depression. It took until World War II and millions of deaths for the Dow to get it back to 381, in 1954.

According to Jim Rickards, in his book *The Great New Depression*, we are currently in a depression.

As Warren Buffett warns:

"You only find out who is swimming naked when the tide goes out."

In his book *The Sun Also Rises*, Ernest Hemingway wrote:

Q: How did you go bankrupt?

A: Two ways. Slowly at first, then suddenly.

Pensions for Government Employees

Before ERISA, government and corporate pension plans were Defined Benefit plans, or DBs. DB plans defined a specific benefit to be paid to a retiree upon retirement. Employees expected that, at retirement, they would receive the "benefit payment" they were promised. Most government employees have DB plans, which is why so many people want to work for the government. The problem is that, today, many of these DB plans are bankrupt.

A few years ago I co-authored a book titled *Who Stole My Pension?* with former SEC attorney and America's leading authority on pension looting Edward Siedle. In the book we explain how Wall Street bankers, pension managers, companies, and governments have systemically looted the DB pensions of workers. The list of looted pensions is a long one and includes labor unions, airline pilots, truck drivers, police, fire fighters, schoolteachers, and public servants.

Q: Are you saying that up until 1971, it was smart to have a job and save money?

A: Yes. Until 1971 saving money was smart because the Fed and U.S. government were not allowed to print money. Savers were winners and, thanks to compounding interest, it was possible for a person to "save their way" to retirement. After 1971, savers became losers.

Q: Are you saying that up until 1974, workers had DB pension plans so they did not need to learn to be investors?

A: Exactly. In 1974, the year ERISA was passed, workers were forced into the stock market. Workers with 401(k)s and IRAs —but no financial education — became gamblers in the stock market... and bankers became billionaires.

A quote often attributed to Lenin ties central banks to communism:

"The establishment of a central bank is 90% of communizing a nation."

As a reminder of the timing on all of this...

In 1913 the Federal Reserve Bank was created.

In 1913, the 16th Amendment was passed. This led to the formation of the IRS, the Internal Revenue Service... the tax man.

Q: Are you saying the Fed and the IRS are Marxist?

A: Yes... but look at the facts and not my opinion.

As Marx said:

"Taxation is the source of life for the bureaucracy, the army, the church and the court, in short, the whole apparatus of executive power. Strong government and heavy taxes are identical."

In 1913, the government now had the power to print money and tax people.

And the American Revolution began in 1773, in Boston Harbor. The event, The Boston Tea Party, was a tax revolt.

I am surprised that there isn't more push back, morer outrage related to the 1619 Project and the campaign to rewrite our history.

As Marx warned:
> *"Take away a nation's heritage and they are more easily persuaded."*

Thomas Jefferson (1743-1826), a Founding Father of America, signer on the Declaration of Independence, and third President of the United States, warned:
> **"If the American people ever allow private banks to control the issue of their currency, first by inflation, then by deflation, the banks and** corporations that will grow up around [the banks] will deprive the people of all property until their children wake-up homeless on the continent their fathers conquered. The issuing power should be taken from the banks and restored to the people, to whom it properly belongs."

Jefferson also warned:
> *"And I sincerely believe with you that banking establishments are more dangerous than standing armies, and that the principle of spending money to be paid by posterity under the name of funding is but swindling futurity on a large scale."*

Congressman Ron Paul, Republican Presidential candidate and author of *End the Fed*, shares these words from a plaque on his desk:
> *"Don't steal – the government hates competition!"*

And Congressman Paul warned:
> *"It is no coincidence that the century of total war coincided with the century of central banking."*

In 1971, the year Nixon took the U.S. dollar off the gold standard, the U.S. dollar became debt and taxes. The U.S. dollar became fiat money, aka "fake money."

These words, from an article by John Maynard Keyes, linking the destruction of capitalism to the manipulation of our currency:

> *"Lenin is said to have declared that the best way to destroy the capitalist system was to debauch the currency."*

And repeating Marx's warning:

> *"A heavy or progressive or graduated income tax is necessary for the proper development of Communism."*

And these words:

> *"The way to crush the bourgeoise is to grind them between the millstones of taxation and inflation."*

Repeating Thomas Sowell's warning:

> *"Hyperinflation can take virtually your entire life's savings, without the government having to bother raising the official tax rate at all."*

Warren Buffett warned:

> *"The arithmetic makes it plain that inflation is a far more devastating tax than anything that has been enacted by our legislature. The inflation tax has a fantastic ability to simply consume capital.*

Buffett also warned:

> *"Inflation feels like an abstract concept, but it hits everyday people the hardest."*

Socialist Points of View

U.S. Senator Bernie Sanders — Democrat, socialist, and Presidential candidate — had this to say about income in equality:

> *"They talk about class warfare – the fact of the matter is there has been class warfare for the last thirty years. It's a handful of billionaires taking on the entire middle-class and working-class of this country. And the result is you now have in America the most unequal distribution of wealth and income of any major country on Earth and the worst inequality in America since 1928. How could anybody defend the top 400 richest people*

in this country owning more wealth than the bottom half of America, 150 million people?"

And U.S. Senator and Presidential candidate Hillary Clinton said this in a speech at a fundraiser in 2004:

"Many of you are well enough off that... the tax cuts may have helped you. We're saying that for America to get back on track, we're probably going to cut that short and not give it (tax cuts) to you. We're going to take things away from you on behalf of the common good."

While I agree with the problems that Sanders and Clinton see, I disagree on the solutions.

During the 2016 U.S. Presidential campaign, both Bernie Sanders and Hillary Clinton, professional politicians, were running against Trump a capitalist. During a debate Hilary Clinton accused Donald Trump of paying no income tax, after he didn't make make his tax returns public.

On global television, Hilary says:

"He doesn't want the American people to know... that he's pad nothing in federal taxes."

Trump replies:

"That makes me smart."

When I heard that I thought: he is a smart guy — and he surrounds himself with very smart people. The tax code offers many incentives for businesses and investors and paying little or no income tax isn't illegal. Or even suspect. It's simply taking full advantage of the incentives in the tax code. These same incentives and tax benefits are available to all American who meet the requirements. Meaning that Trump isn't getting any special treatment or doing things other business owners cannot do.

The New York Times would later report that Trump paid $0 in *income* taxes for 11 years, $750 in 2016, and $750 in 2017, the years he was the President of the United States.

Trump countered by saying the figures were inaccurate and says he paid "a lot" in taxes. Without real financial education and a basic understanding of the tax law, most people would think he's lying if he paid $0 in income taxes for 11 years. There are many kinds of taxes that businesses pay... apart from income tax. The more employees you have the less tax you'll pay. If you're doing what the government wants done and the tax code offers incentives for doing that, you can drastically reduce your tax liability.

In 2019 Amazon was considering building a second headquarters in Queens, New York. Many saw this as a huge economic opportunity that would mean 25,000 jobs and saw how the ripple effect of that could benefit New Yorkers. AOC — Alexandria Ocasio-Cortez — let the charge against the tax breaks and "corporate greed" that resulted in Amazon's decision to pull out of the proposed deal.

In 1996, after the Australian Broadcasting Corporation (ABC) and the Christian Cult Awareness Network labeled my entrepreneurial seminar business a religious cult and effectively shutting down our business, it was time to fight back. The Capitalist Manifesto known as The Rich Dad Company, rose from those ashes.

In 1996, the *CASHFLOW* board game was launched, in Australia, New Zealand, Canada, Singapore, and several cities across the United States.

In 2000, Oprah Winfrey called. I spent an hour on *Oprah!* with one of the most powerful women in the world, and the rest is history. *Rich Dad Poor Dad* went global, running on the power of spiritual infinity.

In 2000, Donald Trump and I began doing seminars to tens of thousands of people across America and Australia. That year I said a silent "thank you" to the Australian Broadcast Corporation and the Christian Cult Awareness Network.

In 2006, Donald Trump and I published our first book together, *Why We Want You to Be Rich.* Five years later, in 2011, we published our second book,

Midas Touch. In that book we answer the question: What's an entrepreneur's most important job? The answer: creating high-quality, stable jobs.

In 2015, we were about to write our third book together when he announced on the Rich Dad Radio Show "I'm going to run for President." All I could say was "Good luck. You have my support." Or, as Marines say, "Semper Fidelis."

I do not know if Oprah and Donald are friends. I have never asked. I mention Oprah Winfrey and Donald Trump, not to drop names but to reinforce the lesson from the previous chapter, the chapter on spiritual Infinite Returns. Oprah, Donald, and I were drawn together as teachers, in support financial education and the mission of The Rich Dad Company:

"To elevate the financial wellbeing of humanity."

As Fuller said to our class in 1983:

"We are called to be architects of the future, not its victims."

Just as Oprah and Donald Trump heeded that call — as entrepreneurs and agents of change.

After reading GRUNCH the pieces of the puzzle, the puzzle I call my life, began making sense. I understood why I had two dads. I understood why I went to military school and studied Marx, Lenin, Stalin, Hitler, and Mao. I understood why I joined the Marine Corps and why I flew behind enemy lines looking for gold, real money. I understood why I dropped out of the MBA program and why I did not fly for the airlines, as my poor dad wanted me to... choosing instead to become an entrepreneur, a capitalist like my rich dad. I understood why I had failed so many times, starting business after business, struggling, being cheated by partners and suppliers, and losing a lot of money.

In words credited to Winston Churchill:

"Success is not final, failure is not fatal: it is the courage to continue that counts."

In 1983 I met Kim. And when Kim, Blair Singer, and I sold everything and moved to San Diego, California in 1985 we trusted we could do what God wanted done. It has not been an easy journey. Our souls and spirits were tested. We met many wonderful people and as well as crooks, conmen, and charlatans. Some of them were our business partners.

Over the years we've learned that Warren Buffett's words are true:
> *"You can't make a good deal with a bad person."*

The good news is, out of every bad deal and out of every bad person Kim and I met great people. You will hear from them shortly. They will all share how we all work to do what God wants done, and support the mission of the Rich Dad Company.

Some of our partners, like Blair, have worked with me for 38 years. Many others, including Ken McElroy and Tom Wheelwright and Mona Gambetta, have been with Kim and me for over 25 years. Together, we have built a strong global business and impacted millions of lives by sharing what we've learned. We've done well, as capitalists and entrepreneurs, but also stayed true to our mission. We've made money; we've paid taxes when and where taxes were due.

As this first section of the book draws to a close, you will meet the rest of our spiritual teammates in business. I introduce them to you, with the intention that you put together your own team of professional and spiritual teammates.

As Gad Saad warns:
> *"In this case the virus is not a biological virus, it's a mind virus. That's why I call them idea pathogens, or parasitic ideas"*

Our world is being torn apart by mind viruses, carcinogenic pathogens of fear and hate, spread through our schools. Building a tight and trusted team around you is one way to fight back.

Another Great Depression

According to Jim Rickards, we are in "the great new Depression." In today's world there will be no greater asset than your team of professional and spiritual teammates. That is why Kim and I want to introduce our team to you. They are our greatest asset. And over the years we have become more selective in who we surround ourselves with... seeking like-minded individuals who share our vision and values and are committed to life-long learning and open to all points of view.

In the years ahead it will not be enough to have a stockbroker, a real estate broker and a financial planner as advisors. You will need a unified team, people who are professional friends you trust, people you can count on. Just like the people my rich dad met with on Saturday mornings, all those years ago.

In the next chapter, you will also find out how capitalists can make millions of dollars and pay $0 in taxes... legally.

The Cancel Culture

The cancel culture is a culture of victims. They love victims. They worship victims. They elevate some victims, not into saints but into martyrs. Martyrs are people who love to suffer. Please do not be a martyr. Or a victim. Instead, become an architect of your future.

Your future will depend upon you and your spiritual team. They will be your bridge into the infinite.

CHAPTER ELEVEN

A MILLION PATHS TO HEAVEN

"There are a million paths to financial heaven...
And billions of paths to financial hell."
— Rich Dad

One of Bucky Fuller's statements that I found most profound was:
"We now have four billion billionaires on board Spaceship Earth who are entirely unaware of their good fortune."

In 1981, there were approximately 4 billion people on planet earth.

Today, in 2021, there are approximately, 7.9 billion.

In 1981, sitting in the audience listening to Bucky speak, the idea of *4 billion billionaires* was outside my reality. I was going broke. My business was going down. How could there be 4 billion billionaires?

Today, I am better able to see the world through Fuller's eyes.

Bucky Fuller devoted his life to exploring one question: What can one average man do to change the world? He called himself "Guinea Pig B" (the "B"... for Bucky). His was "an experiment to discover what a little, penniless, unknown individual might be able to do effectively on behalf of all humanity.

In 1927, after contemplating suicide, he stopped working for money. In 1927, he decided to sit at his kitchen table and follow his "intuition." That led him to becoming one of the greatest geniuses — futurists — in the world. He continued asking himself "What does God want done?"

This new thinking and perspective had a profound effect on Fuller, and he turned his life around. Sitting at his kitchen table, Fuller did not limit himself to one field. He let his intuition guide him. He worked as a 'comprehensive anticipatory design scientist' to solve global problems surrounding housing, shelter, transportation, education, energy, ecological destruction, and poverty. Throughout the course of his life Fuller held 28 patents, authored 28 books, and received 47 honorary degrees.

Freedom in Failure
Rather than say he "failed" many times, Fuller said to our class:
> *"I simply found out what did not work."*

Fuller also said:
> *"Human beings were given a left foot and a right foot to make a mistake first to the left and then to the right, left again, and repeat.*
>
> *"God did not create humans with a right foot and a wrong foot."*

Fuller inspired many others to do what "God wants done."

The discovery of "Buckminsterfullerene," also known as a "Buckyball," was awarded the 1996 Nobel Prize in Chemistry. The scientists who discovered it named it in Fuller's honor.

A "Buckyball" is a highly unusual carbon molecule, distinguished by a triangulated surface like the geodesic dome. Buckyballs are being researched for their potential to be used as superconductors, lubricants, synthetic diamonds, rocket propellant, and an AIDS vaccine, as well as countless other applications.

Teaching Scarcity

As I've stated earlier in this book, Fuller was disturbed with education being based on scarcity. He cited 19th-century economists and philosophers, like Malthus, who promoted the idea that *"economics is the allocation of scarce resources."*

Fuller's point of view was that resources are not scarce. And human ignorance was abundant.

Fuller warned:

"You cannot question an assumption you do not know you have made."

Q: Was he saying that assumptions we do not know we have made...run our lives?

A: Yes. For example, not that long ago, people *assumed,* "The earth is flat." People stood on the seashore, looked out at the horizon, and *assumed* they would sail off the edge, and *assumed* sea monsters would eat them.

It took an explorer like Christopher Columbus to challenge that assumption. He sailed off the edge of the earth... and discovered America, the richest country in history.

The important questions that I think we need to ask ourselves are these: What are my assumptions? And what assumptions were you taught by your parents and schoolteachers? I often ask myself: *What assumptions am I making... that I don't realize I've made?*

I've found that when a person is 'stuck' it is often because of an assumption they don't know they've made. For example, I had assumed that it was impossible for there to be 4 billion billionaires. When I discovered that assumption, I began to see the world through Fuller's eyes, the eyes of a genius.

In a speech he gave to NASA in 1966, Fuller said:

"There is no such thing as genius, some children are less damaged than others."

That is how I began to see the future and decided I had a chance of becoming an architect of the future, my future... not a victim.

One of the first assumptions I challenged was: How can there be 4 billion billionaires? When I challenged my assumption — that there had to be both rich people and poor people in the world — I began to see the future.

Fuller did not agree with Malthus. He especially disagreed with Malthus' assumption that there were too many people and that planet earth had too few resources to support humanity. Fuller was angry at that "assumption" based upon a belief and mindset of "scarcity." The assumption that world had to be either you *or* me... winners *or* losers — never both — and that war was inevitable. War was inevitable because rulers wanted to control the "scarce resources."

Both Fuller and Marx dreamed of a utopia. The difference was how that utopia would be achieved. Regardless of what Marx promised related to an ethically just and classless society, the facts are his road to utopia resulted in the murder of millions of people.

Marx promised:
> *"The Communists everywhere support every revolutionary movement against the existing social and political order of things... They openly declare that their ends can be attained only by the forcible overthrow of all existing social conditions."*

And:
> *"The theory of the Communists may be summed up in the single sentence: Abolition of private property."*

Fuller's Utopia

One of Fuller's more famous books is *Utopia or Oblivion*. That book is a provocative blueprint for the future composed of essays derived from the lectures he gave all over the world during the 1960s. Fuller's thesis is that humanity — for the first time in its history — had the opportunity to create a world where the needs of 100% of humanity are met. This is Fuller in his prime, relaying his urgent message. If we do not challenge our education and assumptions on scarcity, humans will choose "oblivion," even though utopia is possible.

Again, it begins by asking ourselves:
> *"What assumptions have I made... that I do not know I have made?"*

First published in 1969 *Utopia or Oblivion* also includes one of the earliest published discussions of *Fuller's World Game,* a revolutionary educational simulation game that set this lofty as its goal for players: a world that "works" for 100% of humanity and to no one's disadvantage. It challenged players to overlook traditional world units such as nations, states, and other political and economic divisions.

In 1984, Blair, Kim, and I built *Fuller's World Game.* The game was large. It was a map of the world that fit on a regulation-size basketball court. The map was big enough to fit 100 players, each person representing 1% of the world population. There were 10,000 red bingo chips, which represented the number of nuclear warheads in storage.

Utopia or Oblivion
If the 100 participants got the lesson, utopia was achieved. If the 100 participants did not get the lesson... oblivion. Those 10,000 red bingo chips covered the map.

Fuller's lesson for this game was this:
> *"We are not going to be able to operate our Spaceship Earth successfully nor for much longer unless we see it as a whole spaceship and our fate as common. It has to be everybody or nobody."*

For Kim, Blair, and me, the experience of driving around California in a tiny Toyota — with this giant game board, rolled up and strapped to the roof — was an experience. No group ever "won" the game. Utopia was never achieved.

Dropping 10,000 red bingo chips was sobering. Picking them up,10,000 red bingo chips, after each game, was alarming... and deeply disturbing. We all wanted peace... yet we all "nuked" each other. Memories of witnessing the atomic blast as a kid continued to haunt me. Had I seen the future of humanity in 1962?

Fuller wanted the participants to learn that human ingenuity and existing resources could solve global problems. He believed that we could access human ingenuity, as long we committed "egocide." "Selfishness," he declared, "is unnecessary and... unrationalizable. ... War is obsolete."

In 1984, after playing the game for the last time, Kim, Blair, and I realized it was time to move on. It was time to find another way to relay Fuller's warning.

As Fuller said:

> *You never change things by fighting the existing reality. To change something, build a new model that makes the existing model obsolete..*

That wisdom from 1984 guided us in developing the *CASHFLOW* board game in 1996.

Identifying the Enemy
I had an aunt who lived in New York City. She was married to my father's uncle. Aunt Lydia was a prima ballerina in Paris, during World War II. After the war, she married my uncle, a graphic artist, and moved to the Upper East Side of New York City. I always enjoyed taking the train from Kings Point on Long Island and hob-nob with the rich and beautiful on the Upper East Side of the city.

On occasion, my aunt would discuss America's failure to defeat Stalin with me and my classmates. She would tell us stories of how everyone knew that Stalin was going to take Berlin. She also said that everyone knew there was very little difference between Hitler and Stalin — and that the Russians were going to be our real enemy and knew that once Stalin took Berlin, we would never be able to stop the spread of communism to the West.

I vividly remember her comments that it was common knowledge at the time that both General Dwight D. Eisenhower and President Franklin D. Roosevelt were afraid of Stalin. Rather than stop him, they allowed him to continue the advance of communism.

America's Greatest General

My aunt also said that many people thought that George Patton was America's greatest general. She believed if Eisenhower had let General Patton lead the battle against Stalin, we would not be fighting communism in America today. My aunt believed that if Patton had taken out Stalin, millions of people would still be alive. She believed Hitler and Stalin were of the same ilk, both ruthless and cold-blooded... and feared by both FDR and Eisenhower.

For years my aunt fought for the French underground by day and was the prima ballerina of Paris at night. She told me she would spend hours, drinking with Russian generals, gathering information for the war effort. One night, after drinking vodka with the Russians, she got on her bicycle and peddled to the opera house. On her way she fell and broke her ankle. Rather than cancel the show, she had her broken ankle taped and danced her last dance. She was a very courageous woman. My friends and I loved drinking vodka with her in her New York apartment and getting her first-hand insights into the war.

When I'd return to the Academy I would often discuss my aunt's points of view with my economics teacher, the B-17 pilot who was shot down twice in Europe. He agreed. His point of view was that Eisenhower and FDR were intimated by Stalin. Stalin had millions of troops behind him. America did not want to fight a prolonged war in Europe at the same time it was fighting in the Pacific.

"As Progressives," my teacher said, FDR and Eisenhower had tried to "befriend him." They hoped he would join the fight for Democracy. My teacher agreed with my aunt in that everyone knew Eisenhower was already planning to run for President, long before WWII was over. While Stalin was heading west, Eisenhower's campaign for President had already begun.

The Role of History
General George Patton said:
"To be a successful soldier, you must know history."

It was FDR who, in 1933, made own gold illegal. He was debauching the currency, making it illegal for Americans to own real money, aka God's money.

The Social Security Act was enacted August 14, 1935. The Act was drafted during President Franklin D. Roosevelt's first term by the President's Committee on Economic Security. America was opening our doors to the first stage of Marxism-Leninism.

A Promise to the World
In 1944, the Bretton Woods Conference was held before WWII ended. The Bretton Woods Conference was formally known as the United Nations Monetary and Financial Conference. It was a gathering of 730 delegates from all 44 allied nations at the Mount Washington Hotel, located in Bretton Woods, New Hampshire. The purpose of the conference was to regulate the international monetary and financial order after the conclusion of World War II.

As our class at the academy studied history, I thought it was fishy that it was illegal for Americans to own gold, yet we were promising the world that the United States would back each dollar with gold.

On August 15, 1971, President Nixon broke that promise to the world and took the U.S. dollar off the gold standard. At that point the U.S. dollar became fake, aka fiat money.

The Tax Man
In 1942 FDR asked Congress to cap the income any one American could claim and keep. By the end of the war, Congress had raised the tax rate to a record 94% on all income of more than $200,000.

FDR was following Marx's *Communist Manifesto*:

"A heavy or progressive or graduated income tax is necessary for the proper development of Communism."

Marx's *Communist Manifesto* promoted three main ideas:
1. Abolition of private property.
2. Graduated income tax.
3. Abolition of all right of inheritance.

It's pretty obvious, I think, that the "abolition of all right of inheritance" and the "abolition of private property" have the same objective. Everything you worked for will be taken away from you and given back to the state when you die. Between the time you start working and stop working, everything will be taxed.

Marx warned:

"Taxation is the source of life for the bureaucracy, the army, the church and the court, in short, the whole apparatus of executive power. Strong government and heavy taxes are identical."

The Most Respected General
My instructor, the B-17 pilot, said, "Patton was the general my men and I respected the most." He said, *"We respected him because Patton was a general who fought from the front, not from the rear."*

Although General George Patton may have been regarded as America's greatest general, that didn't stop the press from bringing him down.

General Patton was one of the few generals who regularly visited wounded soldiers in field hospitals. On Aug. 10, 1943, during one of those visits to a field hospital, Patton slapped a soldier who was hospitalized for combat fatigue, accusing him of cowardice.

The media had a field day and never let up. It did not matter how many battles Patton had won, all they focused on was his slapping a soldier for being too afraid to fight.

The media did the same to America's fighting men and women during the Vietnam war.

After listening to my aunt and my economics teacher, I began to understand why communism was winning.

As Patton is said to have warned Winston Churchill:
> *"Yet it is America that now commits the unconscionable act of deferring to Russia at the expense of Britain—in effect, killing England."*

Flying over burned-out French chateaux in 1973, and later being spit on by Flower Children, I recalled my conversations with my aunt and my economics teacher. Both fought communism in Europe. Both knew the spread of communism would not stop at Berlin.

Why Bucky's World Game Did Not Work
After sweeping up 10,000 red bingo chips too many times, Kim, Blair, and I realized that using Stalin's threat of nuclear oblivion was not going to work. People still chose Oblivion, over Utopia. It was back to questioning assumptions we did not know we had made.

Kim, Blair, and I realized why Bucky's World Game was not working.

It was Patton's words — "Fear kills more people than death." — that made Kim, Blair and me realize by Bucky's World Game wasn't working.

We realized that terrifying people who were already terrorized, threatening fearful people with more fear, was not going to work. Teaching people what Stalin planned to do to America was not working. Our assumption was that fear might inspire the players to do something different. The problem was, during the Cold War, people were already living in fear. People were already hiding under their desks.

We realized it would be better if followed Patton's lesson on leadership, by inspiring people to:
> *"Live for something rather than die for nothing.*

Different Assumptions

In 1996 we challenged our assumption. Rather than teach with fear, as we were doing with 10,000 red bingo chips, Kim and I created the *CASHFLOW* board game. In 1996 Rich Dad's Capitalist Manifesto was born.

In 1996, after being kicked in the head by the Australian Broadcast Commission and the Cult Awareness Network, the light bulb went on... and the *CASHFLOW* game, a financial education game, was born. The change in our reality was that people wanted to learn to be rich. They did not want to learn to live in fear of tyrants such as Marx, Lenin, Stalin, Hitler, Mao, and Khrushchev. *CASHFLOW* is a capitalist tool that gives everyday people the power to fight back.

The *CASHFLOW* game and our Capitalist Manifesto follows Patton's leadership.

General Patton's Lesson #1:

"Never let the enemy pick the battle site:"

When the *CASHFLOW* game was first launched, a friend immediately said, "I will take this game to Harvard and have it evaluated."

Harvard trashed the game. They mocked it. One faculty evaluator said, "We don't play games at Harvard."

As Einstein said:

"School failed me, and I failed the school. The teachers behaved like Feldwebel (sergeants). I wanted to learn what I wanted to know, but they wanted me to learn for the exam. What I hated most was the competitive system there. Because of this, I wasn't worth anything and several times they suggested I leave."

Bucky Fuller was asked to leave Harvard twice. Although he never graduated from Harvard, Harvard continues to count Fuller as one of its more famous graduates.

When I am asked, "How did I learn to become rich?" my reply is: "Rich dad taught me by playing *Monopoly* with me as a kid, and today, as an adult, I play *Monopoly* in real life."

Repeating Maria Montessori's lesson on learning:
"What the hand does, the mind remembers."

That is why Rich Dad's Capitalist Manifesto is:
How do we fight communism taught in our schools?
We teach capitalism in our homes.

Repeating Thomas Sowell who said:
"Apparently almost anyone can do a better job of educating children than our so-called "educators in the public schools. Children who are home-schooled by their parents also score higher on tests than children educated in the public schools."

Sowell also says:
"The challenge is to provide more escape hatches from failing public schools, not only to help those students escape, but also to force these institutions to get their act together before losing more students and jobs."

General Patton's Lesson #2:
"If you tell people where to go but not how to get there...you'll be amazed at the results."

When I was on *Oprah!* in 2000, a young woman raised her hand and asked me, "What should I do with my money?"

Oprah turned to me and said, "I'll handle this question."

Oprah said to the young woman, "Don't ask anyone to tell you what you should do with your money. Your job is to study and make your own decisions."

I fell in love with Oprah at that moment. The photo below speaks to the kindred spirit I had found in her, a bond forged by our shared respect for education.

As I'm mentioned earlier in this book, I cannot tell you how many times — over the past 25 years — I've been asked these questions:

I have $10,000. What should I invest in?

How do I get out of debt?

Is real estate a good investment?

What stocks do you recommend?

How do I get rich?

I lost patience with the questions at George Gammon's Rebel Capitalist seminar in Miami a few months ago. I was in an elevator filled with people when a young woman asked, "Do you recommend investing in real estate?" My response was quick and pointed: "Don't ask anyone what to do with your money. Learn about money." I had turned into Oprah.

A-Student Behavior

I've come to realize that people who ask what to do with their money are behaving like A students — who believe that memorizing the "right answers" is the formula for success. Thinking for themselves is not part of the process.

Many do not know how to think for themselves. They do not know how to find their own answers. They are terrified of making mistakes. They wait to be told what to do.

The A students goes out into the real world and wait for people to tell them what to do. They make great employees, "brain slaves," waiting to be told what to do. If they make a mistake, they are fired.

Classical conditioning, unconscious learning through association, was discovered by Ivan Pavlov (1849-1936) for his work in classical conditioning of dogs and humans.

These A students get a job, pay taxes, save money, buy a house, get out of debt, and invest for the long term in the stock market. Pavlov showed that when a bell was sounded each time the dog was fed, the dog learned to associate the sound with the presentation of the food. Like Pavlov's dogs, they wait for someone to ring the dinner bell and begin to salivate on command.

John Broadus Watson (1878-1958) was an American psychologist who popularized the Scientific Theory of Behaviorism, aka classical conditioning, based on Pavlov's studies and observations.

From his and Pavlov's research, Watson was able to explain was able to explain all aspects of human psychology.

According to Watson, everything from speech to emotional responses was simply patterns of stimulus and response. Watson denied completely the existence of the mind or consciousness. Watson believed that all individual differences in behavior were due to different experiences of learning. He famously said:

> *"Give me a dozen healthy infants, well-formed, and my own specified world to bring them up in and I'll guarantee to take any one at random and train him to become any type of specialist I might select - doctor, lawyer, artist, merchant-chief and, yes, even beggar-man and thief, regardless of his talents, penchants, tendencies, abilities, vocations and the race of his ancestors."*

Notice the word "specialists," aka brain slaves.

As Einstein said:
>   *"Imagination is more important than knowledge."*

Repeating Lesson #2 from General Patton: "If you tell people where to go *but not how to get there...* you'll be amazed at the results."

Rich dad often said, "There are a million paths to financial heaven... and billions of paths to financial hell."

Kim and I chose the path less traveled:
>   We do not have jobs.
>   We do not save money.
>   We do not live debt free.
>   We do not have 401(k)s.
>   We had no government support.

With financial education, a plan of action, learning from our mistakes, and the desire driven by absolute certainly that we wanted to find a path out of the Rat Race, Kim and I achieved financial freedom in 10 years. Kim was 37 and I was 47.

One of Fuller's principles is:
>   *"The reward for a job well-done is a bigger job."*

All the mistakes Kim and I made on our way to financial freedom were to prepare us for a bigger more important task, that God wanted done.

As we traveled the world, teaching and speaking, people kept asking us how we did it. How we went from nothing to financial freedom in 10 years. We knew that we needed to step up, that there was a bigger job for us.

As Fuller said:

> *"Observation of my life to date shows that the larger the number for whom I work, the more positively effective I become. Thus, it is obvious that if I work always and only for all humanity, I will be optimally effective."*

In 1996, although we were financially free and we could have kicked back and "retired," Kim and I followed Fuller's guidance, repeating over and over to ourselves:

> *"The reward for a job well done is a bigger job."*

Our work was fueled by our belief in Bucky's principle that the more people we served, the more effective we'd become.

Malcom Gladwell is an English-born Canadian journalist, public speaker and one of my favorite authors. His writing and his speaking presentations always make me to think. My favorites among his books are: *Tipping Point, Blink, Outliers,* and *David and Goliath.*

Gladwell has a lot to say on the power of culture. In his book *Outliers* he writes:

> *"Who we are cannot be separated from where we're from."*

Q: Is he saying if we come from a poor culture... we are that culture?

A: Yes. That is why it is very difficult for poor people to learn to be rich in school. School is a culture, a cult of fear and scarcity. That is why "job security" is so important.

Q: Is that why you went in search of different teachers when you were only 10 years old?

A: Yes. I did not realize it at the time, but I knew my family of schoolteachers was always going to be employees, who belonged to the teacher's union. Our family was a culture of academic education, job security, and government socialism. Financial education was not in our family's culture.

At 10 years old, I did not realize I was searching for a culture of capitalism and a life as an entrepreneur, an investor, a person who created jobs and created my own assets. I just knew that I wanted something different that the culture in which I was being raised.

That may be why Donald Trump and I speak about the influence of our dads as our best teachers. Both were rich dads. Our dads taught us to find our own paths to financial heaven.

Gladwell says:
> *"Each of us comes from a culture with its own distinctive mix of strengths and weaknesses, tendencies and predispositions, so difficult to acknowledge."*

That is why he says:
> *"Who we are cannot be separated from where we're from."*

Q: Is that what Pavlov and Watson meant by *classical conditioning?*
A: Yes. When we created the *CASHFLOW* game we wanted to re-create the capitalist culture of my rich dad, not the job security culture of my poor dad.

Q: Is that why Patton said: *"Never let the enemy pick the battle site:"*
A: Yes. And that's why Rich Dad's Capitalist Manifesto is: *"The way to counter communism taught in our schools... is by teaching capitalism in our homes."*

General Patton's Lesson #3:
> *"Where there is fear of failure... there will be failure."*

The biggest problem with going to school is, school is a culture of fear. Academics thrive in a culture of fear. I often think that's why so many entrepreneurs — Walt Disney, Henry Ford, Thomas Edison, Steve Jobs and Bill Gates — dropped out of school.

Modern Education

Post-Modernist education is the educational philosophy in our schools today... which is education based on opinion and emotions rather science, facts, and principals. That should concern all of us, since while we are entitled to our own options we are not entitled to our own facts.

That is why Gad Saad states:

> *"Any system that is built on a false understanding of human nature is doomed to fail. Building a society where the primary objective is to protect one's fragile self-esteem from the dangers of competition will only lead to a society of weakness, entitlement, and apathy. Life is necessarily competitive; society is necessarily hierarchical. It does no one any favors to pursue a utopian vision of society where no one's feelings are hurt."*

A Cult of Victims

Post-modern education is a culture of victims. As a counterpoint: Bucky Fuller's challenge to be "architects of the future, not its victims."

As Gad Saad warns and writes in *The Parasitic Mind*:

> *"These politically correct language initiatives are misguided and harmful. They create highly entitled professional "victims" who expect to be free from any offense, and they engender a stifling atmosphere where all individuals walk on eggshells lest they might commit a linguistic capital crime."*

Victim or Villain

University of Toronto psychology professor Jordan Peterson had had enough of what he saw as a campus culture where "social justice warrior, left-wing radical political activists" ran rampant. He zeroed in on Canadian human rights legislation that prohibits discrimination based on gender identity or expression.

Dr Peterson was especially frustrated with being asked to use alternative pronouns as requested by trans students or staff, like *ze* and *zir*, used by some as alternatives to *he* or *she*. In his opposition, he set off a political and cultural firestorm that shows no signs of abating.

As Lenin warned:

> *"We can and must write in a language which sows among the masses hate, revulsion, and scorn towards those who disagree with us."*

I view Jordan Peterson as a hero, right up there with General Patton. Modern education is a culture of fear and opinions... not a culture of learning. Post-modernism prevents us from learning from history... by changing history.

A Culture of Learning

I've often wondered what our schools would look like if Bucky Fuller ran the educational system. In his words:

> *"If I ran a school, I'd give the average grade to the ones who gave me all the right answers, for being good parrots. I'd give the top grades to those who made the most mistakes and told me about them, and then told me what they learned from them."*

I am inspired by our freedoms... and the spirit of freedom that drove our founding fathers to protect "life, liberty, and the pursuit of happiness." All the signers of the Declaration of Independence knew they were putting *their* life, liberty, and happiness on the line when as they signed that document... a document that defined a new nation, a democracy, not a monarchy, that would one day become the United States of America.

In 2020, the world is on the verge of losing the freest country in world history.

President Ronald Reagan (1911-2004) warned:

> *"Freedom is a fragile thing and it's never more than one generation away from extinction. It is not ours by way of inheritance; it must be fought for and defended constantly by each generation, for it comes only once to a people. And those in world history who have known freedom and then lost it have never known it again."*

The Fight for Freedoms

So, how do we fight for our freedoms? We fight armed with education and by investing in ourselves and our futures.

We fight for freedom in our homes by learning about capitalism, teaching capitalism and practicing capitalism in real life.

The second book the Rich Dad series is *The Cashflow Quadrant*. It introduced this icon and concept:

E   stands for employee

S   stands for Specialist, self-employed, and small business owner

B   stands for big business... and brand

I   stands for investor... and insider

The B and I Quadrants

B stands for Big Business, companies with 500 employees or more and brand. For example, Warren Buffett prefers to invest in brands, such as Gillette and Coca-Cola. He does not invest in startups, in the S quadrant.

I stands for Investors who invest from the inside. Most Es and Ss invest from the outside, generally in stocks, bonds, mutual funds, and ETFs.

There is much less freedom on the left side, the E- and S-side of the quadrant. There is more security, in most cases, but less freedom. It is from the E- and S-side that our freedoms are being stolen.

For example, many people are threatened with being fired if they do not get the COVID vaccine. I see that as Fascism.

Hitler was able to get the Germans to murder Jews by forcing them to wear yellow stars. First little atrocities... then mass murder.

My new Arizona driver's license has a yellow star on the upper right corner. As far as I can tell, nothing else changed on my license.

In 2021, Biden is calling for mass vaccinations. He is saying that the people who are causing COVID to spread and causing more deaths are the unvaccinated.

Repeating Gad Saad's warning:

> *"I argue that contrary to the current pandemic that we're facing with Covid, we've faced another pandemic for the past forty, fifty years. And in this case the virus is not a biological virus, it's a mind virus. That's why I call these idea pathogens, or parasitic ideas. And so, where do these ideas come from? So, if we are trying to find out where the Covid virus came from, we're not allowed to say because to say where it comes from would be racist of course. So where do these idea pathogens come from? They all come from the university eco-system. In other words, as I always remind people, it takes intellectuals and professors to come up with some of the dumbest ideas."*

Q: Are you saying the idea of "go to school, and study hard to get a good job," is a mind virus, an idea pathogen that steals our freedoms?

A: I am.

Q: Are you saying our freedoms are on the B and I side?

A: Yes. If you are on the B and I side, you do not need job security, steady paychecks, high taxes, and live with the fear of market crashes. People on the B and I side are not afraid of being fired for not being vaccinated. You can get to financial heaven on the E and S side, but it's at the price of your freedoms. Es and Ss still need to work and make money. Bs and Is do not need money.

Freedom from Assumptions

We often don't realize all the assumptions we've made without knowing it. Here are a few examples:

> I must have a job.
> I need a paycheck.
> Investing is risky.
> I'm not smart enough.
> I can't do it.

Freedom from Culture

Marx was obsessed with money. He was trapped by his culture. He did not know how to make money and was constantly begging for money. He even failed as a husband, unable to provide for his wife and child, and survived by begging and borrowing from friends and family. Being an intellectual, he believed he was "entitled." That is a part of the entitlement culture of Marxism today. That is education today.

In 2020, billions of people are following Marx's Culture of Entitlement. As Malcolm Gladwell states:

> *"Who we are cannot be separated from where we're from."*

One reason why many professional athletes and lottery winners are bankrupt within five years after earning millions is because money does not separate you from your culture.

Personally, my transition from E and S quadrants to the B and I quadrants meant letting go of my poor dad's academic culture. Today, I respect both cultures, my poor dad's and my rich dad's.

To make the change, I had to travel from poor dad's culture of the classroom to rich dad's culture, working as an apprentice in his business. As I've said, collecting rent for rich dad was a great education in the power of culture.

As Maria Montessori said:

> *"Growth comes from activity, not from intellectual understanding."*

The purpose of CASHFLOW Clubs is to support the transition in culture from poor dad's culture to rich dad's.

Freedom from History

Do not let yourself be a victim of history. In school, when history is studied, the emphasis is on memorizing dates and events. Then students regurgitate those dates and events and, like magic, they are "smart students." But they have learned nothing.

Steve Jobs said:

> *"You can't connect the dots looking forward; you can only connect them looking backwards. So, you have to trust that the dots will somehow connect in your future."*

By studying history — factual historical records, not fiction — and connecting the dots, you *can* see the future.

By studying history, I understood the true intentions of President Franklin D. Roosevelt and President Richard Nixon. In 1933, FDR made it illegal for Americans to own gold. In 1944, the United States promised to back every U.S. dollar with gold. In 1971, President Nixon broke that promise.

And printing fake money began.

In 1972, I flew behind enemy lines, looking for gold. I could see the future of fake money.

In 1999, the Glass-Steagall was repealed. The Glass-Steagall Act was part of the 1933 Banking Act. The 1933 Act separated investment banks from mom-and-pop commercial banks. In 1996, the repeal of Glass-Steagall turned the United States into one giant casino, putting mom and pop at risk.

In 2008, the subprime real estate market crashed. Bankers made billions. Mom and pop lost everything.

In 2008 the U.S. deficit was $1.4 trillion. By 2020 The U.S. deficit had grown to $5 trillion. That means the United States imported $5 trillion more than it exported.

How Much Is a Trillion?
If you were to spend $1 a minute, it would take you 34,000 years to spend a trillion dollars. It takes the Federal Reserve Bank less than a minute to "print" $1 trillion.

The 50th anniversary milestone, in 2021, of Nixon's 1971 decision to take the U.S. dollar off the gold standard is an important one and we are feeling its impact today. Because on August 15, 1971, the U.S. dollar became a creation of debt and taxes. On August 15, 1971, savers became losers. In 2021, it's estimated that the United States will print another $4 trillion to keep the economy from collapsing.

In 1972, I began saving gold, silver, and, more recently, Bitcoin and ethereum. If I need money, I use debt as money. That's because in 1971, the U.S. dollar became debt... and more debt I use as money, the less taxes I pay.

In a letter to investors on July 29, 2020, Pantera Capital CEO Dan Morehead states:

> *"The United States printed more money in June than in the first two centuries after its founding. Last month the U.S. budget deficit — $864*

billion — was larger than the total debt incurred from 1776 through the end of 1979."

As Fuller said:

"Only two things are infinite, the universe and human stupidity, and I'm not sure about the former."

There are approximately 700 employees with PhDs working at the Federal Reserve Bank. How can so many highly educated people be so incompetent? Have they not studied history? Maybe they should get a real job. Better yet, start a business.

New estimates coming out of the Fed are calling for $150 trillion in bailouts. Bailouts are the name of the game. And making the case for socialism under the guise of 'protecting the environment.'

Dinesh D'Souza, an Indian-American author and documentary film maker states:

"Academics think they are the truly smart people. They truly believe they are the most important people in society. When they look at an entrepreneur who owns ten McDonald's franchises, or a pest control business, and they consider those people inferior. A professor of romance languages at Princeton earning $150,000 a year thinks it is outrageous, a pest control entrepreneur is earning $500,000 a year. To the academic, that is not fair. That is where socialism begins."

My take on these points — and bailouts — is that the latest estimates coming out of the Fed are calling for $150 trillion in new government spending (paid for by the taxpayers) under the guise of protecting the environment when in reality it's pushing us toward their vision for a socialist utopia.

Emotions and opinions are at the core of post-modern education. History is not.

In 1983, after reading *GRUNCH of Giants,* I began questioning my assumptions. Assumptions that I did not even realize I had made.

I remember when I heard Fuller say, *"There are four billion billionaires."* My mind immediately said: *"That's impossible."*

I thought Fuller was nuts. How could everyone be a billionaire? Once I challenged my own assumptions, I got to work doing what Fuller suggested we do, which is ask ourselves, "What does god want done?"

Fuller said:
> *"Never forget that you are one of a kind. Never forget that if there weren't any need for you in all your uniqueness to be on this earth, you wouldn't be here in the first place. And never forget, no matter how overwhelming life's challenges and problems seem to be, that one person can make a difference in the world. In fact, it is always because of one person that all the changes that matter in the world come about. So be that person."*

Margaret Mead (1901-1978) an American Anthropologist said:
> *"Never doubt that a small group of thoughtful, committed citizens can change the world. Indeed, it is the only thing that ever has."*

In words often credited to Edmund Burke:
> *"All that is necessary for the triumph of evil... is that good men do nothing."*

In 1983, when Fuller asked "What does God want done?" I decided to question all the assumptions I had made. And I began teaching people what my rich dad taught me: how to be a millionaire — possibly a billionaire — without needing money.

The first word I learned at the Academy, in 1965, was *mission.*

In 1984, Kim and Blair joined me and together we set out to fulfill the mission. We left Hawaii for California and our Capitalist Manifesto began.

CHAPTER TWELVE

DEEDS NOT WORDS

"What can I do, I'm just a little guy?"
— R. Buckminster Fuller

On hot August day, in 1965, after punch and cookies were over, and parents and family departed the Academy grounds, Hell Week began.

Immediately, approximately 20,18-year-old boys were lined up in sections while an upper-classman, probably 19-year-olds, began yelling and screaming at the 20 of us.

Immediately after our bags were dropped off in our rooms, we were marched down to the barber shop and our hair was cut off. Next came the issuing of our dungarees, our uniform for the next month. I began to realize I may have made a mistake.

Hell Week was a living hell. We never knew if we were coming or going. We had very little sleep. Constant jogging. Constant "in your face" screaming if you did not "get it" fast enough. Lights out at ten, bugle at five.

The first Saturday night was our first time off. I walked out to a point of land, overlooking Long Island Sound, framed by lights of mansions along the shore and New York City in the distance, and cried. I was miserable. I was on the verge of requesting to be DOR, Dropped on Request, aka "I quit." In a week, three of the starting 20 students were already gone.

As I stood overlooking the lights on Long Island Sound, my mind was saying "I don't need this BS." The University of Hawaii hadn't started classes yet. I could still get home and not miss a class. Besides, winter was coming, and the surf will be up on the North Shore in a few months. I was preparing to quit.

The only reason I didn't quit was because I knew the purpose of Hell Week was to find the quitters and flush out the weak. I refused to give them the pleasure of having me be one of quitters.

That Saturday night, I met the quitter in me. It was not a pleasant meeting.

I stood alone, in the dark, listening to that quitter — the loser and the wimp in me — telling me all the reasons why I did not have to stay. It wasn't pretty.

One benefit of Hell Week was that it brought out the spiritual power... the staying power and the power to fight back against the quitter in us. The motto of Kings Point was *Acta Non Verba* — Actions Not Words. During Hell Week, that motto was instilled in us... at the same time they were doing their best to have us quit.

As I stood in the dark, listening to the quitter in me whine, the motto, the lesson of Acta Non Verba — *Deeds Not Words* — was fighting back.

As Thomas Sowell warned:
> *"The big divide in this country is not between Democrats and Republicans, or women and men, but between talkers and doers."*

He also said:
> *"Facts are not liberals' strong suit. Rhetoric is."*

Finally, after about an hour, the wimp in me was still giving me all the reasons I should quit. There were some pretty good ones (I told myself) like the fact that there were no women at Kings Point, but many beautiful women in Hawaii. Slowly I turned my body, letting my body do the talking as I took one step at a time, heading back to my room, for one more week... and four more years... of hell.

Bear Bryant (1913-1983), a football coach at the University of Alabama, is one of the greatest coaches in history. Coach Bryant said:

> *"I make practices real hard because if a player is a quitter, I want him to quit in practice, not in a game."*

American entrepreneur Russell Simmons is a record executive, writer, and film producer. He co-founded the hip-hop label Def Jam Recordings and created the fashion clothing lines Phat Farm, Argyleculture, and Tantris. Russell says:

> *"There are no failures, only quitters."*

David Goggins, a retired Navy Seal, is an American ultramarathon runner, ultra-distance cyclist, author, and motivational speaker. Among his prominent works is the book *"Can't Hurt Me."*

David says:

> *"A warrior is not a person that carries a gun. The biggest war you ever go through is right between your own ears. It's in your mind. We're all going through a war in our mind, and we have to callus our mind to fight that war and to win that war."*

Snowflake University

In 2020 our schools were mass producing *everyone-gets-a-trophy* "snowflakes." Rather than develop core strength, curriculum focuses on Critical Race Theory. Rather than build mental strength, schools have "safe spaces" and "safe zones" to protect "marginalized" students from ideas that may "trigger" emotional episodes.

In 2020, the entire academic system became a "safe space," and no longer were institutions of higher learning places where ideas are challenged and debated. Worst of all... freedom of speech was denied.

Warrior Professor

Dr. Jordan Peterson has become an international celebrity, a warrior professor. Jordan stood up against academic and bureaucratic fascists who are requiring that language be changed, thoughts be controlled, and freedom of speech cancelled — all in the name of the entire school becoming a "safe space," a place where everyone (even the losers) get a trophy.

Jordan Peterson is credited with both of these sobering thoughts:
"When you have something to say, silence is a lie."
"If you don't say what you think then you kill your unborn self."

Today the culture of the liberal academic elite elevates *victims into heroes, quitters into critics,* and *losers into leaders.*

To that end, Jordan Peterson warns:
"If you think strong men are dangerous wait until you get a load of weak men..."

Abraham Lincoln warned
"At what point then is the approach of danger to be expected? I answer, if it ever reach us, it must spring up amongst us. It cannot come from abroad. If destruction be our lot, we must ourselves be its author and finisher."

Q: Are you saying our academic institutions are destroying America from the inside?

A: Yes. In 1989, the Berlin Wall came down. Everyone celebrated, believing capitalism had won and communism was dead. Today we know, communism is not dead. Communism had spread via our schools, like a cancer, eating America from the inside.
Marines would say, "They are inside the wire."

The reason I've spent so much time on General Patton, Stalin, General Eisenhower, Churchill, and President Franklin D. Roosevelt is because I believe Patton was right. Patton saw the bigger picture. America and England should have taken on Stalin before Berlin. America should have pushed Stalin back to Stalingrad. Stalin, Hitler, and Mao were ruthless men. Hundreds of millions of people would not have died if Patton had led the charge, from the front.

A Fighting General

My roommate on the carrier was Jack Bergman. We were both lieutenants in Vietnam. Jack went on to become a 3-star general, a feat almost impossible for an air-winger. Stars are generally reserved for ground Marines. I entered the Marines a lieutenant and left a lieutenant

In 2021 Jack continues to lead. This time as a U.S. Congressman from Michigan.

Jack fought in every conflict after Vietnam. He fought from the front, as pilots do. He said in confidence to me, "many Generals are "bunker bunnies."

Watch Jack Bergman...
on the Rich Dad Radio Show...
on RichDad.com

They fight from the back, deep inside a bunker. Eisenhower and FDR lead from the rear. Patton led from the front.

Leading from the Front

President Trump came close to making good his campaign promise to build a wall along the United States' Southern border. Steady progress was made while he was in office.

When COVID-19 reared it ugly head, President Trump ordered Operation Warp Speed on March 30, 2020 and promised to have vaccines produced in less than a year. Producing a vaccine is normally a 10- to 15-year process.

On July 14, 2020, Moderna had initial results from the vaccine's clinical trials. On August 16, 2020, Pfizer's submitted initial results from its vaccine trials. If Joe Biden had been President in 2020, it's impossible to know if we would have vaccines today. He's viewed by many as a weak leader, and certainly not one who leads from the front.

That is what leaders who lead from the front do — they get things done. Leaders from the front are living examples of Deeds Not Words. They let their actions speak, not their words.

Trump gets things done because he is an entrepreneur and a capitalist. He is hated by the press, as was General Patton.

President Biden and Vice President Kamala Harris have stopped construction on the wall at the southern border. Then they opened the borders, inviting anyone to enter. They also invited in COVID-19. Then provided free transportation and hotel rooms all over America for the untested, unvaccinated immigrants.

So far, Kamala has been to the U.S. southern border only once. Both Biden and Harris remain "bunker bunnies" in the White House. Both are adored by the press.

As Stalin warned:

> *"The press must grow day in and day out – it is our Party's sharpest and most powerful weapon."*

You may remember President Trump toured America, speaking to thousands of raving fans, asking for their vote for reelection. Trump leads from the front. Bunker Biden ran his campaign from his basement. He campaigned from the rear, a "basement bunny."

As Jordan Peterson warned:

> *"If you think strong men are dangerous wait until you get a load of weak men..."*

Marx was a weak man. He was an angry man, a financially irresponsible man. When Marx and his wife and their seven children were living in London, a visitor wrote a description of their lifestyle in their 3-room flat. Not only did the Marx children have to endure the hunger of poverty, they were raised in filth, or what his friend described as "a pigsty." Four of his children died in childhood.

Marx blamed the rich for his problems. He did not have the courage to look in the mirror and meet the loser in him. He did not have the internal strength to go past the loser in him. Instead, he chose to blame the rich and let the loser in him win. Today. Marx is the hero of victims, leader of losers.

Post-Modern Education

During a YouTube interview another warrior professor, Gad Saad, was asked: What would you say is an example of a parasitic idea?

Gad Saad replied:

> *"The granddaddy of all idea pathogens is what's called Post-Modernism."*

> *"[Post Modernism] basically purports the following: there are no universal truths, there are no objective truths, we are completely shackled by personal biases, by our subjectivity, by relativism."*

Lenin had many warnings credited to him on the topics of language and free speech:

> *"It is, of course, much easier to shout, abuse, and howl than to attempt to relate, to explain."*

> *"We can and must write in a language which sows among the masses hate, revulsion, and scorn toward those who disagree with us."*

> *"Free speech is a bourgeois prejudice."*

> *"A people without a heritage are easily persuaded."*

> *"The cause of popular freedom is lost when it is entrusted to professors."*

And Hitler wrote in *Mein Kampf*:

> *"The receptivity of the masses is very limited, their intelligence is small, but their power of forgetting is enormous. In consequence of these facts, all effective propaganda must be limited to very few points and must harp on these slogans until last member of the public understands what you want him to understand by your slogan."*

In 2021 a few of the popular slogans are:

    1 – "Black Lives Matter."

    2 – "America is a systemically racist country."

    3 – "Wear your masks."

    4 – "Get vaccinated."

    5 – "America was founded in 1619."

Plato warned:

"The philosopher is in love with truth, not with the changing world of sensation, which is the object of opinion, but with the unchanging reality which is the object of knowledge."

Professor Gad Saad also said this in his YouTube video:

"Post-Modernists fly planes of bull shit on to our edifices of reason and slowly destroy everything that has been made."

Two definitions of edifice are: 1 – *a building, especially a large imposing one;* and 2 – *A complex system of beliefs.*

The number of warrior professors who are fighting back is growing. Two more are Victor David Hanson and Dennis Prager.

Victor Davis Hanson, a Professor at Stanford University, warns:

"Westernization, coupled with globalization, has created an affluent and leisured elite that now gravitates to universities, bureaucracies, and world organizations, all places where wealth is not created, but analyzed, critiqued, and lavishly spent."

Dennis Prager is an American Republican conservative radio talk show host and writer. His initial political work concerned Soviet Jews who were unable to emigrate. He is the founder of Prager University.

Dennis Prager warns:

"If we continue to teach about tolerance and intolerance instead of teaching about good and evil, we will end up with the tolerance of evil."

He also warns:

> *"Compassion without wisdom is dangerous. It's what enables people to support the "underdog" even if the underdog is evil."*

Hillsdale College is a private conservative liberal arts college in Hillsdale, Michigan. Founded in 1844 by abolitionists known as Free Will Baptists, Hillsdale has a liberal arts curriculum that is based on the Western heritage as a product of both the Greco-Roman culture and the Judeo-Christian tradition. Hillsdale requires every student, regardless of concentration of studies, to complete a core curriculum that includes courses on the Great Books, the U.S. Constitution, biology, chemistry, and physics.

A New Model for Public Education

Hillsdale is America's new role model for new public education. Hillsdale staff and faculty have joined the growing number of academics fighting back against racist, Post-Modernist education. Hillsdale College offers free, online, not-for-credit courses taught by Hillsdale College faculty patterned after the education offered on Hillsdale College campus to students enroll in that college.

Hillsdale's mission is to provide students with an education that pursues knowledge of the highest things, provides insight into the nature of God and man, forms character, and defends constitutional government.

These professors join Thomas Sowell, Jordan Peterson, Gad Saad, Albert Einstein, Bucky Fuller, Plato, and many more, warrior professors who have joined the fight against Marxist Post-Modernist teaching. In 2021, the number of these warrior educators is growing.

David Goggins is the only member of the U.S. Armed Forces to complete SEAL training (including two Hell Weeks), the U.S. Army Ranger School (where he graduated as Enlisted Honor Man), and the Air Force Tactical Air Controller training. He is a man of "deeds, long distances, and few words."

Goggins is a warrior's warrior who says:

"A warrior is not a person that carries a gun. The biggest war you ever go through is right between your own ears. It's in your mind. We're all going through a war in our mind, and we have to callus our mind to fight that war and to win that war".

As Lenin warned:

"Our propaganda necessarily includes the propaganda of atheism; the publication of the appropriate scientific literature, which the autocratic feudal government has hitherto strictly forbidden and persecuted, must now form one of the fields of our Party work."

Post-Modern education is based on scientific socialism... opinions, not science.

Fuller, a futurist, also predicted:

"Primarily the individual is going to study at home."

I do not know if Fuller was familiar with Post-Modern education. If he was, I am certain he would have fought back. Fuller was able to predict the future because he believed in Universal Principles, Operating Principles of God, or Generalized principles.

Generalized Principles are principles that are true in all cases, with no exceptions.

Fuller estimated there were approximately 250 Generalized Principles. And they are all important since they operate together. Fuller had discovered about 50 of the 250 before he passed away in 1983. One of his discoveries was *"Unity is plural... and at minimum two."*

Q: Unity is plural... not one?

A: Correct. By observing the universe Fuller realized that universe was at minimum two, not one. For example, God designed humans to have two eyes, two feet, two arms. In the physical universe, there is an *up* and a *down*.

Q: Up cannot exist without down?

A: Correct. You're getting it. Neither can *in* exist without... *out*. *Rich* would not exist without *poor*. The same goes for *happy* and *sad*, *young* and *old*, *man* and *woman*.

Q: Does that mean someone will always say they are *right* and someone else is *wrong*?

A: Exactly.

God's operating principles of the universe, Generalized Principles guide us to be — in Bucky Fuller's words — the "architects of the future... not its victims." Generalized Principles are what Fuller used to become recognized as a futurist, a man John Denver called The Grandfather of the Future.

Fuller died in 1983 and a few of his predictions have come true. Fuller predicted a new technology would be available before 1990. In 1983 he said:

"A new technology will become available on planet earth before the end of this decade. This technology will change the world."

The internet was born in 1989... the same year the Berlin Wall came down.

Fuller also predicted Bitcoin. He said:

"Computers make it practical to electronify wealth distribution games that accomplish the movement of goods in services in more channeled, designed structures. Not big brother though, since no central planning authority – just lots of dial-in ''games" with costs and rewards, likely to attract those with a self-interest in playing. Those are the details."

Fuller predicted free education taught by real teachers. He said:

"From a distance, it looks like a planet full of professors on tenure, working hard, doing more metaphysical stuff than before."

Today YouTube and social media teach more people, for free, than all the university professors in the world.

That is what Hillsdale College, Prager University, Rich Dad's CASHFLOW Clubs, and teachers such as the Rich Dad Advisors, George Gammon, Mark Moss, Max Keiser, Peter Schiff, the Real Estate Guys, Richard Duncan, Patrick Bet-David of Valuetainment, Jim Rickards, Chris Martenson Adam Taggert, Daniela Cambone of Stansberry Research, Dr. David Lim of Kitco News, Raoul Pal of Real Vision, Brian Rose of London Real, Jay Martin of Cambridge House, Gerald Celente, and many others. I listen to them religiously, for free. These are the men and women we will go to war with... Parabellum.

In my opinion they are all teachers who "practice what they teach." They personify "deeds not words." As Fuller predicted *"professors on tenue, working hard, doing more metaphysical stuff than before."*

Teaching metaphysically is teaching out of love. Most college professors teach for money. At the same time that there is so much free education available, traditional education models leave students saddled with massive student loan debt, the worst type of all debt.

That said, there are also many con artists and fake teachers on YouTube.

We All Know Talk Is Cheap
As Thomas Sowell warned:
> *"One of the common failings among honorable people is a failure to appreciate how thoroughly dishonorable some other people can be, and how dangerous it is to trust them."*

Generalized Princple:
Unity is plural, and at minimum two

All Coins Have Three Sides
In an insane world where everybody wants to be right it is insane to argue. I've found that it's best to stand on the edge of a coin and decide which side is best for you. There are three sides to every coin — heads, tails and the edge.

In a previous chapter, I wrote about the word *cult*, and that it is short for *culture*. And a culture can be a group dedicated to study. For example, Jews are a religious culture, as are Muslims, Morons, Catholics, Protestants, and Buddhists.

INTELLIGENCE IS THE ABILITY TO SEE BOTH SIDES OF THE COIN

E   B

S   I

ALL COINS HAVE 3 SIDES
HEADS, TAILS, AND THE EDGE

Just because we are from different cultures, it does not mean we have to kill each other. As The Generalized Principle of 'Unity is Plural, at minimum two' means there will always be another religious culture. There will never be one religion. The idea of one religion, violates the God's operating principles. That idea — of only one of anything — is insane thinking... and a fascist idea. Because the definition of *fascist* is: a person who is extremely authoritarian and intolerant of others.

As Gad Saad warns:
> *"Anyone who is willing to end a relationship because of a reasoned difference of opinion is not worthy of your friendship."*

He also said:
> *"Every one of us prefers talking with people who share our opinions. That is an indelible part of human nature. But our minds are elevated when we discuss opposing points of view respectfully."*

How Intelligence Grows
That is why standing on the edge of a coin is important. The edge is intelligence, and your intelligence grows when you are able to listen to another point of view.

The primary reason Kim and I created the CASHFLOW board game was to empower people to start their own cult — their culture of capitalism.

So, as Bucky asked, what can a little person do? A little person — which, to me, means each and every one of us — can start a CASHFLOW Club in his or her home and be connected to Rich Dad's teachers via YouTube. And as Fuller predicted:

> *"From a distance, it looks like a planet full of professors on tenure, working hard, doing more metaphysical stuff than before."*

Through the power of the mantra Deeds Not Words, you become a doer, not a talker or complainer... or a victim. And via the magic of YouTube and technology our real Rich Dad teachers will come and guide your group in study. There are CASHFLOW Clubs in cities around the world

What do they study? They play the game and learn to become financially free on the B and I side of the Cashflow Quadrant.

Q: What if we want to become rich on the E and S side of the quadrant?
A: That's your choice, of course. But it's a harder path because the roadmap for that — go back to school, get a job, work hard, pay taxes, save money, buy a house, get out of debt, and invest for the long term in the stock market — becomes more and more obsolete each year.

The lesson here is this: all coins have three sides. It is a Generalized Principle. There is always another side to every coin. Stand on the edge and choose the side that is best for you. If you choose the E and S side, you choose the specialist side, the "brain slave" side.

To repeat Fuller's words:

> *"Specialization is in fact only a fancy form of slavery, where in the expert is fooled into accepting a slavery by making him feel that he in turn is a socially and culturally preferred-ergo, highly secure-lifelong position."*

Freedom vs. Security
Those on the E and S side of the quadrant have the least freedom. They trade freedom for security. You can migrate to the right side, the B and I side — the warlord side — and fight for your freedoms. One of them being the freedom from taxes.

In 1974, I chose the B and I side... the side where my rich dad operated. It was harder. I could have made other choices, like flying for an airline, as an employee, or going back to my job with Standard Oil as a tanker officer, again a high-paid employee.

The problem was I had seen too much in Vietnam. I knew my teacher's lessons on Marxism was real. Flying along the burned-out French mansions, I could see the future of America.

In 1974, I stood on the edge of the coin and chose the B and I side, my rich dad's side of the coin. I do not recommend that choice for everyone, but I am glad I chose the B and I side, the side of maximum personal freedom.

In 1983, after Fuller's death and after reading *GRUNCH of Giants,* I knew what I had to do. As I've said, it was then that I knew what God wanted done.

In 1984, I met Kim. In 1984, I remembered the lesson from Hell Week: *Deeds Not Words.*

That year Kim, Blair, and I sold everything and left Hawaii for California.

CASHFLOW Clubs are not "get rich quick" clubs. They are not "Let's make a deal" clubs. No one is allowed to raise money or pitch their latest investment. They're also not "Let's make a date" clubs." The purpose of CASHFLOW Clubs is the same as military school... to create leaders

CASHFLOW Clubs are capitalist cults and places where like-minded people gather, people who share a common culture, body of study, values, and priorities — places of study, places to learn, and places to expand your infinite.

CASHFLOW Clubs are designed to be places where people come to study, to share, grow, and become leaders of capitalism by becoming stronger mentally, emotionally, physically, and spiritually.

The purpose of CASHFLOW Clubs is to prepare participants for real game of money. It's a tough game, the game of money, when it's played in real life… with real money.

So What's Next?
You will also meet my team of real teachers, every entrepreneur and capitalist's true assets.

CHAPTER THIRTEEN

TEACHING CAPITALISM AT HOME

"Plans must be simple and flexible.
They must be made by the people who execute them."
— General George Patton

In 1981, during the 5-day conference with Fuller, he said something that disturbed me. In fact, what he said shocked me. Paraphrasing from memory, he said:

"I speak about the future, and I speak in words, most people do not use or understand... because if 'they' knew what I was saying 'they' would kill me."

I sat there wondering why anyone would want to kill a sweet 86-year-old man. All he did was use strange words and speak about the future.

Then I remembered the 1968 song, sung by Dion, *Abraham, Martin, and John*, which I mentioned in an earlier chapter.

A few words are:
Anybody here seen my old friend Abraham?
Can you tell me where he's gone?
He freed a lot of people,
But it seems the good they die young
You know I just looked around and he's gone."

The song continuing to ask the same questions about John Kennedy, Martin Luther King, and Bobby Kennedy. All great people who were murdered.

The more important questions posed in the song were:
> *Didn't you love the things that they stood for?*
> *Didn't they try to find some good for you and me?*

Who Murders Our Great Leaders?

In 1981, listening to Fuller, I wondered what Fuller knew? What did he know that would cause someone kill him? Why would someone want him dead? From all indications, he was a very good man, often called "the planet's friendly genius."

He then said:
> *"It will be your generation that will take on the people who want to kill me today."*

Again, I am paraphrasing his message. He did not use those words, but that was the message I got.

As I've said, in 1983, the year he died, his book *GRUNCH of Giants* was released. I thought it was interesting that GRUNCH stood for **Gro**ss **Un**iversal **C**ash **H**eist. It was a tiny book and I wondered what might be in the book that I didn't grasp or couldn't fathom.

Again, Fuller used words and stories that spoke around a subject, without ever naming names or speaking in specifics. Much like most of his talks and writing, *GRUNCH* was "big picture."

The reason I found *GRUNCH* interesting was because it was a book very different from Fuller's normal messages. He usually wrote and spoke of math, science, the universe, and far-out metaphysical ideas.

GRUNCH was about the bigger picture of money, power, and greed. A subject I was familiar with... yet I wondered if there was more to *GRUNCH* than met the eye.

Rich Dad's Warning

In 1972, soon after arriving in Vietnam, rich dad sent me a letter. It was via snail mail since, in 1972, that was how we communicated.

Rich dad warned:

> *"President Nixon took the dollar off the gold standard. Watch out – the world is going to change."*

I did not know what he meant, but I trusted rich dad and heeded his warning.

A few weeks later, my co-pilot and I were flying behind enemy lines in search of a gold mine. We thought we could buy gold at a discount if we bought gold at the mine. The reason we were behind enemy lines is because America was losing the war. The North Vietnamese were rolling South. The gold mine we were looking for was now in enemy hands. Of course, being Marines, that fact did not stop us.

I have written and spoken a number of times about meeting a tiny Vietnamese woman, the sales rep for a gold mine. When we tried to negotiate a better price on gold she would smirk and say, "spot."

Although we were college graduates, my copilot and I had no idea what the word *spot* meant. A few moments, later, our crew chief began screaming bloody murder, the negotiations broke down, and my co-pilot and I ran through the tiny village, expecting to meet the enemy at our aircraft.

The reason our crew chief was screaming was because our helicopter was sinking. I had parked the aircraft on an old rice paddy. As I said, Marines are not known for our academic genius.

Flying back to the carrier, covered in mud, I kept wondering what the word *spot* meant. The more I thought about it the more I realized that it was the Vietnamese woman's smirk that disturbed me most. Was she telling us how stupid we were? Probably. Was she saying, "How can you not know what is really going on?" Did she wonder why we were risking our lives, behind enemy lines, negotiating for a better price on gold?

In 1983, after reading *GRUNCH of Giants*, I could see the future and Fuller's warning with greater clarity. Fuller and the Vietnamese woman were making more sense.

Since 1972, I have traveled the world — South America, Africa, Mongolia, Canada, and across America — looking at little holes in the ground. These little holes were dug by ancient humans who intuitively knew where to dig for gold or silver. Ancients did not need to go to college or be told "dig here for gold." They intuitively knew gold and silver are God's money.

Spot Price

The word **spot** *means the price, in this case of gold, on that day all over the world. Gold is real money because gold is God's money. Gold is God's money because God put it here, not humans.*

In the 1989, I was in Peru to buy a gold mine. I remember standing in the South American Andes Mountains, as high as 17,000 feet, light-headed and hallucinating without oxygen, looking at tiny holes in the ground.

As I stood there, gasping for breath, my mind drifted back to my 5th grade class, and my favorite teacher, Mr. Ely who taught us about the Incas, one of the most advanced cultures in history. I remember Mr. Ely recounting the story of Spanish explorer Francisco Pizarro. In the 1500s, Pizarro was more than an explorer. He is best known as a conquistador who conquered the Incas and executed their leader Atahuapla before stealing all their gold and returning to Spain.

In 2021, I have a better understanding of why Fuller said:

> *"It will be your generation that will take on the people... who want to kill me today."*

In 2021, more and more people are feeling the effects of GRUNCH.

In 2021, more and more people are realizing their wealth is being stolen via their money.

In 2021, I better understand why COVID-19 appeared, mysteriously out of China, a few weeks after the Repo Market crashed on September 17, 2019.

And I think about socialism and Marx's words in *Communist Manifesto*:
"Thus, in 1847, Socialism was a middle-class movement, Communism a working-class movement. Socialism was, on the continent at least, 'respectable'; Communism was the very opposite."

I wondered if Fuller's 1981 warning was coming true in 2021, the year that marked the 50th anniversary of Richard Nixon's broken promise to the world in 1971... the promise that the U.S. dollar would be backed by gold.

Today, Fullers warning seems more urgent and more imminent. These are some of my concerns:

- The milestone of the 50th Anniversary the day President Nixon took the U.S. dollar off the gold standard and the most disruptive economic period in history
- The fact that there are very few bankruptcies. Many companies are zombies kept alive on fake money
- The problem of debt being solved with more debt
- Trillions being spent without returns
- Wall Street cheering on the insanity chanting "Don't fight the Fed!"
- The $100 trillion-plus entitlement problem we face
- The anger at the rich growing richer

I do believe Fuller was correct. The problems he foresaw coming from GRUNCH will wipe out the Baby-Boom generation... the generation that has, for the most part, enjoyed an easy life. The hammer of GRUNCH will soon fall.

With that thought in mind, here are some questions to consider:

> When GRUNCH drops the hammer, is that when Stage One of Marxism Leninism comes to an end... and rioting begins?

Does Fuller's warning coincide with the 50th Anniversary of Nixon closing the gold window... the the beginning of the end of free market capitalism?

Will the rioting and unrest that we're experiencing pave the way for Stage Two of Marxism-Leninism... and usher in communism?

Is that why Fuller said it was our generation that would take on the challenges he saw coming... back in 1981?

Is that what Fuller could not talk about? That he saw the future?

My answers to these questions are that I don't know. I do not have answers to these questions. No one does, with absolute certainty. As I've said, there was something fishy about September 17, 2019, the crash in the Repo Market, and something fishy about COVID-19 coming suddenly out of China.

Q: Was the first thought in your head that GRUNCH, the Gross Universal Cash Heist, was taking place... that the bank robbery was on?

A: Yes. But I have no proof. I only have personal experiences of fighting communists in Vietnam, being spit on in California, and years of study, meetings, coincidences, suspicions, and unanswered questions. I have a friend who has been impeached twice, had his friends arrested, now have a yellow star on my driver's license... and recall Fuller's warning to my generation.

As stated at the beginning of this book, I have more to lose than to gain by writing this book.

These words attributed (or, as others say, misattributed) to Edmund Burke haunt me and motivate me:

"The only thing necessary for the triumph of evil... is for good men to do nothing."

Here I present to you my interpretation of what GRUNCH looks like in 2021:

GRUNCH

THE SWAMP = CRONY CAPITALISM
THE MONEY NEVER REACHES "WE THE PEOPLE"

Q: Are you saying GRUNCH runs the world from the shadows?

A: Yes. That is why the pipes and plumbing — all the inner workings below the surface — are known as the Shadow Banking System.

Q: Are you saying GRUNCH has people killed?

A: I do not know the answer to that question. And even if I thought it might be true, I have no proof. Yet, throughout the ages, people have mysteriously died.

In 2019, Jeffry Epstein, billionaire and convicted sex-offender, died in his jail cell. The official report states he committed suicide by hanging himself. People suspect he was murdered. Too many important people in high places, flew to his island illicit activities.

As you know, the world is filled with conspiracy theories. Are they true? I don't know.

I suspect Fuller knew too much, which is why he was careful with his words. Fuller did know that we the people are ripped off via our money, our banks,

Wall Street, the government, and the shadow banking system. Fuller and my rich dad agreed on many things.

Q: Is that why rich dad's Lesson #1 is "The rich don't work for money"?

A: Yes. Remember from previous chapters that Fuller spoke about warlords creating an educational system to produce "brain slaves." In 1903 the General Education Board was formed by John D. Rockefeller and incorporated by an Act of Congress. Not much has changed. In 2021 there is still not real financial education in schools. It doesn't take a rocket scientist to figure out why: War lords do not want brain slaves to become war lords.

As Fuller said:

"The things to do are the things that need doing, that you see need to be done, and that no one else seems to see need to be done."

All of us have different "warlords" to take on. There is no scarcity of of them... no scarcity of things that need to be done. I chose GRUNCH.

The warlord I personally take on is called the education system. That is why Kim and I began our Capitalist Manifesto with the CASHFLOW board game in 1996.

Q: And those who takes on the war lords are murdered?

A: In the extreme, yes. And in many different ways. I think of my friend Donald Trump. He went through character assignation after character assignation. Trump will go down in history as the only U.S. President impeached twice.

Both Trump and Patton, in my opinion, were great leaders. Yet Patton will be remembered for slapping a soldier in a hospital and Trump will be remembered for being impeached twice and allegedly fueling the attack on the U.S. Capital.

As Gad Saad warned:

"An analysis of political campaign donations across a broad range of industries uncovered that the four most liberal professions, in decreasing

order, were the entertainment industry, academia, online computer services, and newspapers and print media."

"A 2013 study from Indiana University's School of Journalism revealed that American journalists were nearly four times more likely to be Democrats than Republicans."

Q: Is that why you recommend teaching capitalism in our homes?

A: Yes. Socialist media will still eavesdrop on you, using your own private property, your devices, such as Alexa and Siri.

During World War II, America had the CIA, Russia had the KGB, and Germany had the Gestapo. These organizations spied on its own citizens. Today, you and I purchase our spies, and put them in our homes.

As George Orwell warned in his book, *1984:*
   "Big Brother is watching you."

Q: In spite of Big Brother, you still recommend teaching capitalism at home?

A: Why not? Aren't you smarter than Silicon Valley's Big Brother? Besides there is nothing wrong with teaching capitalism... and certainly not in our own homes. Teaching capitalism at home is far safer than teaching capitalism in school.

The Rich Dad Company has been teaching capitalism in plain sight since 1996.

The goal of capitalist entrepreneurs is to make life easier for people. For example, the computer made life easier for billions of people. The same is true for the automobile, airplane, and McDonald's. McDonald's serves nearly 6.48 million burgers every day, plus shakes and fries, to millions (70 million, in 2021) of people every day at affordable prices, making life easier. McDonald's jingle and first real tagline, introduced in the early 1970s, was 'You deserve a break today.'

The problem with socialism, Marxism, and communism is that they make life harder and more expensive, because socialist do not produce. They consume, which is why most grocery stores are empty in socialist countries.

Think about education. Today a college education leaves millions of students deep in debt. On the flip side, many capitalists teach for free. Just as Fuller predicted, millions of real teachers teach for free, via social media platforms, podcasts, and YouTube.

Just as Fuller predicted Bitcoin, decades before Bitcoin was introduced, Fuller also predicted the greatest teachers would be teaching for free.

Traditional schools and schoolteachers are becoming obsolete. Why? Because they make education boring... as schools make life harder, more expensive, and don't teach the practical skills and subjects that people use in their everyday lives.

Financial education is practical, useful... and essential. Yet, with rare exceptions, it's not a subject taught in schools. Most teachers are like Marx. He was a poor person because he did not know how to make money or manage money. He couldn't support his wife and children. That is why I say Marx's ghost walks the halls of higher education.

If you have ever been to a socialist country, I expect you would have seen that government bureaucracy is a mess, that there is no food on the shelves, and that the people are poor. Taking from the rich and giving to the poor just creates more poor people.

The purpose of a capitalist entrepreneur is to make life easier and more affordable, and to raise personal standards of living. The capitalist who does that gets richer and richer.

Jeff Booth, in his book *The Price of Tomorrow,* revisits and refines Bucky Fuller's view of the future. If you are an entrepreneur and a capitalist, Jeff's book is a must-read. He explains why true capitalists bring prices down and make life easier and less expensive. Socialists make life harder and more expensive. Socialists are the cause of the growing gap between the rich and everyone else.

The differences between socialism and capitalism are extreme. Schools teach socialism. Socialists raise taxes, increase debt, expand entitlement programs, and label the rich are greedy.

It is hard to learn to be a capitalist in a socialist and entitlement culture. Socialism make life harder. Capitalists make life better.

People leave socialist schools looking for a job, afraid of making mistakes, seeking job security, and waiting to be told what to do with their money. That's one side of the coin.

> **Rich Dad's Capitalist Manifesto:**
> *Make learning capitalism fun, affordable, and inspiring, teaching capitalism at home.*

The other is the Rich Dad philosophy and a capitalist culture of learning. It is a culture of becoming inspired to live a life of lifelong learning... a life of lifelong service to fellow humans and our planet.

Rich Dad accomplishes this by producing capitalist tools for lifelong, multi-generational, inspired learning. We don't believe in learning by memorizing answers, just to pass a test. That is not learning. We promote learning through experience and applying what you learn to your life to improve it and enhance it.

Great entrepreneurs such as Thomas Edison, Henry Ford, Jeff Bezos, Steve Jobs, Elon Musk became extremely wealthy by seeing the needs of the future and ways to make life better. They did not sit around waiting for a government "stimulus check."

CAPITALIST TOOL #1: *The CASHFLOW Board Game*
First beta-tested and played in 1996, the CASHFLOW game was launched that same year.

There are two crucial points of learning in the game: the game board and the financial statement.

Both of these **Capitalist Tools** are pictured below.

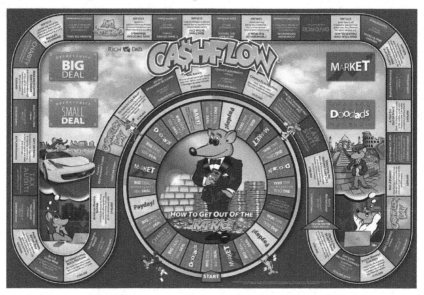

Games Are Great Teachers

There are many things you'll learn my playing the CASHFLOW game.

The game board has two tracks: the Rat Race and the Fast Track. The Rat Race is the track that most schools train students to live on. The Rat Race is where Es and Ss earn their money. And where the terms "trapped in the rat race" and "living paycheck-to-paycheck in the rat race" came from.

The Fast Track is where the *accredited investors* live. Accredited investors are individuals or business entites that meet specific requirements regarding income, professional experience, and other standards. They have attained some degree of wealth and are financially educated. The Fast Track is for capitalists — and where the Bs and Is invest. Most Fast Track investments are closed to Es and Ss, who for the most part, do not qualify as accredited investors. It takes real financial education to become a real accredited investor.

The objective of the CASHFLOW game is get out of the Rat Race and win the game on the Fast Track.

The reason games are better teachers than teachers in schools is because games involve all four intelligences. For example, no one has learned to play golf from a book or lecture. To be successful at anything in life requires engaging all four intelligences.

The Four Intelligences

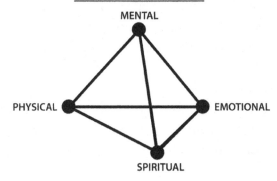

The problem with schools is that academics prey on students' fear of failing, fear of looking stupid, and fear of being ostracized because they're different.

It's hard to be an entrepreneur if you are afraid of failing and afraid of being different.

Neural Pathways

Games retrain the neural paths in your brain. For example, let's say you brush your teeth with your right hand. If for some reason you had to learn to brush your teeth with your left hand, the relatively simple process of brushing your teeth would require the retraining of all four intelligences... which is not simple.

That is what the CASHFLOW game does. It retrains the patterns of your brain's neural pathways. The good news is that retraining your neural pathways is like learning to ride a bicycle. Once you learn to ride a bike, you can do it forever.

Changing Cultures

The best news about the CASHFLOW game, in my opinion, is that it has the potential, the power, to change cultures... and mindsets.

As Malcolm Gladwell writes in his book *Outliers:*
  "Who we are cannot be separated from where we're from."

By challenging and engaging all four intelligences, the odds improve for a person from a poor or middle class culture to enter the culture of the rich. And that's done best by inspiring and motivating and teaching — not by giving people answers, not by telling people what to do or what to invest in. True teachers inspire new and higher levels of learning.

The Financial Statement

My banker has never asked me for my report card. My banker has never asked me what my GPA, Grade Point Average, was. My banker has never even asked me what school I went to or if I have a college degree.

The only document my banker has asked me for is my Financial Statement. And herein lies the problem. Most people do not have a financial statement. Nor do they know how one works... or even why their banker wants to see their financial statement.

Pictured again here is the financial statement from the *CASHFLOW* board game.

Capitalist Tool

When I am asked how we borrowed $300 million after the 2008 subprime mortgage meltdown, the reason was the banker liked our "report card," our financial statements.

People without strong financial statements should be cautious about borrowing money.

One reason for playing the game or joining a CASHFLOW club is to practice investing — with play money — and make as many mistakes as possible. You'll engage all four intelligences, train your neural pathways, and learn to keep your cash flowing inside your financial statement. The more mistakes you make playing CASHFLOW the smarter you become... and you can do it with play money. The game prepares you to invest your *real money* with more knowledge and confidence and experience. The CASHFLOW game is infinite because you can make an infinite number of mistakes — without losing a dollar of real money.

I think these words, attributed by some to Albert Einstein, track perfectly with both the power of the game — and how we can learn from trying something new and learning from the mistakes we'll make along the way:
> *"A person who never made a mistake never tried anything new."*

And, in a similar vein, Winston Churchill reportedly said:
> *"All men make mistakes, but only wisemen learn from them."*

And Fuller taught:
> *"Mistakes are only sins, when not admitted."*

Accounting Can Be Boring
I know that from personal experience. The most boring class I have ever taken was accounting. Which isn't a good thing because accounting is a very important subject. The problem with my experience was the teacher was boring and he punished us for making mistakes.

Why did I take an accounting course? Because rich dad told me that the three foundational courses for entrepreneurs are accounting, business law, and sales. He also said that you don't have to go to Harvard to learn those foundational subjects.

What Real Entrepreneurs Do
When Kim and I designed the CASHFLOW game we wanted people to have fun learning new things and be excited about taking risks, making mistakes, and learning from them. We learn by admitting or acknowledging that we've

made mistakes and then finding the lessons in those mistakes so we're less likely to make the same ones in the future.

That is what real entrepreneurs do. In school, you are punished for making mistakes and often labeled "stupid."

The real purpose of the CASHFLOW game is to give people a way to stop lying to themselves.

It's a tool and a path to taking a long hard look at yourself and your finances — as well as what you know, or still need to know, about money. It's also about a mindset shift... in how you think about money. When you show your banker your financial statement, your report card in the real world, and you can prove how smart you are with your money, the banker will be happy to give you the money you need... to become richer.

That is how Kim, Ken, and I borrowed $300 million after the crash of 2008. We showed our banker our report card.... our financial statement which tells the banker all he or she needs to know about our credit-worthiness, experience, and strength as a borrower.

CAPITALIST TOOL #2: *Rich Dad Poor Dad*

In 1996, after Kim and I had created the CASHFLOW board game, we faced another challenge — how to sell it. So I wrote *Rich Dad Poor Dad*. Most people don't know that *Rich Dad Poor Dad* started out as a sales brochure... and wound up as a book.

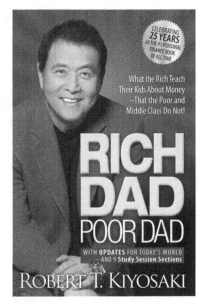

In 1997 *Rich Dad Poor Dad* was self-published because, apparently, my rich dad's lessons on money were too foreign to the New York editors, who were people more like my poor dad.

Financial Literacy

Rich Dad Poor Dad is a book about financial literacy and Financial IQ. Financial literacy is the ability to read, study, and make sense of financial words and numbers.

As an example, from the core principles of *Rich Dad Poor Dad*, let's look at the words *assets* and *liabilities*. Rich dad definitions of these words are different from the ones you'll find in a standard dictionary.

The definition of *asset:*
   "Something that puts money in your pocket whether you work or not."

The definition of *liability:*
   "Something that takes money from your pocket."

The biggest mistake people make, in my opinion, is calling their house, car, or college education an asset. In most cases they are liabilities.

A Picture Is Worth 1,000 Words

As promised... We're KISS-ing here.

I'm Keeping It — the Financial Statement — Super Simple:

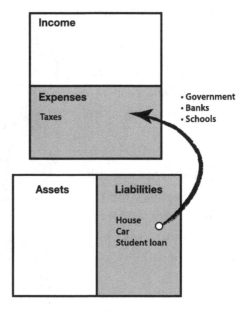

Q: Are you saying, many people who look rich might really be on the verge of bankruptcy?

A: Yes. They work hard, make more money, buy a bigger house or a new car. They may have more money and they may look good, but they grow poorer.

Some say these are Marx's words... but regardless of who said them I believe the warning clear:

> *"Owners of capital will stimulate working class to buy more and more of expensive goods, houses and technology, pushing them to take more and more expensive credits, until their debt becomes unbearable. The unpaid debt will lead to bankruptcy of banks which will have to be nationalized and State will have to take the road which will eventually lead to communism."*

Q: Is that what you got from reading *GRUNCH of Giants*?

A: Yes. That was one of the lessons. Fuller simply said:
> *"Our leaders are playing games with money."*

Q: What did Fuller mean by "playing games" with money?

A: The game of making the rich richer, at the expense of the working class, the Es and Ss.

Q: The people who work for money?

A: Yes.

Q: Is that why *Rich Dad's* lesson #1 is The Rich Don't Work for Money?

A: Yes. In 1971, the year Nixon took the U.S. dollar off the gold standard, the U.S. dollar became a function of debt and taxes.

In 2021, the poor and middle class grow deeper in debt, work harder for money, and pay higher percentages in taxes.

Q: And those in the B and I quadrants earn more money and pay less taxes?

A: Yes. All legally, based on a tax code that incentivizes business owners and investors.

Q: Is that why financial education is not taught in our schools?

A: That's part of it... What do you think?

Real Assets

Pictured below are real assets.

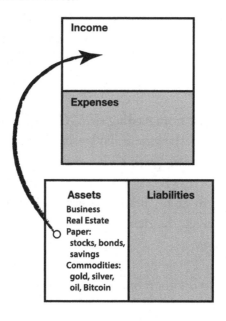

Millions of people spend money on big homes, nice cars, luxury vacations, and private schools for their kids... and believe they are assets when, in fact, they're buying liabilities that they *think* are assets. They're buying things that take money out of their pockets. And all the while they believe they are rich.

Ernest Hemingway (1899-1961), author and winner of the Nobel Prize in Literature, warned in his 1926 book *The Sun Always Rises* alluded to the perils of confusing the two and the dire consequences when the house of cards collapses. When the character was asked: *How did you go bankrupt? The response: "Two ways... Gradually and then suddenly."*

And I'm sure you've heard these words:

> *"There are decades where nothing happens, and there are weeks where decades happen."*

Jim Rickards, author of *Currency Wars, Aftermath,* and *The New Great Depression,* warned:

> *"It's an avalanche waiting for the last snowflake."*

I've found that it's best to study capitalism at home, with a cult of capitalists... people who love to study and share that common culture. That is what rich dad did with his advisors on Saturday mornings and what we do at Rich Dad... every Thursday via Zoom.

Financial IQ

So what *is* Financial IQ? We talk a lot about it and it's good to be clear on how we define it. In simplest terms, Financial IQ measures the size of financial problem you can solve. Just before COVID-19, it was widely reported that nearly half of American families would struggle to come up with $400 to cover an unexpected expense. In that case, their Financial IQ is $400.

CAPITALIST TOOL #3: *The CASHFLOW Quadrant*

Many readers of my book *The CASHFLOW Quadrant,* the book that followed *Rich Dad Poor Dad* in the Rich Dad Series, tell me that it was the book that changed their lives. Pictured below is the Cashflow Quadrant.

Repeating this explanation from earlier in this book and in other Rich Dad books:

E stands for Employee

S stands for Specialist or Small business owner

B stands for Big Business owner 500 employees... and for Brand

I stands for insider Investor. (Es and Ss invest from the outside.)

My poor dad wanted me to be an employee, in the E quadrant.

My mom wanted me to be a doctor, in the S quadrant.

Most entrepreneurs are small business owners in the S quadrant

People like Elon Musk are in the B quadrant. And people like Warren Buffett are in the I quadrant. As I've stated earlier in this book, Buffett does not invest in S quadrant businesses, or "start-ups." Buffett invests in Brands, such as Apple, Visa, Kraft Heinz, and Coca-Cola.

> Q: I remember you saying that freedom is on the B and I side of the quadrant...
>
> A: Yes. Just look at taxes:

TAX PERCENTAGES PAID PER QUADRANT

Q: So people who work for money, as Es and Ss, *do* pay the most in taxes?

A: They do. And that's why Margaret Thatcher said:

> *"Socialist governments traditionally do make a financial mess. They always run out of other people's money."*

And governments keep raising taxes...

I'm often asked what drove me to change quadrants, to move from the left side — working as an E and an S, to the right side. I remember my poor dad constantly saying, "tax the rich." When I told my rich dad what my poor dad was saying, rich dad just shook his head and said: *"That is how little your dad knows about money and taxes. Somebody should educate him on the facts."*

The facts are that governments never tax the rich. Governments need rich capitalists to do what the government cannot do. And they're given tax incentives to do it. Governments only tax the people who work for money.

Paraphrasing a warning from Marx in *Communist Manifesto:*

> *"A heavy or progressive or graduated income tax is necessary for the proper development of Communism."*

Schools are Marxist. Marxists believe in taxes. So we should find it surprising that schools churn out Es — employees — and Ss, who can be counted on to keep a steady stream of tax revenue coming into government coffers.

CAPITALIST TOOL #4:
The B-I Triangle

The Introduction of this book is about my decision to go to military school, versus a traditional college or university. The B-I Triangle defines the differences between military school and a traditional school.

The outer triangle — *Mission, Team,* and *Leadership* — is the focus of military school. The purpose of military schools is to develop leaders. During Hell week, the outer triangle was all we focused on: mission, team, and leadership.

The inner triangle represents "brain slaves," the focus on traditional, "specialist" education.

One reason a person would start a CASHFLOW Club in their home is to develop the skills of the outer triangle. Traditional schools do a pretty good job producing specialists for roles inside the B-I Triangle, but put little emphasis on leadership or team building or mission.

We have seen how those who start and teach CASHFLOW Clubs grow and develop into strong leaders. Their minds were opened to different points of view about money, about how people learn, and about what it takes to get out of the Rat Race. Many of them have been successful in applying all that they've learned to their own lives.

CASHFLOW Club leaders, guided by Rich Dad via YouTube, set the culture and put a high priority on mindset and learning from mistakes. They nurture and support new leaders as they emerge within the club.

Great leaders produce great cultures. Take sports for example. Certain countries such as Jamaica have developed a culture of great sprinters. The same as Kenya has a culture of long-distance runners. Some may say it is genetics, but the world is filled with individuals with great genetic gifts. Once a culture takes hold, the spirit of the culture spreads and young people are inspired to be part of that culture.

As a CASHFLOW Club leader grows stronger and more skilled as a teacher, he or she develops a strong culture that will shape the club's growth, strength, and expansion. A few words of warning: CASHFLOW Clubs have very clear rules. If Club members find leaders violating the rules we encourage them to contact The Rich Dad Company.

We've seen the CASHFLOW Club culture spread because it is aligned with one of Fuller's Generalized Principles:

"The more people I serve... the more effective I become."

One reason why The Rich Dad Company does so well with a very small core team is because we follow that one specific fundamental of God's Operating Principle of the Universe.

Again, requoting Indian Guru Sai Baba:

"Some say knowledge is power, but it is not true. Character is power."

Following that principle and with a focus on "serving more people," our company did nearly 50 percent more business during the during the pandemic than in the prior year. Many people have told us that they discovered a silver lining in having to 'shelter in place' with family and found the time that had so often eluded them to read, study, play games as a family. And the spirit of the Rich Dad culture continued to spread throughout the world via Zoom, even though no one was traveling.

The Secret to Our Success

Being a leader does not mean Kim or I are in charge. We are not the leaders. The Rich Dad company is a team of leaders. Long ago I learned to only work with people who are smarter than I am. No one leads from the top down. The Rich Dad organization is lead from the inside out.

As General George Patton said:

"Plans must be simple and flexible. They must be made by the people who execute them."

And then there are our Advisors... each one of them a leader. Rich Dad has created, over time, a great team on the inside and a great team on the outside.

Warlords

Just as the B-I Triangle illustrates, The Rich Dad Company operates as a B-I Triangle. That is what students are taught to do in military school. We are taught to be warlords. We are taught to lead from the inside and lead from the outside. That is why, despite the COVID-19 pandemic, we got stronger, more efficient and did better financially than the year before.

Investing Is Not Risky
There is risk in everything. For example, when a baby is learning to walk, risk is very high. Yet once the child can walk, he or she naturally wants to run, ride a bicycle, drive a car, fly a plane. More risks…

While there will always be risk, the learning process for managing and mitigating it does not have to be risky. Risk can be controlled. And control is the opposite or risk.

When I was in flight school, we took ground school classes, learned to parachute, met our instructor, climbed into the plane, and learned how to fly. Like magic, after 10 hours I was flying solo. Three years later, I was flying in Vietnam.

That is the power of real education. That is the power of joining a cult — a culture of learning — that in this example was a culture of military pilots.

The same is true with money, investing, business, entrepreneurship… all dedicated to learning, in a culture of capitalism.

Every Thursday, as a core piece of the Rich Dad culture, the team gets together on Zoom for one hour and studies together. We are a cult in the very best sense of the word — a culture that values education and study.

What is risky is hanging around the water cooler with a cult of critics and complainers… people who paint themselves as victims.

A Winning Formula
One key aspect of how our team operates is keeping an open mind to other points of view. We appreciate that there are those on a path to financial freedom who are still operating as Es… and may have (or still be) funding

401(k)s or other investments in the markets. As as an entrepreneur on the B and I side of the quadrant, I create my own assets.

That is what real entrepreneurs do. They create their own assets. Entrepreneurs who are in the S quadrant, work for money. Entrepreneurs in the B and I quadrants create their own assets.

Let me be clear: This does not mean you should not invest in stocks, bonds, mutual funds, or ETFs. You probably *should* buy these paper assets, especially if you do not want to be a student on the B and I side of the quadrant.

Debt Is Money
I love debt. I am nearly a billion dollars in debt. I make more money and pay less in taxes because I use debt as money. Please know that I do not share this information to boast — only to provide a real-life example of how using debt — once you've invested in your financial education to learn and understand how to use debt responsibly — can build wealth. Keep in mind that on August 15, 1971, the U.S. dollar became a function of debt and taxes.

The Other Side of the Coin
Dave Ramsey and Suze Orman promote living debt-free. And, for most people, this is sound advice. People should live debt free, especially if they do not want to be a student on the B and I side of the quadrant. Both...

My Winning Formula
The following is a simple diagram on how I use debt to get richer and richer and to pay less and less in taxes.

You may recall that I wrote about taking my first real estate investment course in 1974. My homework was to look at 100 properties in 90 days, writing a brief one-page assessment on all 100 of them. Like the lessons I learned from the Vietnamese gold merchant, that 90-day/100-property exercise made me the multi-millionaire I am today.

This is what I do today. This is one of my winning formulas. And one reason why I do not invest in the stock market, why I do not have a 401(k), and why I do not cut up my credit cards.

As rich dad said:
"*There are a million paths to financial heaven.*"

The following three steps are one of my paths. There are many more. The good news is you do not have to go to Harvard to find your winning formula, or your paths to financial heaven.

STEP #1

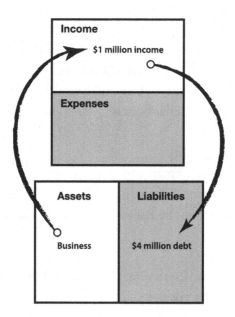

My business generates $1 million in income after expenses. I borrow $4 million in debt.

STEP #2

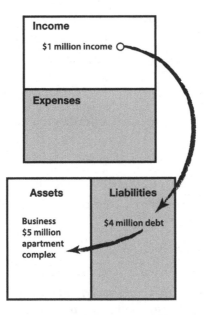

With the $1 million in income and $4 million in debt, I buy a $5 million apartment complex.

STEP #3

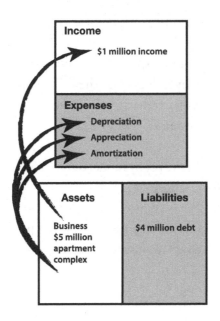

The $5 million apartment complex generates cash flow into my income column. Tax laws allow me to pay very little or even zero in taxes via depreciation on $5 million. In addition, there is appreciation, the increase in value on $5 million, and amortization, the $4 million debt that is paid off by the tenants, not me.

Depreciation, appreciation, and amortization are all forms of tax-free incomes.

If you're interested in learning more on the details and strategy of this winning formula, I encourage you please read these books in the Rich Dad Advisor Series:

Tom Wheelwright's *Tax-Free Wealth*

Ken McElroy's *ABCs of Real Estate Investing*
ABCs of Property Management
ABCs of Buying Rental Property
ABCs of Advanced Real Estate Investing
ABCs of Raising Capital

CAPITALIST TOOL #5: *A Team of Leaders*
My favorite sport is rugby. rugby is a team of leaders.

American football is a corporate sport. There is a quarterback, a CEO, who calls the plays, and every player does what the CEO tells them to do. Once a play is over, the CEO, the quarterback, calls meeting, a huddle, and tells the team of Es and Ss what to do next.

Both models work. I prefer the rugby model of business and working with — playing with — a team of leaders.

Soccer and basketball teams are like rugby. Golf is a pure S-quadrant sport, much like doctors and lawyers in private practice.

Our Best Assets

In the next section, Part Two, you will meet Rich Dad's team of advisors, our leaders on the outside of the B-I Triangle. They are all leaders in their own businesses.

We all come together, not just for money but to support the mission of the Rich Dad company, which is: *"to elevate the financial well-being of humanity."*

Many of our team of advisors have been with The Rich Dad Company for over 20 years. Blair Singer has been with me since 1980, 41 years.

I introduce them to you to use as guides... as real-life examples of the Rich Dad team of leaders and so that you can build your team. Your team is one of your most important assets and a powerful Capitalist Tool.

PART TWO

Teams and B-I Triangle

Rich dad said:
"Business and Investing are team sports."

INTRODUCTION
TO PART TWO

EDUCATION:
WE WERE WARNED

Education has always played a role in how groups and organizations and ideologies move agendas forward and take control. *Forbes* called the NEA, the National Education Association, the National Extortion Association.

Marx warned:

> "*The education of all children, from the moment that they can get along without a mother's care... shall be in state institutions.*"

Lenin warned:

> "*Whenever the cause of the people is entrusted to professors... it is lost.*"

Hitler warned:

> "*Let me control the textbooks... and I will control the state.*"

Thomas Sowell warned:

> "*Before so many people went to colleges and universities... common sense was much more widespread.*"

Here's a short Q&A to get us all thinking...

Q: How do Schools Teach People to be Poor?
A: 1 – Schools Teach: No Financial Education
A: 2 – Schools Teach: Mistakes Make You Stupid
A: 3 – Schools Teach: Asking for Help Is Cheating

Q: How do We Counter the Communism Taught in Schools?

A: 1 – Teach: Real Financial Education at home

A: 2 – Teach: Mistakes make people smarter

A: 3 – Teach: Cooperation is not cheating.

Q: What Is an Entrepreneur's Greatest Asset?

A: Their team... their Band of Brothers, Sisters, and Angels

Real Financial Freedom

Kim and I designed the *CASHFLOW* game in 1996, *after* we had achieved financial freedom. Kim was 37 and I was 47. We created the game because we found it was almost impossible to explain, with words alone, the process of how we achieved financial freedom. Once again, these are our Capitalist Tools.

Rich dad taught his son and me how to become entrepreneurs and investors by playing *Monopoly*.

I am often asked about the differences between *Monopoly* and *CASHFLOW*. And there are quite a few.

Two of the most important ones are:

> Difference #1: The *real* game board in the *CASHFLOW* game is the financial statement. There is no financial statement in the game of Monopoly.

Difference #2: There are two tracks in *CASHFLOW* — *The Rat Race* and *The Fast Track*. The primary teaching lesson in the game is how to get out the Rat Race and on to the Fast Track.

Trapped in the Rat Race
In the real world, there really is a Rat Race. And a Fast Track. Simply stated, Es and Ss are in the Rat Race — trapped, some would say — living paycheck to paycheck. When a player's monthly cash flow exceeds his or her expenses... they're out of the Rat Race and have achieved financial freedom. The Bs and Is find freedom, and fulfillment of their dreams, on the Fast Track.

In the *CASHFLOW* game and in real life, the way to escape the Rat Race is by "proving" you know what you're doing when it comes to money. The "proof" comes when your passive income exceeds your expenses. And that's where the financial statement comes in.

A financial statement proves a person knows how to manage their money and make their money work hard for them... rather than them working hard for money."

That's what rich dad taught his son and me. That "your financial statement is your report card when you leave school." He spoke from experience when he told us, "My banker has never asked me for my report card. My banker wants to see my financial statement."

The problem, today, is that most students leave school without ever knowing what a financial statement is. Or why it's so important to their financial future.

That even applies to students who graduate with PhDs. Look at the Federal Reserve Bank. There are over 700 employees there who hold PhDs. And look at the mess those academic elites have caused in the United States and in the world economy. In 2021, the world is on the verge of a global depression, a depression caused academic elites, with advanced degrees but no hands-on experience, in position of decision-making power.

The picture below explains the big difference between my rich dad and my poor dad:

The Gap Between the Rich and the Poor

The real problem, in real life, is that without real financial education in our schools, 99% of high school, trade school, and college graduates leave school without knowing what a real financial statement is.

I am very concerned about the gap between the rich and the poor. As well as the financial struggles of the middle class as inflation, or the threat of inflation, looms. Social unrest occurs when a person's upward mobility is thwarted and their standard of living declines. When I see homelessness spreading, I am reminded of Marx's warning:

"Revolutions are the locomotives of history."

It has long been my position that the lack of real financial education is one of many reasons why the gap between rich and poor grows. A bigger problem that I see is most schoolteachers are like my poor dad and Marx. Most teachers are good people, but without a real financial education they are cannot really prepare students for the real world. And most teachers and academics are not capitalists. Most academics are socialists in terms of financial philosophy. They believe in giving people fish rather than teaching people to fish.

In my opinion, the future belongs to those who buck the system of traditional education and find ways to enhance their FIQ, their financial IQ, so they can be prepared for whatever the future holds. And learning about and having a financial statement is good first step. At the very least a financial statement will give you a snapshot of where you are, financially, at any given point in time. It's a great tool and you begin to take an honest, maybe even brutal, look at your finances.

As you move into the B and I quadrants, if that's the path you choose, your banker will want to see your financial statement. It'll prove that you're a capitalist, and a capitalist knows how to have money and people work for them. A capitalist knows how to make money and use the tax laws and the incentives within them to pay very little in taxes.

It has always struck me as interesting that capitalism, the vehicles that afford jobs to those in the E quadrant, so angers the socialists like Marx who was supported by Engels. Most socialists work for capitalists... capitalists who have created these jobs that allow them to earn a living, feed their families, and put a roof over their heads. Yet Marx's anger toward capitalism is why he said:

"Workers of the world unite; you have nothing to lose but your chains."

A strong financial statement is your ticket to a world of money and opportunities, a world very few people see. Without real financial education most people are not even aware of the Fast Track. Without a strong financial statement, most people are not qualified or allowed to invest on the Fast Track.

I'm often asked why I don't invest in the stock market, since that's where most people in the Rat Race invest. They may have a 401(k) program at work or get the rush from acting on a "hot tip" that's similar to a gambler at a casino. The barrier to entry is low... and virtually anyone can own shares of stock. I don't invest in stocks because I invest on the Fast Track, where I can use debt as money and pay less in taxes. That is true capitalism.

This is what 'what I do' looks like on my financial statement:

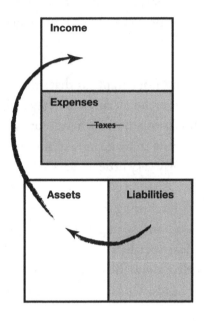

Marx warned:

> *"A heavy or progressive or graduated income tax is necessary for the proper development of Communism."*

To learn more about how capitalists make money and can pay next to nothing in taxes, legally thanks to government incentives, I recommend Rich Dad Advisor Tom Wheelwright's book, *Tax-Free Wealth*. And although learning how a financial statement works is important, if you earn all of your income as an employee, in the E quadrant, Tom Wheelwright cannot help you.

Freedom from taxes is found on the B and I side of the Cashflow Quadrant. And when you have a financial statement, you better understand Bucky Fuller's Generalized Principle of "Unity is plural... at minimum of two."

The notes on this simple diagram will help explain the differences:

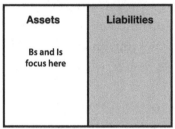

It's long been my position that the reason most schools teach Marx's philosophies is because that education opens their eyes to the E and S side of the quadrant but blinds them to the B and I side.

If you accept the fact that all coins have three sides, it's easy to see why and how keeping an open mind and learning what you can from multiple points of view makes sense.

Intelligence vs. Ignorance

I'll choose intelligence every time… even if it means I'll hear some things that I might disagree with or respect points of view that are different than mine. A financial statement — knowing what your financial picture looks like — gives you the power to stand on the edge of the coin and see both sides. The need to be "right" or make someone else "wrong" is wasted energy. I try to ask myself: why do they think the way they do… and what can I learn from that?

Today, in the tinderbox of emotion and outrage that is our world, I've found it's best to rise above who is right and who is wrong, rise above politics, rise above racism, rise above gender identity, and rise above victim mentality. When you stand on the edge of the coin, you can see both sides. And everyone's opinion and point of view deserves respect, whether we agree with it or now.

Standing on the edge of the coin and rising above the fray and the emotional rhetoric is where freedom is found. The freedom that gives you the power to choose which side is best for you.

Remember: post-modernism education is based on opinions and emotions. The financial statement is based on facts.

I choose to be a capitalist. If you want to choose to be a communist, that is your choice. That is freedom. And being able to see both sides — and understand both sides — gives you power. That is intelligence, versus ignorance.

When you stand on the edge of the coin you can decide if you want to be a capitalist or a communist. You will see and weight the pros and cons of both sides. That is freedom. Standing on the edge, understanding both sides, you find more personal freedom. You do not have to play the game of *"'I'm right' and 'You're wrong.'"*

And that is why rich dad often advised his son and me: "Choose your teachers and education wisely."

And you don't need to argue or debate… and you don't have to play the game of "I'm right and you're wrong." Because the power lies in having an open mind. As rich dad often said: *"If you argue with an idiot, there are two idiots."*

Why Poor Dad Was Poor

My poor dad never saw the other side of the 3-sided coin. Without a financial statement, most people just don't understand why there is a growing gap between rich and poor. Most socialists and communists blame capitalists for the gap between rich and poor. Most socialists blame capitalists for the problems that the liberal-left, academic elite socialists have caused.

Without real financial education, without a financial statement, people play Karl Marx's "oppressor and victim" game. Rather than educate, Marxists sought a utopian society where everyone is equal.

For Kim and me, our financial statement was like our "secret door" to the B and I side of the Cashflow Quadrant. Once we escaped from the Rat Race we knew we needed to up our game for the Fast Track.

When you look at a financial statement, you can see the secret doors.

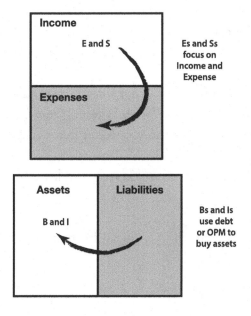

Q: The *CASHFLOW* game changes the players focus from Income and Expense to Assets and Liabilities?

A: I've always found it interesting that Marx makes this distinction: *"The way people get their living determines their social outlook."*

The reason is that the Cashflow Quadrant illustrates the options on where people derive their income — "the way people make their living." It's important to point our that anyone can have income coming in from any, or even all, of the quadrants. Earning paycheck income as an E does not prevent you from also owning a small business in the S quadrant... and owning stocks, in the I quadrant, that pay quarterly dividends.

And if a person changes their income from working for money as an E and an S to income from assets on B and I side, it's likely that their social outlook will change.

Personally, I never wanted my poor dad's job security in the E and S quadrants. I wanted my rich dad's financial freedom that's found in the B and I quadrants. Financial freedom requires personal control and taking personal responsibility over your personal financial statement.

As you change quadrants, you're likely to give some thought to specialization,,, and the need to be more generalized in your thinking in some areas. As Einstein warned:

"Specialization is in fact only a fancy dorm of slavery wherein the 'expert' is fooled into accepting a slavery by making him feel that he in turn is socially and culturally preferred-ergo, highly secure-lifelong position"

Es and Ss are specialists. Bs and Is are generalists. Opposite sides of the same coin.

Everything on your path to financial freedom starts with education. So I'll recap a few points here:

1 — the lack of financial education in our schools creates generations of Es, people who see only one side of the coin of life and will need to take the initiative to seek out the education they'll need if they choose to pursue the path of financial freedom.

2 — education's biggest mistake is teachers punishing students for making mistakes and humans have been deceived into thinking that mistakes make you stupid. They are opportunities to learn and are not something to hide or be embarrassed about. It's how we learn. And that's the key: finding the lesson in the failure or the mistake ... and learning from it.

The Capitalist Manifesto teaches students how to make mistakes and learn from their mistakes. And the purpose of the CASHFLOW board game is for you to learn by making mistakes with play money. I'll even take this a step farther: People who make mistakes and learn from their mistakes get smarter.

How would a baby learn to walk if they didn't try to walk, fall down, pick themselves up and keep at it until they're running around. They'll follow the same process when they learn to ride a bicycle, drive a car, fly a plane — and get rich — if they aren't afraid of making mistakes.

As Maria Montessori teaches:
"Growth comes from activity, not from intellectual understanding."

Your Four Intelligences

Education's biggest mistake is in the realm of emotional intelligence. Most teachers have a high IQ, but leave school with a low EQ. Most teachers are terrified of making mistakes.

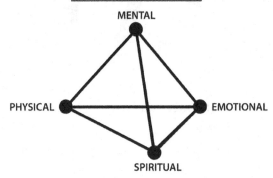

If we live fear of making mistakes, it doesn't matter if we're mental geniuses. If we are underdeveloped emotionally and or physically, we don't take risks. The results of that is that we fail to develop our genius using all four intelligences. As Nelson Mandela taught:

> *"Do not judge me by my success, judge me by how many times I fell down and got back up again."*

The *CASHFLOW* game allows you to make mistakes — and learn — using play money. It takes the risk out of play — but keeps the lessons intact. That's why rich dad used the game of *Monopoly* to teach his son and me to be entrepreneurs and investors on the B and I side of the CASHFLOW Quadrant. The primary reason I make more money and pay less in taxes than most professors is that I have made more mistakes, with play money, than they have. Most people are poor because they are afraid of making mistakes with real money.

3 — life and business are team sports but teachers punish students for cooperating. In school, cooperating is considered cheating.

Our Capitalist Manifesto teaches cooperative learning and taking on business and investing with a team of like-minded people. Rich Dad makes our Advisors available via YouTube for free.

The Calm Before Storms...

The most peaceful time on the aircraft carrier was just before flying into battle. Every night, before a battle, I would sit at the bow of the carrier and meditate. I wanted to make peace with myself before the morning.

After a 5 am breakfast, in silence, aircrews would go for a briefing. We would sit in the ready room until the ship's captain said:

"Pilots, man your planes."

I still vividly recall how I felt walking out on the flight deck with my crew — a co-pilot, a crew chief, and two young gunners. We were beyond fear. We were at peace. We were a band of brothers flying into battle.

A core lesson of this book is the difference between military academy education and snowflake university education. From day one, at Kings Point, we were taught to operate as teams united by a mission — to lead, follow, and operate as a unified band of brothers. Being a hero was frowned upon. Being a leader was everything.

At Snowflake University, the opposite is true. At Snowflake University, dog-eat-dog competition is everything. Cooperation is cheating. Helping a classmate in need ruins your chances of academic success, and the ultimate high-paying job.

Once the pre-flight of our gunship was compete, the crew of five strapped in. Pilots brought the engines up to speed, gunners checked and recheck our guns and rockets, the crew chief gave the two pilots a thumbs up. Pilots then gave the launch officer a thumbs up. The launch officer waved us down the flight deck following the aircraft ahead of us. As our aircraft lifted, the launch officer saluted us as we flew into the battle ahead.

Once in the air, there was silence. There was no cheering. There was no more rank, no more college degrees, no grade point averages, or racism. We were a band of brothers. Although many brothers did not return, never did a flight crew turn back. Once in the air, God was our co-pilot as we flew into battle.

The Most Important Part of the B-I Triangle

From the age of 10, Rich dad was preparing his son and me to be entrepreneurs and investors on the B and I side of the Cashflow Quadrant.

A Team Under Pressure

After arriving at the academy in 1965, I began to realize that rich dad's education on the B-I Triangle was military education.

One reason why so many people leaving the military and first responders such as police, firemen, and Emergency Medical Technicians (EMTs) like nurses and corpsmen become successful entrepreneurs is because military and first responder education is four-intelligences education, the elements of the outer triangle of the B-I Triangle.

In battle, I was most inspired by Navy Corpsmen who would jump out of the aircraft unarmed to bring a wounded Marine back to the aircraft, then keep the wounded Marine alive as we flew back to the hospital on the carrier. We were a band of brothers, guided by angels.

Military personnel, police, fire fighters, and medical first responders must have very high Mental IQs, Emotional IQs, Physical IQs, and Spiritual IQs. How else does a police officer stop domestic violence, in a neighborhood where police are hated, or a nurse stop the hemorrhaging from a knife wound, or a fireman walk into a burning building? In the real world of entrepreneurial capitalism, emotional, physical, and spiritual IQs are more important than mental IQ, a person's GPA, their Grade Point Average, or what Ivy League school they graduated from.

The Biggest Problem
It's Democracy turning into fascism.

Hitler warned:
> *"How fortunate for governments that the people they administer... don't think."*

The biggest problem is most of our teachers, corporate and political bureaucrats, our so-called "public servants," may have high mental IQs, but lack emotional, physical, and especially spiritual IQs.

Hitler also warned:
> *"Pacifism is simply undisguised cowardice."*

Most teachers and corporate and political leaders today lack courage. Courage is spiritual and emotional; it comes from our heart and our convictions.

In 2021, we have seen many corporate leaders bowed to supporting Black Lives Matter, out of fear. Many corporate leaders fired employees for refusing to be vaccinated. This is not freedom. This is fascism.

I believe that we fight for freedom with facts. We fight fake news with facts. And we fight fascism with facts. Here are a few related to Black Lives Matter and parts of the false narrative that has driven the $10 billion (with a 'b') BLM has raised for its causes in the past seven years. One: The accurate number of unarmed black people who have been killed by police officers is 14.

Fourteen too many, certainly, but a small number when put into a factual context. Two: For every one of those shootings there are 270 blacks killed by other blacks. That's 3,780 deaths... with only 14 at the hands of police. "That is the reality," said Robert Woodson at a forum on the Black Lives Matter Movement and Civil Rights hosted by Hillsdale College. He added: "Perceptions have more of an impact than facts."

All of this begs yet another question: Why is this "fantasy narrative" being perpetuated and why are the other 3,766 other deaths — and the fact that these are black people killing other black people — not receiving news coverage? Media bias... at its best. And a horrific statement on how division and hate are being fueled by selective reporting, emotion, bias, and fiction-based narratives. Why this "fantasy narrative" at all? Many would say, as Jack Nicholson's character Col. Jessup said in *A Few Good Men*, we "can't handle the truth."

Education... for Free
I encourage you to watch this YouTube video, presented by Hillsdale College, in which the speakers set the record straight — in terms of facts — about the BLM movement, civil rights, and false narratives.
You can access it at RichDad.com/capitalist-manifesto

I was in Honolulu in August 2021. I had already had COVID and I probably have antibodies. Because I refused to be vaccinated. I was told:
"People who refuse to be vaccinated are killing other people."

As Hitler warned:
"The greater the lie, the greater the chance that it will be believed."

Respect and Courage
I did not always agree with my poor dad, but I gained a lot of respect for him when he gave up his high-paying job, his steady paycheck and his retirement, to run against his boss, a very corrupt Governor of the State of Hawaii, obviously a Democrat. He had the courage to stand up to corruption and take action at great personal risk. When he lost that election, a Republican running against an incumbent Democrat *in Hawaii,* he was so ostracized and

blackballed that he and my mom where planning to leave Hawaii. Then my mother died, and he was crushed.

In a 2021 Rich Dad Radio interview with Congressman and Presidential Candidate Ron Paul, a Constitutionalist, he reminded our listeners that the U.S. Constitution has no power without the power of the Ten Commandments, ancient words of wisdom from the Old Testament.

After that interview with Ron, I took another look at the Ten Commandments. The following are the essence of those Commandments.

1. *You shall have no other gods.*
2. *You shall not make idols.*
3. *You shall not misuse the name of the Lord.*
4. *Keep the Sabbath day holy.*
5. *Honor your father and your mother.*
6. *You shall not murder.*
7. *You shall not commit adultery.*
8. *You shall not steal.*
9. *You shall not lie.*
10. *You shall not covet.*

Our political leaders should repeat those Ten Commandments when they put their hand on the Bible and promise to God that they will be legal, ethical, and morally strong people... before promising to defend the Constitution of the United States.

Fake Fauci

The point Ron Paul makes is that the U.S. Constitution is powerless with leaders lacking a moral and spiritual backbone. Representative Ron Paul, a medical doctor himself, has been critical of Dr. Anthony Fauci's legal, moral, and ethical codes. Simply put, Fauci may be a doctor, but he lacks backbone and moral strength.

I write about ancient religious wisdom because modern education, aka post-modernist education, is based on the teachings of Marx, who was racist and anti-religious. Post-modernist education is tearing apart the heart and soul of the world.

Post-modernist education is based upon opinions and emotions. Not facts.

That's why the financial statement that I've written about just a few pages back is so important. A financial statement is based on facts.

The Divided States of America

Post-modernist education is the perfect breeding ground for Critical Race Theory, Cancel Culture, and the Woke movement as well as the divisiveness that can build around issues of diversity, inclusion, social justice, and gender pronouns.

Post-modernist education is not about diversity or inclusion. It's about dividing and conquering. It's not about the United States of America, it's about the Divided States of America.

Professor Gad Saad, author of *The Parasitic Mind,* warns:

"...These politically correct language initiatives are misguided and harmful. They create highly entitled professional "victims" who expect to be free from any offense, and they engender a stifling atmosphere where all individuals walk on eggshells lest they might commit a linguistic capital crime."

Reviewing this tetrahedron diagram of the Four Intelligences, it's easy to see how "strength" — in this case the structural integrity of the tetrahedron itself — is based on the connections between the Four Intelligences.

AWAKEN YOUR FINANCIAL GENIUS
YOUR 4 INTELLIGENCES

MENTAL

PHYSICAL

EMOTIONAL

SPIRITUAL

Q: Are you saying post-modernist education focuses only on keeping people stirred up emotionally?

A: I am.

Q: And when that happens, they have lower EQ, lower emotional intelligence?

A: Exactly. EQ is often thought to be the most powerful of our intelligences. When people are riled up emotionally, their Mental IQ drops and the person cannot process data, facts, logically. When a person's EQ goes down, their Physical IQ is also lower and they often do or say things they later regret.

In my experience, when emotion goes up... intelligence goes down.

Q: So... Critical Race Theory, Cancel Culture, the Woke movement... all the things you're writing about... They thrive in low-EQ post-modernist education?

A: Yes. And the NEA, the National Education Association, the national teachers union, is the pillar of post-modernist education.

Quoting this from an Opinion piece in the July 5, 2021 edition of the *New York Post*:

> *"The political left wants critical race theory in every school district in the nation.*

> *"The nation's largest teachers union has approved a plan to promote critical race theory in all 50 states and 14,000 local school districts.*

> *"Over the weekend, the National Education Association (NEA) held its annual Representative Assembly, with delegates from across the United States voting on priorities and allocating funding for the upcoming school year, with the ideology of critical race theory — a form of race-based Marxism — taking center stage.*

> *"The union, which represents 3 million public school employees, approved funding for three separate items related to this issue: "increasing the implementation" of "critical race theory" in K-12 curricula, promoting*

critical race theory in local school districts, and attacking opponents of critical race theory, including parent organizations and conservative research centers.

"This is a significant reversal. For the past month, liberal pundits and activists have insisted that critical race theory is not taught in K-12 schools. This was always a bad-faith claim — critical race theory has made inroads in public schools for more than a decade — but the NEA's official endorsement is the final nail in the coffin."

And according to Fox News, on July 4, 2021:

"The National Education Association, which boasts 2.3 million members, recently passed a resolution claiming it is "reasonable and appropriate" to include CRT in curriculum — and pledged to create "a team of staffers" to help teachers "fight back against anti-CRT rhetoric."

And this from the NEA website: *"To boost the effort, the NEA will work to publicize 'an already-created, in-depth study that critiques white supremacy, anti-Blackness, anti-Indigeneity, racism, patriarchy ... capitalism ... and other forms of power and oppression.'"*

"We oppose attempts to ban critical race theory and/or The1619 Project," the NEA said.

Here are how these terms are defined: **CRT** asserts that racism is not just about individual bias but systemic in society and government policies and institutions, including the legal system. **The 1619 Project** refers to efforts to focus on when the first African slaves arrived in America and their contributions to the country.

In a tweet by Senator Ted Cruz, he cut to the chase: "Critical Race Theory is a Marxist ideology that sees the world as a battle, not between the classes – as classical Marxism does – but between the races. It's bigoted and should not be supported by the federal government."

Q: Aren't parents fighting back against CRT, gender pronouns, and vaccine mandates?

A: They are. I've seen signs held by protestors, playing off the CRT acronym, that read:
   Creating Racial Tension.

Q: How do *we* fight back?

A: We fight back by rising above. By standing on the edge of that 3-sided coin, and doing our best to see both sides, before taking a side. I think the following diagram helps illustrate that.

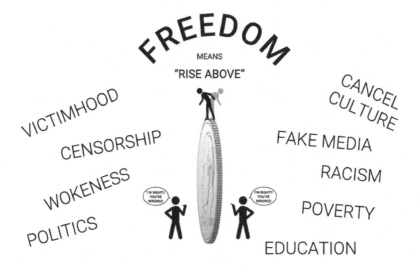

I know I'm repeating myself here, but... Post-modernist education is not about facts. Post-modernist education is about opinions and emotions. Post-modernist education is tearing America apart. We are no longer the *United* States of America. To repeat another related thought: When emotion goes up, intelligence goes down.

And, again... Professor Gad Saad's words of warning:
   "Similarly, social justice warriors and their ilk are intellectual terrorists, and they can wreak havoc on reason and our public life, limiting people's willingness to speak and think freely, without ever constituting a majority."

Lenin, too, promoted this division:

> *"We can and must write in a language which sows among the masses hate, revulsion, and scorn towards those who disagree with us."*

Q: How do we protect ourselves from post-modernist education?
A: I will repeat what I wrote earlier.

> *"Every night, before a battle, I would sit at the bow of the carrier and meditate. I wanted to make peace with myself before the morning.*
>
> *"After a 5 am breakfast, in silence, aircrews would go for a briefing. We would sit in the ready room until the ship's captain said: 'Pilots man your planes.'*
>
> *"I still vividly recall how I felt walking out on the flight deck with my crew, a co-pilot, a crew chief, and two young gunners. We were beyond fear. We were at peace. We were a band of brothers flying into battle."*

Fighting for Freedom

We — Kim and I and The Rich Dad Company, along with our trusted Advisors — continue to fight what we believe is the good fight... with advocacy for education, especially financial education. Our mantra is Parabellum — If you want peace, prepare for war.

We will stand up for freedom... and for all those who fight for our freedoms. There are many types of freedom... and they are all under attack today.

In the following chapter, I will introduce you to the Rich Dad team of advisors... brothers, sisters, and angels. You will find out who they are, and why they are so important to our future and yours.

We call ourselves the Infinite Team, because with a strong and tight team anything is possible.

Finding our team was not easy. Kim and I found that we had lessons to learn about people, and about teammates. We learned that all "good people" have a good side and a dark side. We've dealt with deceit and greed as well as lawsuits and lies. We learned quickly that more people were drawn to the money they could make by working for or with Rich Dad... than the mission. For us, from day one, it's been mission over money. And that priority has served us well.

Along the way we've used lessons from both Bucky Fuller and rich dad...
Partnership Lesson #1: "You can't do a good deal with bad partners."
Partnership Lesson #2: "From every bad partnership comes good partners."

Everyone on The Rich Dad Company team and our Infinite Team of advisors you are about to meet, came from bad partners and horrible business dealings. The good news is that out of the bad deals and the bad partners came great partners, coaches, and professional advisors. Today, Rich Dad is a tight band of brothers, sisters, and angels who all embrace our mission:
"To elevate the financial well-being of humanity."

As I've said, we are a band of brothers, sisters, and angels. If you support our mission, you are invited to join us via a Cashflow Club near you. All we ask is you co-operate by respecting our published Code of Honor, our rules, club leaders, and our teachers. Mission is more important than money. Just like good partners, money is a derivative from following a spiritual mission.

It's time for you to meet *our* co-pilots, our Advisors.

CHAPTER FOURTEEN

AN ENTREPRENEUR'S MOST IMPORTANT ASSET
MEET ROBERT AND KIM'S TEAM

The difference between my rich dad and my poor dad was the word *team*.

The difference between rich dad's wealth and poor dad's wealth was *team*.

The difference between military school and snowflake education is *team*.

Mayday, Mayday, Mayday
One early morning, off the coast of Vietnam, my crew and I were flying what is known as a "racetrack pattern" at a 1500-feet altitude, about a mile from the carrier group of seven ships. The racetrack pattern is a holding pattern. We were waiting for the other aircraft in the group to launch, before we flew a strike into Vietnam.

Out of the corner of my eye, I saw the N-G gauge flicker. The N-G gauge measures the speed of air flowing through the aircraft's jet engine turbines. As student pilots, we are taught that "when the N-G gauge flickers, to stand-by, prepare to kiss your ass good-bye."

Immediately the engine quit, alarms went off, the lights on the control panel lit up like Times Square on New Year's Eve. The aircraft began to fall from the sky.

Emotion Overload

The most important first step in a crisis situation is to override your emotions. Immediately, when the aircraft stops flying and falls, the overriding mental, emotional, and physical desire is "pull up," and climb for altitude. Pulling back on the "stick," to pull the aircraft up, would kill us faster.

Q: Is that why so many pilots crash when the engine stops?
A: Yes. They "pull back" rather than "push forward."

Q: Is it frightening to push forward?
A: It's terrifying. One of the most important lessons in flight school is to "push forward" when everything in the pilot wants to "pull up." It takes discipline to do what you know you need to do. And lives hang in the balance.

This is known as EQ, emotional intelligence. EQ also runs financial intelligence.

The Eyes of Death

Immediately I pushed the nose of the Huey forward and put the aircraft into a dive. Pilots call this "staring into the eyes of death." Pilots who panic and "pull up" — flying in response to their emotions — die.

Simultaneously, I begin broadcasting "Mayday, Mayday, Mayday! Marine Echo Whiskey 96. Engine failure. Going down two miles from carrier."

Without being told what to do, the two gunners and crew chief began jettisoning the rockets, machine guns, and ammunition. There was no talking. No panic. No blame. No yelling and screaming. Everyone knew what to do.

We had done this at least a thousand times before. On every training flight, pilots practice crashing over and over, again and again, starting at flight school in Pensacola, Florida.

In snowflake school, IQ is most important. In military school, EQ is more important than IQ. Those brave men and women in our military, first responders, and police must manage all of their intelligences. They, like Marines, train for this. Most academics cannot manage fear because their focus is on intelligence or IQ.

The Beginning of the End

The final 30 seconds was flown in deathly silence as we watched the ocean rising to meet us. Just before hitting the water, all there was was SQ... Spiritual Intelligence. Everything else was silent.

As we had practiced time and time again, just before impacting the water I slowly raised the nose of the aircraft, bleeding off airspeed, gliding, then stopping about 100 feet above the waves.

Just as the aircraft ran out of air speed, I pulled the nose up, stalling the aircraft to zero, rotated the nose forward and, when the aircraft was level, I pulled up on the 'collective' which controls the blades. The aircraft settled gently on the waves. I was not thinking. There was no IQ. It was 100% PQ, muscle memory, Physical IQ, developed after years of practicing a crash scenario over and over again. A perfect 'autorotation' practiced repeatedly, faithfully, religiously... again and again.

On the day my engine quit, I was ready to do the real thing. Doing the real thing, was all EQ, Emotional Intelligence, PQ, Physical intelligence, SQ Spiritual Intelligence, and only a tiny bit of IQ, Mental Intelligence, the intelligence that academics run on.

Immediately, the helicopter lurched violently to the right, the blade cut through the cockpit, and the jet engine exploded when sea water hit the white-hot turbine blades. The Huey rolled to the right, sea water flooded the cabin, the aircraft began sinking faster than a lead balloon. School days were over. Real life survival began.

As we escaped from the sinking aircraft, panic increased with the memory of another aircrew that had gone down a few months earlier. Sharks got to them... before they could be rescued.

The combat mission continued. The mission had priority over our rescue and it went on without us. About four hours later, a Navy rescue boat picked up our crew of five. Five Marines happy to be alive. We had all done our specific jobs as a team. We had trained to work as a team and it had saved our lives.

I have carried the lessons learned at the Academy and in the Marine Corps into my businesses.

You can see those elements, the 8 Integrities of a Business, in my rich dad's B-I Triangle:

The outer triangle represents what military school and rich dad taught me about mission, team, and leadership. Those inside the triangle are specialists. Military schools teach leadership, how to be generalists... how to work as a team. Kings Point was once honored as one of the top schools for teaching leadership. The Marine Corps is infamous for teaching young men and women to be leaders, regardless of rank. If a leader goes down, another Marine steps up as leader. We are trained to think and operate that way. That is why one of the sayings among Marines is "all Marines carry a gun." Although a Marine may be a specialist, such as a lawyer or a cook, they are all trained to lead, and to shoot.

Mission vs. Money

The first word I learned in the Marines, and the most important word at the Academy, was *mission*. When I went to business school, the most important word was *money*. Most of the students had the same question: "How much money can I make?" I soon dropped out of my MBA program. Something was missing... SQ, Spiritual Intelligence.

One of the reasons an entrepreneur in the S quadrant stays small, is because the S quadrant businessperson performs all 8 functions of the B-I Triangle. Most S-quadrant entrepreneurs may be very smart, and highly educated "specialists" such as a medical doctor or a dentist, but they lack leadership skills. They do not know how to lead other specialists.

Busy-ness Is Not a Business

Another reason 95% of all business startups fail or fail to grow is because the entrepreneur is responsible for all the components that make up the B-I triangle. Most S-quadrant entrepreneurs own a "busy-ness" not a B-quadrant business."

The mantra of an S-quadrant entrepreneur is:
"If you want it done right... do it by yourself."

The thinking of a B- and I-quadrant entrepreneur is:
"I only work with people better and smarter than me."

And:
"I work as a team."

Q: Is everyone in the Rich Dad B-I triangle better and smarter than you?
A: They are. If they weren't smarter than me, or could not do something much better than I can... why would I hire them?

Q: Was your crew on your gunship all better and smarter than you?
A: Absolutely. We all had different jobs, but in the Marine Corps, respect is far more important than rank or college degrees. I was a pilot for two Marine Generals in Vietnam. They treated everyone — regardless of rank, from privates to generals — with tremendous respect.

The Power of the Rich Dad Team

KIM KIYOSAKI

Kim is the leader, the CEO of the Rich Dad Company. Kim greets everyone with a smile and treats everyone with respect. If you did not know who she was, you would never guess she was "the boss," the owner of a multi-million-dollar, global business.

Kim keeps the inside triangle humming and coordinates the outside triangle, the team of advisors who support the Rich Dad Company.

Kim and I met in 1984. Over the years I have watched her grow into a powerful, accomplished, and respected woman, a global entrepreneur and investor. Hence her books, *Rich Woman* and *It's Rising Time!*

I can assure you she did not marry me for my money, because when we met I had no money. Although I had nothing, she still held my hand and took a leap of faith with me into the unknown in 1985. We were homeless for a while, living in a brown Toyota, parked at a public beach in San Diego, California.

If not for Kim, I would not be who I am... or where I am... today.

MONA GAMBETTA

My favorite sport is rugby union. I love rugby because it is not a game of physical size. For example, in basketball it's best you're tall. If you are a jockey, it is best you are small and light. If you play soccer, it is best you be thin, fast, agile, and physically coordinated.

In rugby, no matter your size, height, or weight there is a position for you. All that is required is the love of the game. In rugby, the most important player is the 'scrum half.' The scrum half on a rugby team is like the quarterback on an American football team.

I call Mona my scrum half. Mona coordinates the "inside" of The Rich Dad Company with the outside world. For example, when I write a book, Mona takes a pile of scribbles, misspelled words, a jumble (most times) of ideas and messages and chapters and turns it into a finished book.

True to her title of scrum half, Mona then spins a finished book out to publishers all over the world, who license and translate the book into more than 58 different languages. Mona is responsible for all publishing, distribution, contracts, and publicity for our books and our games. She is priceless. If not for Mona, all the Rich Dad books and the Rich Dad Advisor books — and especially this book, *Capitalist Manifesto* — would never have been published. She tells me that I'm exaggerating when I say that, but the longer I work with her the more certain I am that it's true.

Within the B-I Triangle, her work integrates into every area: Product, certainly, but also Communications and Systems, Legal, and Cash Flow. She works with dozens of partners around the world to spread the Rich Dad messages and support our global network. Today — just shy of 25 years since *Rich Dad Poor Dad* was first published — the book still consistently holds the top spot as #1 in Personal Finance on Amazon and

ranks among Amazon's all-time Top 20 Books. Our books are also sold in tens of thousands of stores around the world, from the major booksellers and the big-box stores to the beloved Indies, the independent bookstores around the world.

Mona has been with the Rich Dad Company since 2000.

GARRETT SUTTON, ESQ.

Garrett will tell you: "The poor and middle class want to own everything in their name. The rich want nothing in their name. The rich want everything in the name of a corporation... that they control."

Garrett Sutton is Rich Dad's corporate attorney, specializing in asset protection. He says, "The 'S' in S-quadrant stands 'Sole Proprietor.'" Garrett also says, 'SOLE' stands for: *Someday You'll Lose Everything*. He would support the legal and asset-protection strategy that B-quadrant entrepreneurs want nothing in their name.

Garrett warns:

"As the gap between rich, middle class and poor widens, lawsuits will increase. As the economy worsens, for more and more people will decide that the best way to get rich, is to 'sue the rich.'"

The good news is that when Garrett puts a business into a corporate entity, the corporate entity also protects the entrepreneur from government taxes. When a private citizen loses money, the losses are personal. When a corporation loses money, the losses are tax losses.

Garrett serves as our corporate counsel." If we need a more specialized attorney, an IP or trademark attorney, for example, we call Garrett and he makes recommendations or assists with vetting.

Rich dad warned:

"What would happen if some drivers drove on the right side of the road and others drove on the left? If drivers did not obey the laws, traffic would stop, and a demolition derby would begin."

The Constitution and the laws are the backbone of the United States of America. If the Constitution and our laws are broken, the nation is paralyzed.

That's why The Rich Dad Company, our advisors, and the businesses we associate with do our best to obey the laws. "When in doubt we check it out."

If anyone or company or CASHFLOW Club does not obey the laws, the Rich Dad company ceases doing business. It is easier to make money, with legal, honest, and moral people.

I call Garrett our "guard dog." That is why he is an essential member of the Rich Dad team.

One of Garrett's books is *Start Your Own Corporation.*
Why work for someone else's business when you could own and run your own corporation?
Oher Rich Dad Advisor Series books by Garrett include:

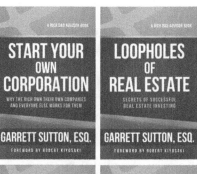
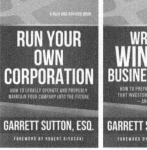

> *Run Your Own Corporation*
>
> *Loopholes of Real Estate*
>
> *Writing Winning Business Plans*
>
> *How to Buy and Sell a Business*
>
> *ABCs of Getting Out of Debt*
>
> *Veil Not Fail*

Garrett is a Rich Dad Advisor who has worked with us since 2000.

TOM WHEELWRIGHT, CPA

Rich dad often reminded his son and me that America was born as a "tax-free nation" Ever since then, people have been taking away our freedom via taxes. Rich dad reminded us that America was born as a tax revolt, the Boston Tea Party, in 1773. Tom's Rich Dad Advisor Series book is titled *Tax-Free-Wealth* and he is our advisor on taxes.

One reason rich dad encouraged his son and me to become capitalists is to be patriots, capitalists and minimize the taxes we pay, legally

Tom warns:
> *"There are two ways to pay less in taxes: legally and illegally."*

If you want to pay less in taxes legally, I suggest you read Tom's book *Tax-Free-Wealth*.

Reading and studying Tom's book is a lot less expensive than hiring an attorney to defend you in court.

Tom uses the Cashflow Quadrant when he talks about taxes:

TAX PERCENTAGES PAID PER QUADRANT

Tom has said, *"The biggest tax cheats are in the E and S quadrants."*

The tax laws are written against Es and Ss... and in favor of Bs and Is. Bs and Is don't have to cheat. Tax laws allow them to avoid paying taxes legally.

Those in the B and I quadrants have the power to do what governments want done. Tom explains that tax breaks are not "tax loopholes — they are government tax incentives. For example, governments offer B-quadrant entrepreneurs tax breaks because B-quadrant entrepreneurs create thousands and thousands of jobs.

Taxes are your life's greatest expense. Tom's book could save you more money than any other book you read. You may make a lot more money and pay less taxes. Tom's book will beat going to school to get a higher paying job or become a high paid doctor or lawyer, only to leave deeper in student loan debt and pay more in taxes.

Best of all, give Tom's book to your accountant. If they disagree with Tom, find a new accountant.

How does Tom guide you and me? In the real world of entrepreneurship, there are two kinds of numbers.
> Forecasts (projections)
> Actual (facts)

Tom guides Kim and me by educating us how to project future earnings. He guides us to focus on what types of income we want to earn in the future.

There are three types of income: ordinary, portfolio, and passive. Es and Ss work for ordinary income that's taxed at the highest rates. Bs and Is work for portfolio and passive income. Kim and I want I want more "portfolio income" and "passive income" which comes from our investments. Those two incomes are income from people, assets, taxes, and money... all working hard for us.

Capitalists just want to know the facts. That is why your banker asks for your financial statement, not your report card. And that's why accountants look at the numbers.

All B- and I-quadrant capitalists want to know is how to turn their *forecasts* into *facts* and pay less taxes legally. That's why Tom Wheelwright is an essential member of the Rich Dad team.

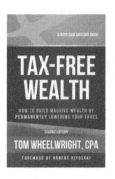

Tom's book in the Rich Dad Advisor Series is:
Tax-Free Wealth

Tom is a Rich Dad Advisor who has worked with us since 2000.

KEN McELROY

Ken is our Advisor on debt and real estate:
> *"Your house is not an asset... but my apartment houses are. On top of that your house does not offer many tax breaks, but my apartment houses offer massive tax breaks."*

The primary reason why tax percentages noted on the Cashflow Quadrant look like this is because of real estate and debt. Es and Ss who invest in the stock market are will always pay the most in taxes.

TAX PERCENTAGES PAID PER QUADRANT

Q: Could people in the E and S quadrants really pay 0% in taxes?

A: Yes. Absolutely. But they would have to start seeing the world from the B and I quadrants.

Q: Is that why your rich dad suggested you take real estate investment courses when you returned from Vietnam?

A: Yes. And if I would have followed my poor dad's advice and worked for the airlines or gotten my Masters, I might have been a slave to taxes, trapped in the E and S quadrant for life.

The first copy oof *Rich Dad Poor Dad* was sold, not in a bookstore, but in a car wash in Austin, Texas. The first book was purchased by Dr. Tom Burns, who was also building an Amway network marketing business at the time. Although the academic elite of the publishing world rejected my books, the public loved them.

In 2020, Dr. Tom Burns, an orthopedic surgeon and physician for the U.S. Olympic Ski Team, an Amway distributor and real estate investor, published his book *Why Doctors Don't Get Rich*.

Dr. Burns became rich following much of the same real estate investment model Ken McElroy teaches.

Q: Can anyone do what Ken McElroy and Dr. Tom Burns do?

A: It's possible, but not likely. Not for everyone. This may sound strange, especially with homelessness increasing and low-interest rate financing so easy. The easy part of real estate investing is buying and financing the property. The hard part is doing what Ken and Tom do *after* they secure an investment property.

If you are serious about becoming a professional real estate investor and taking advantage of the tax incentives the government offers, I suggest you start with Ken's books. Like Tom Wheelwright's book *Tax-Free Wealth*, Ken's books focus on the B-I side of the Cashflow Quadrant.

Most Es and Ss can buy a home. The problem is a home is a liability. Keep in mind the definitions of liability and asset. Liabilities take money from your pocket; assets put money in your pocket. Understanding that difference and the language of money is financial literacy.

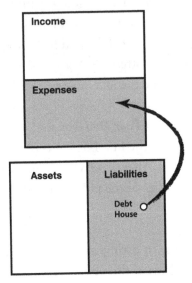

Very few Es and Ss can buy, secure financing, and manage apartment complexes and commercial buildings. Remember the strategy in the game of *Monopoly*. Players start with green houses before investing in red hotels.

Ken is in the red hotel game.

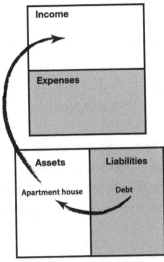

For more than 20 years, Ken, Tom, Garrett, and I have traveled the world, explaining real estate investing from the B- and I-side of the quadrant. We teach investing in red hotels rather than investing in the four green houses, which is where most investors get stuck in.

At most seminars, I start by asking Ken how much debt he took on in the last few months. He often says something like, "Last month, I borrowed $300 million in debt financing."

There is often a gasp from the audience. A number like $300 million is outside the reality and mindset of most Es and Ss. That is why they are stuck investing in four green houses.

In our live seminars, Tom Wheelwright then explains why such large amounts of debt are essential for capitalists, Bs and Is, to make millions and pay little to nothing in taxes, legally. The tax laws are written for the Bs and Is, investors and capitalists who get tax incentives for doing what the government needs done.

Ken got into real estate investing as a property manager. He put himself through college managing large apartment complexes — 'red hotels' in the game of *Monopoly*. Ken quickly realized he was managing properties for the rich.

Small real estate investors lack the property management experience, skills, and business teams to manage red hotels. Ken has over 400 employees in his business. He could not do what he does on his own.

I suggest you read Ken McElroy's, Tom Wheelwright's, Garrett Sutton's, and Dr. Tom Burns' books, before investing in red hotels and especially before you avoid paying taxes. The government does not like tax cheats. Keep in mind: Es and Ss are must prone to cheating on their taxes. Bs and Is do not have to cheat because the tax laws are written for Bs and Is.

Ken's books in the Rich Dad Advisor Series are:
  ABCs of Real Estate Investing
  ABCs of Property Management
  ABCs of Advanced Real Estate Investing
  ABCs of Buying Rental Property
  ABCs of Raising Capital

Ken is a Rich Dad Advisor who has worked with us since 2000.

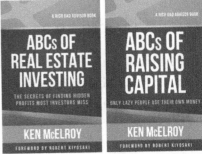
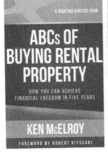

ANDY TANNER

Andy is our Rich Dad Advisor on paper assets and a kindred spirit in his love for teaching.

Andy often says:
  "I make money when the stock market goes up. I make more money when the stock market crashes."

There are two basic types of investors:
  1. Fundamental investors
  2. Technical investors

Fundamental investors invest off financial statements. They invest based on facts. Technical investors invest using trends, the ups and downs of a stock or business. They look at lines not numbers.

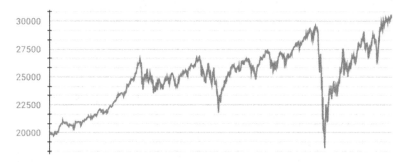

I am concerned that a major stock market crash is imminent. The crash will be caused by CEOs using their company's corporate debt to inflate their company's stock prices. If and when the house of cards comes down, millions of baby boomers will be in dire straits, in old age.

I recommend reading both of Andy's books. Understand why 401(k)s or any retirement plan dependent upon a rising stock market are in trouble. Once you understand why retirement plans based on paper assets are at risk, then study Andy's second book, *Stock Market Cash Flow*. If you study Andy's second book, you will not care if the stock market goes up or down. If you practice, make mistakes, and learn, you could become just like Andy Tanner, a person who can make money regardless of whether the markets are going up or crashing. In fact, you could make the most money in a market crash.

If baby boomers will study Andy's books, it might give them strategies they can use instead of moving in with the kids.

Andy's book in the Rich Dad Advisor Series is:
   Stock Market Cash Flow

He is also the author of
   401(k)aos

This book is especially important for anyone who is counting on their 401(k) for long-term financial security.

Andy is a Rich Dad Advisor who has worked with us since 2008.

JOHN MacGREGOR

Although John is a lot younger than I am, he has been a neighbor a friend and neighbor in Hawaii for years. We both played for the same rugby team, the Hawaii Harlequins, at different times.

John and I share the same financial concerns. Millions of baby-boomers who were rich during their working years, will suffer during retirement. That is why I asked John to join our team of Rich Dad Advisors, write a book sharing his concerns, personal experiences of once rich clients who went broke, and solutions.

John has shared his wisdom with our teams countless times:

> *"The baby-boomers have had it easy. It was easy getting rich from the 1960s to 1990s. Housing prices went up and the stock market went up. Times have changed. In 2000 If a major stock market crash comes, many baby-boomers will be poor, after their working days are over."*

Everyone, rich or poor, needs a financial planner. John has trained financial planners. John is one of the best at what he does — one of the most knowledgeable and most experienced.

Financial education from Rich dad is generally for people who want to be entrepreneurs on the B and I side of the Cashflow Quadrant. John is best for people who are in the E and S quadrants. That is why I asked him to write his book and join our team of advisors.

John and I know many of the same people from Hawaii. In fact, John went to the same school Barack Obama attended, Punahou, in Honolulu. We all know what happened with Obamacare. It got more expensive for the people who could least afford it.

Again, Ken McElroy, Tom Wheelwright, Garrett Sutton are guides for entrepreneurs, on the B- and I-side, Es and Ss need a financial planner like John MacGregor on their team.

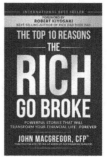

John's book is:
> *The Top Ten Reasons the Rich Go Broke*

John has worked with us since 2012.

JOSH AND LISA LANNON

Josh and Lisa are social entrepreneurs and Rich Dad Advisors on social capitalism. They have built their business on this principle: *Social capitalists can do a lot of good for humanity — and do very well financially.*

Josh and Lisa often recount Josh's story — years of feeding his addiction, alcoholism, during the years he ran night clubs in Las Vegas to acknowledging and defeating his addiction — that led them to become social capitalists. Today, Josh and Lisa operate an addiction counseling and rehabilitation business, a 501(c)3 that they founded in 2015 called Warriors Heart. It serves military veterans and first responders, such as police officers, fire fighters and EMTs. These warriors understand the word mission. It is in their warrior's heart, their sense of mission and high Spiritual Intelligence, that gives them the power that fight and defeat their addictions.

An important lesson I've gained from Josh and Lisa is:
> *"Everyone has addictions. Addictions rob us of life. The bigger problem is most people deny that they have a personal addiction. Denial empowers the addiction to rob them of life... for life."*

Politicians, veteran service organizations, and the more truthful media outlets report that 22 veterans commit suicide each day. The liberal *Washington Post* claims that number is less than 1 veteran suicide a day. What is the truth? The truth is that many veterans returning from war may not commit suicide but are torn apart by addictions.

Josh and Lisa are authors of the Rich Dad Advisor book, *The Social Capitalist, Passion and Profits – an Entrepreneurial Journey*.

Josh and Lisa built their business on the B- and I-side of the Cashflow Quadrant, utilizing many of the same Rich Dad Advisor's that Kim and I use. Josh and Lisa utilized Tom Wheelwright, Ken McElroy, and Garrett Sutton to guide them building their business and use their business to acquire real estate.

And Josh and Lisa use the McDonald's formula. As I wrote about in *Rich Dad Poor Dad*, when Ray Kroc, founder of McDonald's asked the MBA students at the University of Texas, "What business is McDonald's in?" the students replied, "Everyone knows McDonald's is in the business of hamburgers."

Ray Kroc laughed and replied, "McDonald's is in the real estate business." Today, McDonalds owns more real estate than the Catholic Church. Josh and Lisa's business is real estate.

Their business is both socialist and capitalist. A financially smart combination of opposing economic philosophies.

If you want to learn how to do well financially by doing good for humanity, please read their book, learn from their inspiring story and consider joining their growing family of supporters.

If not for Josh and Lisa, I would not have had the courage and honesty to face my personal addictions and move beyond them.

Josh and Lisa's book in the Rich Dad Advisor Series is:
   The Social Capitalist

They have been students of the Rich Dad philosophies since 2001 and Rich Dad Advisors who have worked with us since 2012.

DR. RADHA GOPALAN and DR. NICOLE SREDNICKI

We were warned... in this case by Vladimir Lenin:
"Medicine is the keystone of the arch of socialism."

The Affordable Care Act (ACA), formally known as the Patient Protection and Affordable Care Act and colloquially known as Obamacare, is a United States federal statute enacted by the 111th United States Congress and signed into law by President Barack Obama on March 23, 2010. Among the goals of that act are to make affordable healthcare available to more people and to expand the Medicaid program.

I met Dr. Radha Gopalan, a cardiologist and heart transplant specialists, in 2007 when I was looking for a doctor. I was desperate. My heart was struggling. I knew something was wrong but could not find a cardiologist who would take the time to explain why my heart was failing.

Two previous cardiologists I consulted with only wanted to operate, no education or explanations. One high-profile cardiologist in Phoenix told me I needed to have open heart surgery that night — or I would die. I smelled a rat and left immediately.

Fortunately, a chiropractor friend called his friend, a cardiologist in London, and asked for his recommendation on the best cardiologist in the world. The chiropractor told his friend, "Robert will travel anywhere."

The cardiologist in London said, "You won't believe this. The best heart transplant surgeon in the world just moved to Phoenix." Since I did not die that night, as the esteemed cardiologist in Phoenix had predicted, I made an appointment and met Dr. Gopalan two weeks later. It was the beginning of a love affair between patient and doctor — because I had found the medical education I was looking for.

I got along with Dr. Gopalan immediately because he is a doctor of both Eastern and Western medicine. He was born in Sri Lanka, trained as a doctor of acupuncture. Then he traveled to the West to become a medical doctor and today is a highly respected cardiologist specializing in heart and organ transplants.

In preparation for my open-heart surgery, Dr. Gopalan had me practice yoga, meditation, and receive regular acupuncture treatments. During his acupuncture treatments, he took the time to explain both the Eastern and Western philosophies concerning my ailing heart.

Since that surgery and his East-West medical guidance, my health has gotten better and better.

And as my health was improving, I encouraged Dr. Gopalan to write his book, *Second Opinion*. For those seeking answers to health issues from both an eastern and a western perspective, Dr. Gopalan's book is that guide.

Dr. Nicole Srednicki has a laser focus on health and her business is Ultra Healthy Human. Her passion is the latest and greatest in medical, health, anti-aging technology.

In 2020, I was infected with COVID-19. It was a blessing in disguise. I had the attention of two doctors. I was treated with hydroxychloroquine, IV-vitamin drips, mega-doses of Vitamin C... and sunshine. I have not taken the vaccine. I pass all swabs and tests. Apparently, I still have antibodies.

The good news is that COVID-19 was my wake-up call. As both doctors have been trying to get into my head for years, the best medicine, the best vaccine, is good health.

In August of 2020 I committed to becoming an Ultra Health Human and put my health in Radha and Nicole's hands for guidance.

The first process I went through was a 21-day organ detox. It was tough for 10 days. I wanted to quit, every day. As Josh and Lisa teach, we all have addictions. Mine is food. I eat when I am bored or stressed.

As Nicole explains, our organs are like filters on a car. Cars have oil, gas, and hydraulic filters. The difference is auto mechanics change a car's filter. Humans allow their organs to become toxic and, over the years, the toxicity builds up in the body. This impacts both healing and health, making people more prone to diseases like cancer and viruses like COVID-19.

When I asked Radha and Nicole "Why 21 days?" their answer was that it takes 21 days to change the neuroplasticity of the human brain. In other words, as Josh and Lisa teach, beat the addiction.

Since I began Radha and Nicole's program, I am in better shape at 74, than I was as a Marine at 24. On top of that I meditate, do yoga and Pilates with an instructor two days a week, work out with a former NFL trainer two days a week, and go to spin classes. I am at the gym, five days a week. And I can attest to this: 21 days of cleansing did transform my neuroplasticity.

I thank COVID-19 for the kick in the butt, and I thank my two doctors for their love, wisdom, and guidance.

Radha is the author of the book *Second Opinion*.

Radha has worked with us since 2008 and Nicole since 2013.

BLAIR SINGER

I saved Blair for last because he was my first friend in this group of friends. I knew Blair before Kim. I met Blair right after spending a week with Bucky Fuller in 1981. We have been friends — studying, learning, and making mistakes together — ever since.

Here's the question that is key to this book... and the freedom found on the right side of the Cashflow Quadrant:

"How does an entrepreneur go from E and S to B and I?"

That is Blair Singer's super special technology. Blair is the expert at guiding entrepreneurs from S to B. (I often tease Blair that S and B are his initials...)

When you look at the B-I Triangle, Blair is a super star on the communication line.

Why is the Communication line so important? That's a great question. The answer is that the Communication line is right above the Cash Flow line. If Communications are strong, Cash Flow is strong. If an entrepreneur's communication skills are weak, it'll be reflected cash flow.

Blair Singer is internationally recognized as one of the best sales and leadership trainers in the world. His book, *Sales Dogs* is a must read for anyone who wants to be an entrepreneur. Sales Dogs is an essential training tool for network marketing and direct sales companies.

Blair's greatest technology is PERT — Project Evaluation Review Technique. PERT was created by the U.S. Navy in the 1950s to develop the first submarine-based Polaris missile system. And it's a tool that can help Es and Ss become Bs and Is.

Blair has been teaching PERT for years. Blair has used PERT to teach me how to grow from an S, a small entrepreneur, into a B, a big-business entrepreneur.

In 2020, The Rich Dad Company brought Blair in to teach the whole company how to go from S to B. Pictured below is the actual PERT chart our company developed under Blair's guidance.

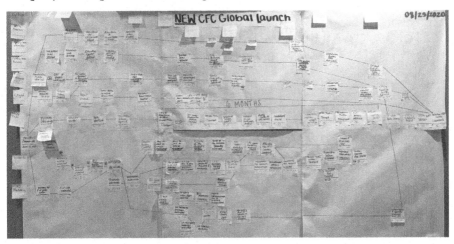

2021, even though the world economy was shut down, 2021 has been the biggest and best year in Rich Dad's 25-year history, thanks in part to my friend Blair Singer.

Blair is currently developing PERT as a commercial product, so more Es and Ss can find their path to becoming Bs and Is. Freedom is found on the B and I side of the Cashflow Quadrant.

Blair's books in the Rich Dad Advisor Series:

> SalesDogs
> Team Code of Honor
> Summit Leadership

He is also the author of *Little Voice Mastery*.

Blair is a friend and Rich Dad Advisor who has worked with us since 1982.

Final Words on Team

Post-modernist education is built upon opinion and emotions to keep people and our country divided.

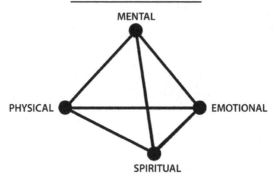

The best way I have found to take on this Marxist ideology is to stay cool and strong and engage all four intelligences. One way to stay cool by having a team you trust. As Marines say, "Semper fi"... always faithful.

That is how Marines are trained. We are trained to fight as a team, a band of brothers, sisters, and angels. This is how Marines find SQ, spiritual intelligence, spiritual courage when facing a fanatical enemy.

That is what my crew and I did when we were going down, staring into the "eyes of death" as we prepared to crash into the ocean.

This why The Rich Dad Company and our team of advisors have thrived during the COVID shut down. Like all business and families, we've had our share of challenges. But we faced them together, found answers together, and found ways to execute our plan within whatever the current protocols or requirements were. That is what teams are for — to help us be our best, to support us when we're facing tough times, and work from a foundation of facts, not opinions.

I'll close with some ancient wisdom that, for me, resonates with our lives today...

We're living in a world where attacks are becoming more and more commonplace... attacks on our institutions, our beliefs, our freedoms. We're attacked for what we do — and what we don't do. For how we think... for how we act... for how we speak. Or don't speak. Ironically, we are attacked for what we love.

When I realize I'm arguing with someone or being attacked, I do my best to stay cool. I take a breath. I slow down. I try not to react emotionally. Instead, I choose to be respectful, even if it is the last thing you want to do or what I think the other person deserves. I do my best to rise above the argument, and hope you do as well, trying to see their point of view, their side of the coin. And who knows? By having an open mind, we might just learn something we didn't know...

Rich dad often said that "when you argue with an idiot, there are two idiots." All too often, I have been the 'idiot.' I become an idiot when I must be right. When I realize I have been an idiot, I do my best to regain humility. From humility, I can gain respect, get smarter... develop wisdom... even apologize. Apologies don't cost much... just a bit of ego. That is real education. That is real learning. Learning begins with humility.

Wisdom begins when we realize that we don't know all the answers... when we realize we don't know everything. None of us are God... or possess infinite wisdom. When we realize that we can become a student... and a child of God.

PART THREE

Freedom vs. Power

INTRODUCTION TO PART THREE

Consider these words from Abraham Lincoln on freedom: "America will never be destroyed from the outside. If we falter and lose our freedoms, it will be because we destroyed ourselves."

Q: What is the difference between freedom and power?
A: Not much.

The definition of *power*:
> *The ability to do or act.*

The definition of *freedom*:
> *The right to act, speak, or think without restraint.*

Simply put, people with more freedom have more power.

On October 2, 2021, I left my home in Phoenix to visit my home in Hawaii. From the moment my driver dropped me off at the Phoenix airport until the time I got to my home in Hawaii, I was bombarded with signs warning:
> *Federal Mandate: Everyone must wear a mask and stay six feet apart.*

Hawaii has implemented additional Marxist mandates such as:
- Football games are played in empty stadiums.
- I cannot eat in a restaurant unless I have a COVID-19 vaccination card
- Private parties are limited to 10 people.

The dictionary definition of *mandate* is:
> *An official order or commission to do something.*

My personal definitions of *mandate* are:
  A loss of freedom. And a loss of power.

The biggest problem with Hawaii is that it is heavily influenced by the Japanese culture. Japanese are the second-largest ethnic group in Hawaii and they are genetically trained not to think... only to bow and obey. I know this. For although I am fourth-generation American, I feel my heritage and the Japanese culture in my soul.

On a trip to Japan, I was put in a group of American tourists who were led by a tour guide with a whistle and a tiny white flag. He blew his whistle, raised his small white flag, and demanded we follow him on the tour. I refused and left the tour to explore on my own. Again, I am fourth-generation Japanese American. I have battled my genetic and ethnic heritage every day, as an American capitalist.

The Miracle of Japan

After World War II Japan rose from the ashes of an atomic bomb blast to become a world mega-power. The resurrection of Japan, after a devasting war, was due to the culture of the people of Japan, the willingness to be led and controlled. The willingness to acquiesce... and not challenge the status quo or those in power.

In the 1970s, the Miracle of Japan re-invaded the United States — this time with dollars, not bombs — buying everything from skyscrapers in New York City to golf courses in Pebble Beach, California... and Waikiki Beach in Hawaii.

By 1990, the Miracle of Japan was going down in flames, this time destroyed by the destructive power of the U.S. dollar. The Japanese had sold too many Sonys and Toyotas to America. The problem was Japan's banking system could not handle the influx of billions of U.S. dollars.

A great book that explains how billions of U.S. dollars destroyed Japan is *The Dollar Crisis,* by macro-economist and friend Richard Duncan. Richard explains how the U.S. dollar destroyed what was known as the Miracle of Japan and how the U.S. dollar is destroying both the United States and the world economy.

In 2021, Japan has the world's worst economy, the highest per capita savings rate, the oldest demographics, and the worst debt-to-GDP ratio in the world.

This is what happens when you have extremely intelligent, highly educated, hardworking people, a mono-culture, trained to obey, to do as they are told... rather than think for themselves.

This is what is happening to the world when good, highly educated, hardworking, productive people lack real financial education.

Japan is known for extremely high-quality cars and electronics, but what have they invented since the Sony Walkman? Japan is a culture that replicates and improves great products and makes them available at great prices, but they do not innovate. They do not create.

The Japanese are a great people and a great race. I am grateful for the Japanese blood flowing through my veins, for that heritage and culture. Yet as a culture, the Japanese win by following. They smile, bow, obey... and follow.

Hawaii puts up with what some see as draconian Marxist Mandates, because the Japanese culture loves mandates... more, it seems, than they love their freedoms.

I know some may say that this thinking makes me a racist, yet many other peoples of different races know exactly what I am saying, because they say it, too. My advantage is I am 100% Japanese, and therefore I can say what other races may think... but dare not say.

I am proud of my Japanese heritage. I am proud of my family's samurai heritage. I am a samurai, which is why I joined the U.S. Marines. I state this because too many of us, regardless of race, follow politically imposed mandates, at the price of our freedoms... and say nothing.

As Lenin warned:

"Fascism is capitalism in decay."

One of my "tweets" was recently taken down because I referred to Dr. Anthony Fauci as "Fascist Fauci."

Fascists love mandates. And Fascist's love stealing our freedoms.

What Is Courage?

The word *courage* is derived from the French word *le coeur,* which means *the heart.* I write about courage because people need en*courage*ment. People today need to find their courage, the courage that beats in their hearts.

Part Three of this book is about how our freedoms are being stolen via fascist government mandates while for years, if not decades, people say nothing.

People are being trained to follow the little man with the whistle and little white flag, to obey—and to say nothing.

Ayn Rand warned:

"We are fast approaching the state of ultimate inversion: the stage where the government is free to do anything it pleases, while the citizens may act only by permission, which is the stage of the darkest periods of human history, the stage of rule by brute force."

A Marine in Solitary Confinement

On August 30, 2021, Ryan Morgan Stuart Scheller, the U.S. Marine lieutenant colonel who was relieved of his command for posting a video calling out military leadership over their handling of Afghanistan, said in a new video that he's not backing down.

As I write, in early October, Lt. Colonel Scheller is in solitary confinement for speaking out.

More Mandates

On September 9, 2021, President Biden issued an Executive Order (EO) mandating all executive branch federal employees to be vaccinated against COVID-19. From the moment the EO was issued, the National Border Patrol Council (NBPC) instructed its seven attorneys to drop all other matters to study the issue and develop strategies to attack the EO. After spending several days reviewing all pertinent laws and relevant case law, the attorneys determined the EO was legal and that there was no viable avenue of challenge.

Ironically, Border Patrol Officers will be fired if they are not vaccinated, yet thousands of undocumented — and quite likely unvaccinated — aliens enter our country each day.

Healthcare Workers on the Front Lines

We've all seen the sobering headlines and news stories in the wake of 2021 COVID-related decisions...

> NEW YORK, Sept 27 (Reuters) – New York hospitals on Monday began firing or suspending healthcare workers for defying a state order to get the COVID-19 vaccine and resulting staff shortages prompted some hospitals to postpone elective surgeries or curtail services.

On October 4, 2021, New York hospitals announced that 100% of their staff are vaccinated. They fail to report that they fired 1,400 workers who refused the vaccine.

Repeating Ayn Rand's warning:

> *"We are fast approaching the state of ultimate inversion: the stage where the government is free to do anything it pleases, while the citizens may act only by permission, which is the stage of the darkest periods of human history, the stage of rule by brute force."*

It seems to all come down to power versus freedom.

In Part 3 we will look at how we can stop losing our power and our freedoms... to the powers that be who are herding us with their whistles and their little white flags... their mandates and decrees and EOs. All in the name of governance. And how we are, in many ways, like the Japanese people who are reluctant to push back or challenge the status quo or the agendas of the academic elite. Every day I think about how today's reality —"*Masks are federally mandated.*"— impacts both our freedoms and our power.

CHAPTER FIFTEEN

AMERICA WOKES UP

Language, as I've stated earlier in this book, is more than simply a means by which we communicate. And being crystal clear on how we define the words we use to communicate is essential.

A definition of *woke*, according to Wikipedia and other sources is:

"Woke (WOHK) is a political term originating in the United States referring to a perceived awareness of issues concerning social justice and racial justice. It derives from the African-American Vernacular English expression "stay woke," whose grammatical aspect refers to a continuing awareness of these issues."

Merriam-Webster's definition it as: aware of, alert, conscious, and actively attentive to important facts and issues (especially issues of racial and social justice).

An urban dictionary defines woke as "being aware of the truth behind things 'the man' doesn't want you to know." Meanwhile, a concurrent definition signals a shift in meaning to "the act of being very pretentious about how much you care about a social issue."

A Stranger in a Strange Land
In January of 1973, I returned to America from Vietnam. I felt like a stranger in a strange land. I had just left one of the most horrifying man-made environments in history, the Vietnam war. Vietnam was a testing ground for new technology and a new type of war, high-tech warfare versus guerilla warfare. The United States on one side, China and Russia on the other.

I was now at home in Hawaii, land of palm trees, hula girls, and Mai Tais. No one seemed to care about what I had just experienced. The Vietnam war was far away and out of mind for most people. I wondered what it was all for...

I had lost close friends... friends who would never return to their homes. Two friends, one a Marine and the other a Navy pilot, both flew the A-6 Intruder. Both were MIA. Their planes or their bodies have never been found. I had one classmate, an Air Force F-4 Phantom pilot, a POW, who was a prisoner in the Hanoi Hilton. He was released after the war ended.

I had three classmates who were drafted, fought on the ground, and returned alive, yet "troubled" from all that they experienced.

One high school classmate, Louie, a gentle soul, was a draftee not a volunteer. He was reportedly shot in the back. As the story goes, he turned and ran when the shooting started and his own lieutenant shot him, as a warning to the rest of the troops. Louie should never have gone to war. He should have worked in a pet shop.

Most of my male classmates dodged the Vietnam war with student deferments. They stayed in college or went on to graduate school.

My point here is that, when I returned home, from one of the most horrifying environments anyone could face, and no one seemed to care. No one talked about it. There was no "welcome home." No "Thank you for your service." It wasn't so much that we expected it. More that there was just no acknowledgement that Americans were putting their lives on the line for their country and the freedoms we stood for.

In 1973, after four years at the Academy, studying Marx, Hitler, Stalin, Lenin, and Mao, then flying, and fighting communism in Vietnam, buying gold after Nixon took the U.S. dollar off the gold standard, and returning home only to be spit on by peaceful hippie protestors, I "woked" up.

As Khrushchev warned in 1959:

"You Americans are so gullible."

America Goes to Sleep

In 1974, I drove out the main gate of the Marine base for the last time, returned my last salute, and entered the world of business. Immediately I began to see Marx's *Communist Manifesto* and Khrushchev's warning playing out all around me.

Working in downtown Honolulu for the Xerox Corporation, I sensed people were being taught to be Marxist... but did not know it.

I sensed that most people had no idea what was going on... or, for that matter, what was coming in the future. I remembered my teacher at the academy who had us discuss Lenin's warning:

"There are decades where nothing happens, and there are weeks where decades happen."

Marx had a long-term plan:

    1 – Democracy
    2 – Socialism
    3 – Communism

Marx warned:

"Democracy is the road to socialism."

Once socialism was in place, communists would kill the socialists.

Q: Is that why the death tolls are in the millions?

A: Yes. Vilfredo Pareto (1848-1923) was an Italian engineer, sociologist, economist, and libertarian capitalist, famous for Pareto's 80/20 Rule. He warned: *"When it is useful to them, men can believe a theory of which they know nothing more than its name."*

Q: Do you mean most people do not know the differences between democracy, socialism, and communism?

A: Correct. Pareto also warned: *"Whoever becomes a lamb will find a wolf to eat him."*

Q: Is that why socialists are killed by communists?

A: Yes. That is what history tells us. Lenin, Stalin, Hitler, and Mao were all mass murderers who got their own people to do their killing. All were socialists first.

Little Atrocities

Earlier in this book I wrote about Hitler's use of "little atrocities," such as mandating that Jews wear yellow stars. Today, as I've said, I have a yellow star on my driver's license and everyone is being pressured into wearing a mask and getting vaccinated.

Remember, Nazi stands for National Socialists German Workers Party. And USSR stands for Union of Soviet Socialist Republics. China is the PRC, People's Republic of China.

America Wokes Up

By April of 1975, I was in the "rat race" of Honolulu, learning to sell and climbing the corporate ladder. I stayed in touch with the war through friends who were still in Vietnam. One friend, a Marine Lieutenant "grunt," a ground Marine, was shot in the head on his second tour, and fortunately recovered. On April 30, 1975, the Vietnam War finally ended when a NVA tank broke down the gate to the U.S. Embassy in Saigon.

It broke my heart to see these pictures while I was working in downtown Honolulu.

A co-worker at Xerox, standing in a bar with a beer in hand, shook his head in disbelief and said, "How can this be happening? I thought we were winning the war."

As Khrushchev warned:
"You Americans are so gullible."

In 1975, photos as the ones above were everywhere in the news. The photos showed a helicopter being pushed over the side of the roof to make room for other helicopters. The helicopters were flown by South Vietnamese Army pilots, fleeing death or torture at the hands of the communist North Vietnamese.

As they say, a picture is worth a thousand words. The helicopter on the right in the photo on the previous page is not a military helicopter. It is an Air America (aka CIA) helicopter. The CIA aircraft obviously could not carry all the panicked military personnel who wanted a ride to freedom. The Air America pilot is pushing people back, waiting for VIPs... American diplomats, aka "spies."

Today, in 2021, we have the debacle in Afghanistan with a chaotic mass evacuation that put American lives at risk and left billions of dollars in military equipment purchased with U.S. taxpayer dollars behind in Afghanistan in the hands of our enemies. The world has witnessed an erosion of both confidence and trust in the United States by its allies... and the world.

Jobs for "Boat People"

When America abandoned the people of Vietnam, thousands became "boat people." Between 1978 and 1983, my little nylon surfer wallet company provided jobs for about 35 of those boat people. They were by far the best workers we ever hired. They were grateful for freedom and a job.

Today, in 2021, millions of small business owners cannot find workers because our government pays people *not* to work. If that is not Marxism, I don't know what is. Many people know that MMT, Marxist (I mean Modern...) Monetary Theory or UBI, Universal Basic Income is coming.

Another little atrocity?

As Marx warned:
   "The last capitalist we hang shall be the one who sold us the rope."

And Jordan Peterson said:
   "Marx did not love poor people. Marx hated rich people."

Happy 100ᵗʰ Birthday

The year 2021 marks the 100th anniversary of the Chinese Communist Party.

On August 14, 1945, Japan surrendered. Japan gave up Korea and on August 15, 1948, the Republic of South Korea is formed. The Democratic People's Republic of Korea was formed less than a month later. World War II ended, and the Cold War began.

And Marx's *Communism Manifesto* was spreading across the world.

The Domino Theory of Communism

On April 7, 1954, President Eisenhower warned that if Vietnam fell to communism, the rest of Southeast Asia would soon follow.

Dwight D. Eisenhower, a 5-Star General and 34th President of the United States, warned:

> *"Finally, you have broader considerations that might follow what you would call the 'falling domino' principle. You have a row of dominoes set up, you knock over the first one, and what will happen to the last one is the certainty that it will go over very quickly. So, you could have a beginning of a disintegration that would have the most profound influences."*

Marx warned:

> *"The Communists everywhere support every revolutionary movement against the existing social and political order of things... They openly declare that their ends can be attained only by the forcible overthrow of all existing social conditions."*

In 1962, my family and I witnessed the detonation of an atomic bomb from our kitchen window. It looked like someone had poured blood in the sky.

In August of 1965, I left Hawaii for the U.S. Merchant Marine Academy where I studied Marx, Lenin, Hitler, Stalin, and Mao. In 1966, I sailed into Vietnam on board an old, World War II Victory Ship carrying bombs for the war in Vietnam.

In January of 1972, I was flying off a carrier in the South China Sea. In 1975, I watch on television as helicopters were being pushed off the side of a carrier in the South China Sea.

History Repeats Itself

In August od 2021, my heart breaks and my gut churns as I watch history repeat itself in Afghanistan. I feel for the thousands of men and women who lost their lives or limbs. I feel for their families. I feel for the millions of Afghanis who supported the US. Many loyal Afghans have been or will be killed, tortured, or placed in re-education camps.

Afghanistan is another notch in communism's belt.

A Tale of Betrayal

In 2021, America once again betrayed the people who trusted us. Millions of Afghans, especially the Northern Alliance, fought fearlessly for America. The Northern Alliance, officially known as the United Islamic National Front for the Salvation of Afghanistan, has fought against the Taliban for decades.

In 2021, the Northern Alliance was abandoned by America. Then Americans wonder: Why does America lose to communism? After Vietnam and, now, Afghanistan... can America be trusted?

With America out of that war, I am concerned that the spread of communism will accelerate.

What Will Be Next?

My concern is that Taiwan, South Korea, Mexico, El Salvador, Peru, Argentina, South Africa, Zimbabwe, Ukraine, Poland, Bulgaria, and Estonia may be next.

Here are some of Marx's thoughts on freedom:

"Do not be deluded by the abstract word Freedom. Whose freedom? Not the freedom of one individual in relation to another, but freedom of Capital to crush the worker."

Marx's position:

"The theory of Communism may be summed up in one sentence: Abolish all private property."

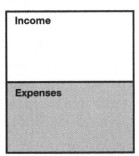

When I asked my rich dad what "the abolition of private property" looked like he simply drew this familiar diagram.

Marx warned:

"Landlords, like all other men, love to reap where they never sowed."

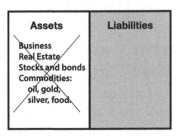

My rich dad was rich because he was a landlord. My poor dad had no assets. He was a government employee and was counting on the government for medical and retirement benefits.

Q: Is this what Marx wants? To keep people dependent? Is this why there is no financial education in our schools?

A: My job it to pose questions... questions that get you thinking — and then ask more questions. These are some of questions you should be asking yourself.

In 1975, after witnessing the fall of Vietnam, I began telling close friends that I could see communism seeping into our lives. Most did not want to listen to my warning. A few accused me of McCarthyism.

McCarthyism is named for Senator Joseph R. McCarthy, a little-known junior senator from Wisconsin until February 1950 when he claimed to possess a list of 205 card-carrying Communists employed in the U.S. Department of State. From that moment Senator McCarthy became a tireless crusader against Communism in the early 1950s, a period that has been commonly referred to as the Red Scare. As chairman of the Senate Permanent Investigation Subcommittee, Senator McCarthy conducted hearings on communist subversion in America and investigated alleged communist infiltration of the Armed Forces. His subsequent exile from politics coincided with a conversion of his name into a modern English noun *McCarthyism*.

Senator McCarthy was censured by the U.S. Senate on December 2, 1954 and died May 2, 1957.

In 1974, I was advised to keep my political views to myself. But I refuse to be censored. I continue to exercise my freedom of speech.

These words often attributed of Edmund Burke heralded a warning:
"All that is necessary for the triumph of evil... is that good men do nothing."

In 2021 America began "woking up" to people doing nothing.

Professor Jordan Peterson warned:
"And if you think tough men are dangerous, wait until you see what weak men are capable of."

Today millions of weak men and women—dubbed *"the mob"* and the *"cowardly cancel culture"*— attack from behind the safety of a computer screen. Cowards have gained power thanks to social media. They exercise their freedom of speech... yet deny you that same freedom.

These are the weak men and women of whom Jordan Peterson warns.

Cancer in Education
In 2021 America is also "woking up" to the cancer in education.

In 2020, I was listening to a talk by Professor Gad Saad discussing:
1 – Black Lives Matter
2 – Critical Race Theory
3 – Antifa
4 – Post-Modernist Education

All four organizations openly acknowledge their Marxist roots.

These are not Professor Saad's exact words, but I am stating what I heard. Fundamentally he is saying:
> "*Marxism is a cancer... a cancer that is metastasizing throughout America and the world.*"

The definition of metastasize is when something spread to other parts of a body, a culture or an institution.

In 2020, Professor Gad Saad warned:
> "*So where do these idea pathogens come from? They all come from the university eco-system.*"

As Gad Saad warns:
> "*An analysis of political campaign donations across a broad range of industries uncovered that the four most liberal professions, in decreasing order, were the entertainment industry, academia, online computer services, and newspapers and print media.*"

As Lenin warned:
> "*Whenever the cause of the people is entrusted to professors, it is lost.*"

The cancer that is metastasizing is the cancer professor Gad Saad calls "idea pathogens" or "parasitic ideas."

I call them socialist, Marxist, and communist idea pathogens. These cancers are spread from schoolteachers to children.

Marx warned:
> *"The education of all children, from the moment that they can get along without a mother's care, shall be in state institutions."*

Lenin warned:
> *"Give us the child for eight years and it will be a Bolshevik forever."*

What is a Bolshevik? Here's a definition: A Bolshevik is a member of the majority faction of the Russian Social Democratic Party, which was renamed the Communist Party after seizing power in the Bolshevik Revolution of 1917.

Education's Cancer Spreads into Religion

Marx had this to say about Christianity:
> *"The democratic concept of man is false because it is Christian. The democratic concept holds that... each man is a sovereign being. This is the illusion, dream, and postulate of Christianity."*

He warned:
> *"We know that violent measures against religion are nonsense; but this is an opinion: as socialism grows, religion will disappear. Its disappearance must be done by social development, in which education must play a part."*

Barack Obama's Minister

Think about this... from *The Moguldom Nation*, July 29, 2019:
> *"The Reverend Jeremiah Wright is the former pastor of Trinity United Church of Christ in Chicago, which he began to lead in 1971. He is credited with transforming the church of 250 members into the largest in the United Church of Christ denomination. Wright is known for*

incorporating Black liberation theology into his sermons, and this among other things attracted the likes of Barack Obama and Oprah Winfrey."

"The title of Obama's 2006 memoir, The Audacity of Hope, was inspired by one of Wright's sermons. This sermon also inspired themes for Obama's 2004 keynote address to the Democratic National Convention."

A video surfaced of one of Reverend Wright's sermons in which he said:

"Let me leave you with one more thing... Not 'God Bless America'; God damn America! That's in the Bible, for killing innocent people. God damn America for treating her citizens as less than human. God damn America as long as she keeps trying to act like she is God and she is supreme!" [Emphasis added.]

It was Vladimir Lenin who warned:

*"We can and must write in a **language** which sows among the masses hate, revulsion, and scorn toward those who disagree with us."*

And Thomas Sowell who said:

"Over the generations, black leaders have ranged from noble souls to shameless charlatans."

Understandably, Obama and Oprah had to sever ties with Reverend Wright, even though he married Michelle and Barack and baptized their daughters. Although Wright has retired, he has stayed in the media spotlight off and on. In 2010, Wright countered the distancing by saying Obama "threw me under the bus" and added that Obama was "toxic" to the White House.

In 2021, we see many churches advertising they support Black Lives Matter.

Although Marx warned:

"The social principles of Christianity preach cowardice, self-contempt, abasement, submission, humility, in a word all the qualities of the canaille."

Canaille means the common people, the masses. Its origin is French, from the Italian word *canaglia*, meaning 'pack of dogs.'

Education's Cancer Turns the Human Race… into "Racism"

Growing up in Hawaii, a multi-racial culture, I was taught that all lives matter. A melting pot for many cultures and ethnic backgrounds and home to lush and abundant plant life and oceans filled with living creatures of all shapes and sizes, the environment in which I grew up put a value on all forms of life. All *life* mattered.

In 2020, rather than showing respect for the human race, I see Black Lives Matter turning humans into racists. That is why I find it interesting that many proponents and those in leadership with Black Lives Matter and the Critical Race Theory movement, report to be followers of Marx. I think most would agree that Marx was a racist.

Q: How do you know Marx was a racist?

A: I listen to his own words. After he was turned down by "a friend," a fellow Jew… Marx's racial bias came to the surface. He said:

"The Jewish nigger Lassalle who, I'm glad to say, is leaving at the end of this week, has happily lost another 5,000 talers in an ill-judged speculation. The chap would sooner throw money down the drain than lend it to a 'friend,' even though his interest and capital were guaranteed. … It is now quite plain to me—as the shape of his head and the way his hair grows also testify—that he is descended from the negroes who accompanied Moses' flight from Egypt (unless his mother or paternal grandmother interbred with a nigger). Now, this blend of Jewishness and Germanness, on the one hand, and basic negroid stock, on the other, must inevitably give rise to a peculiar product. The fellow's importunity is also nigger-like."

In our families, Kim and I were forbidden to use the "n-word."

In 1965, at the Academy, my roommate was Thomas W. Jackson III, an African American from Washington, DC. In Hawaii, I had no black classmates because there was only one black family in Hilo, and their children were younger than me. Having Tom Jackson as a roommate for a year was an eye-opening education into the spiritual disease known as racial prejudice.

Ironically, Tom broke up with his girlfriend soon after starting at Kings Point. Tom let me read her "Dear Tom" letter to him. She broke up with Tom because he was not attending Howard University, a private, federally chartered historically black university that she was attending. According to his girlfriend, "Tom was not black enough."

Tom and I spent many hours, over that year, discussing race.

Are You a Racist?

In today's "woke" culture, if you say you're *not* a racist… you're a racist. If you say nothing… you're a racist. And if you're white and say nothing… you're a racist and a white supremacist.

I've been accused of being both, a racist and a white supremist, which I find interesting. And sad, in many ways. Especially since those labeling me do not know me and, in some cases, have personal agendas that are supported by that narrative. I ask myself time and again: How did we get to this point?

Thomas Sowell warns:
> *"The word 'racism' is like ketchup. It can be put on practically anything — and demanding evidence makes you a 'racist."*

Candace Owens warns:
> *"Play the black card expertly, and you can win awards, make millions — all the while claiming that the people who got you there somehow hate you."*

In August of 2021, Larry Elder, an American conservative talk radio host, author, politician, attorney, and African American candidate for Governor of California, was accused by the *Los Angeles Times* of being "the white face of black supremacy."

Larry Elder says:

> *"The formula for achieving middle-class success is simple. Finish high school, don't have a child before the age of 20; and get married before having a child.*

Who Is a Racist?

In my opinion, in our world today, it is the person who accuses someone of being a racist who is racist.

Thomas Sowell also warned:

> *"Racism is not dead, but it is on life support – kept alive by politicians, race hustlers and people who get a sense of superiority by denouncing others as 'racists'"*

Education's Cancer Spreads into our Freedom of Speech

Marx did not have much to say about "free speech." He was more focused on class struggles and the overthrow of society. Lenin, on the other hand, had a lot to say about free speech.

Lenin warned:

> *"Free speech is a bourgeois prejudice."*

Bourgeois is another word for middle-class capitalist.

Rather than allow other people to voice their points of view, Lenin advised:

> *"It is, of course, much easier to shout, abuse, and howl than to attempt to relate, to explain."*

And Professor Gad Saad warns:

> *"These politically correct language initiatives are misguided and harmful. They create highly entitled professional 'victims' who expect to be free from any offense, and they engender a stifling atmosphere where all individuals walk on eggshells lest they might commit a linguistic capital crime."*

Professor Jordan Peterson warns:

> *"Intolerance of others' views (no matter how ignorant or incoherent they may be) is not simply wrong; in a world where there is no right or wrong, it is worse: it is a sign you are embarrassingly unsophisticated or, possibly, dangerous."*

Teaching racism is not "free speech." Teaching racism, disguised as CRT, Critical Race Theory, is teaching hate, and CRT is teaching and promoting division, not diversity. Teaching CRT is a Marxist agenda, dividing the United States of America.

It's time America "woke up" to what teachers are teaching. And time we look into the NEA, the National Education Association, and the AFT (American Federation of Teachers), the richest and most powerful labor unions in America.

Because Karl Marx warned:

> *"Without the presence of class warfare, trade unions would be hard put to justify their existence."*

America is not systemically racist. America is systemically capitalist, a democratic Republic, dedicated to the freedom of speech, free enterprise, life, liberty, and the pursuit — not the guarantee — of the American Dream. America is not a Marxist Utopia, the land where everyone gets a trophy.

In the words of Vilfredo Pareto:

> *"The assertion that men are objectively equal is so absurd that it does not even merit being refuted."*

If all men were created equal, I would look like Brad Pitt, play golf like Tiger woods, and sing like Sting of The Police. It's time for America to "woke up" to what our teachers are teaching in our schools.

Education's Cancer Spreads into the Press

Joseph Stalin warned:

> *"The press must grow day in and day out – it is our Party's sharpest and most powerful weapon."*

The 1619 Project

The New York Times ran a special 100-page edition of its August 2019 issue of its Sunday Magazine, promoting the "1619 Project. "The Project" presents and interprets American history entirely through the prism of race and racial conflict. The occasion for this publication is the 400th anniversary of the initial arrival of 20 African slaves at Point Comfort in Virginia, a British colony in North America. On the very next day, the slaves were traded for food.

"The Project," according to the *Times*, intends to change history. *The New York Times* goal is to "reframe" America's history. The Times promotes 1619 as America's true founding.

The 1619 Project places the consequences of slavery and the contributions of black Americans at the very center of America's founding. That is why statues of Christopher Columbus are being desecrated.

The New York Times intends to change history by writing a "new narrative."

And it was Marx who warned:

> *"Take away a nation's heritage and they are more easily persuaded."*

"The Project" is so full of lies, emotional untruths, and opinions that the World Socialists Website: WSWS.org: warned:

> *"Despite the pretense of establishing the United States' "true" foundation, the 1619 Project is a politically motivated falsification of history. Its aim is to create a historical narrative that legitimizes the effort of the Democratic Party to construct an electoral coalition based on the prioritizing of personal "identities"— i.e., gender, sexual preference, ethnicity, and, above all, race."*

Education's Cancer Spreads into the Second Amendment

Whenever I hear this battle cry — "Defund the police!" — I ask myself if anyone of the protestors has considered the consequences of doing that.

Lenin warned:

> *"One man with a gun can control 100 without one."*

As did Mao:

> *"All political power comes from the barrel of a gun. The communist party must command all the guns, that way, no guns can ever be used to command the party."*

Lenin also stated:

> *"You must act with all energy. Mass searches. Execution for concealing arms."*

Arming the Taliban

While liberals in America want to defund the police and deny Americans their Second Amendment rights, the Biden Administration's disgraceful retreat from Afghanistan placed over a half-million weapons into the hands of the Taliban. This is not a political statement, merely a statement of fact that has been well documented.

You and I know those same U.S.-made weapons will be smuggled back into the United States and into countries around the world, potentially murdering millions of innocent people.

Lenin warned:

> *"One of the basic conditions for the victory of socialism is the arming of the workers (Communists) and the disarming of the bourgeoisie (the middle class.)"*

Education's Cancer Spreads into Hollywood

As an actor, Ronald Reagan was known as a staunch anti-communist. Many people are unaware that this anti-communist reputation began years before he became President of the United States. President Reagan began his anti-communist crusade as the President of the Screen Actors Guild of America.

Interesting, in my opinion, that Lenin referenced 'cinema' when he cautioned:
 "Of all the arts, for us, the cinema is the most important."

Hollywood's Screen Actors Guild was a breeding ground for Marx and his propaganda. The more Reagan spoke out against communists in Hollywood, the more acting jobs coming his way began to dwindle. Eventually he was forced into television.

The political sentiments in the entertainment industry inspired Ronald Reagan to run for Governor of California and eventually President of the United States.

One Reagan's of most powerful "roles" was as President of the United States. And on June 2, 1987, President Reagan stood at the Brandenburg Gate in Berlin and issued an international challenge to Communist Party Secretary Mikhail Gorbachev.

Reagan warned:
> *"Behind me stands a wall that encircles the free sectors of this city, part of a vast system of barriers that divides the entire continent of Europe. ... Standing before the Brandenburg Gate, every man is a German, separated from his fellow men. Every man is a Berliner, forced to look upon a scar. ... As long as this gate is closed, as long as this scar of a wall is permitted to stand, it is not the German question alone that remains open, but the question of freedom for all mankind. ...*
>
> *"General Secretary Gorbachev, if you seek peace, if you seek prosperity for the Soviet Union and Eastern Europe, if you seek liberalization, come here to this gate.*

"Mr. Gorbachev, open this gate!
"Mr. Gorbachev, tear down this wall!"

Two years later, in 1989, the Berlin Wall came down. Today, not surprisingly, there are still some who say that Communists still run Hollywood.

Many liberals work for government organizations, NGOs (Non-Government Organizations), charities, Political Action Committees, and many other types of non-profit do-good/feel-good organizations.

Most do-gooders actually do good work, but, like Marx, most do not know how to make money. So, who are more generous, liberals or conservatives?

Thomas Sowell found:
"People who identify themselves as conservatives donate money to charity more often than people who identify themselves as liberals. They donate more money and a higher percentage of their incomes."

Unfortunately, many ultra-rich donate to radical liberal causes. For example, mega-billionaire George Soros's money and fingerprints are all over organizations that support initiatives like defunding the police.

According to records filed with the Federal Election Commission and the Washington Free Beacon, billionaire George Soros regularly backs Democratic congressional candidates and attorneys general, donated $1 million to the Color of Change PAC, a defund the police Political Action Committee. The PAC describes itself as the nation's largest online racial justice organization. Soros continues to fund defund-the-police organizations all over the world, although violent crime escalates. And then there's Jeff Bezos and his ownership of *The Washington Post*...

Education's Cancer Spreads into the Economy
Communists blame capitalists for the gap between rich and poor. Communists blame capitalists for income inequality. Communists blame capitalists for homelessness.

These are the lies of socialists, Marxists, and communists. Socialists, Marxists, and communists are the cause of income inequality, the gap between rich and poor. For Marx's *Communist Manifesto* to succeed, economic and social unrest are essential.

Socialists, Marxists, and communists are the real people who cause the real poverty in the world.

Keeping it simple — KISS: Capitalists create prosperity. Communists create poverty.

Q: Why do Marxists want poverty?

A: Two reasons, as I see it:

Reason #1: Marx was a poor, angry academic-elite intellectual. He needed someone to blame for his financial poverty.

In his own words, Marx was a loser. On January 8, 1863 he wrote: *"The devil alone knows why nothing, but ill-luck should dog everyone in our circle just now. I no longer know which way to turn either. My attempts to raise money in France and Germany have come to naught, and it might, of course, have been foreseen that £15 couldn't help stem the avalanche for more than a couple of weeks. Aside from the fact that no one will let us have anything on credit—save for the butcher and baker, which will also cease at the end of this week—I am being dunned for the school fees, the rent, and by the whole gang of them. Those who got a few pounds on account cunningly pocketed them, only to fall upon me with redoubled vigor. On top of that, the children have no clothes or shoes in which to go out. In short, all hell is let loose."*

Q: Is this why Marx hated capitalist and capitalism? Because he was a financial loser?

A: I suggest you reread Marx's own words and decide for yourself. Then it's your informed opinion, not mine.

Reason #2: Marx needed people to be poor and angry, like he was, so he could cause a revolution.

Marx warned:

> *"The class struggle necessarily leads to the dictatorship of the proletariat."*

The definition of proletariat is:

> *Workers or working-class people. The lowest class of citizen in ancient Rome.*

    Q: Was Marx proposing a government run by poor people?
    A: Yes, poor people, academic intellectuals, just like him.

Who Causes Poverty?

Why do I say that socialists, Marxists, and communists are the cause of income inequality, the gap between rich and poor? That's an easy answer: Bailout is the name of the game. Earlier in this book I mentioned *The Creature from Jekyll Island,* aka The Fed. I stated that bankers of the world can "bail out" if they get into trouble. The poor and middle class declare "bankruptcy."

As Bucky Fuller warned:

> *"They're playing games with money."*

The rules of the game of money are different for the rich, poor, and middle class. The question is, who designed the Creature from Jekyll Island?

Jim Rickards writes:

> *"In 2008 the central banks and bailed out Wall Street. In the next crisis, who is going to bail out the big banks? In other words, each crisis gets bigger than the one before. Each bailout gets bigger than the one before. We're now to the point where we've exceeded the capacity of the central banks to 'save the day.'"*

Lenin warned:

> *"The establishment of a central bank is 90% of communizing a nation."*

In 1913 The United States Federal Reserve Bank was formed. The Fed is a central bank. The Fed is America's third central bank.

Keep in mind that The Fed is not U.S., nor is it a bank. It is a "central bank." The Fed is part of a global banking cartel.

Communism begins with "central control" of the economy. That is why The Fed is essential to Marx's *Communist Manifesto.*

The Declaration of Independence
Thomas Jefferson (1743-1826) was the 3rd President of the United States. And not only was Jefferson a signer on the Declaration of Independence, he is also considered the primary driver behind the Declaration of Independence.

Thomas Jefferson warned:
> *"If the American people ever allow private banks to control the issue of their currency, first by inflation, then by deflation, the banks and corporations that will grow up around [the banks] will deprive the people of all property until their children wake-up homeless on the continent their fathers conquered. The issuing power should be taken from the banks and restored to the people, to whom it properly belongs.*

> *"**I sincerely believe** that banking establishments are more dangerous than standing armies, and that the principle of spending money to be paid by posterity under the name of funding is but swindling futurity on a large scale."* [Emphasis added.]

Congressman and Republican candidate for President of the United States, Ron Paul agrees. In his book *End the Fed* Paul warns:
> *"First reason is, it's not authorized in the Constitution, it's an illegal institution. The second reason, it's an immoral institution because we have delivered to a secretive body the privilege of creating money out of thin air; if you or I did it, we'd be called counterfeiters, so why have legalized counterfeiting? But the economic reasons are overwhelming: the Federal Reserve is the creature that steals value."*

In the words of George Washington:
> *"Paper money has had the effect in your state that it will ever have, to ruin commerce, oppress the honest, and open the door to every species of fraud and injustice."*

In her book *Fed Up: An Insider's Take on Why the Federal Reserve is Bad for America.*

Danielle Di Martino Booth warns:
"The Fed's relatively enhanced standing among the public has been aided by the fact the Fed has always paid a great deal of attention to soothing the people in the media and buying up most of its likely critics."

Another important book is by Nomi Prins. Her book is titled *Collusion: How Central Bankers Rigged the World.* (2018)

Nomi writes:
"I quit Wall Street and decided that it was time to talk more about what was going on inside it, as it had changed. It had become far more sinister and far more dangerous?"

I know Nomi personally. She has more brains, guts, and tenacity than most of the men I have done business with on Wall Street. She is a woman of *deeds, not words*. She quit her job as a Wall Street insider and traveled the world investigating and interviewing central bankers. Her findings support Bucky Fuller's 1983 book, *Grunch of Giants*. Her book. *Collusion.* is both infuriating and alarming.

Q: Is that why the Fed and the tax department were created in 1913?
A: Yes. Fake money cannot exist without fake taxes. Fake money is why the stock market is at all-time highs, after the outbreak of COVID-19. CEOs are using fake money to keep their share prices high.

Q: Is that why you and former SEC attorney Ted Seidel co-wrote *Who Stole My Pension?* in 2020?
A: It is. That book goes behind the scenes of labor union officials, government officials, and Wall Street. If you or someone you love has a pension, *Who Stole My Pension?* is an eye-opening book. Best to prepare now.

My fellow Marines who got jobs flying for United Airlines lost everything in United's union pension. Too old to continue flying, many are still struggling financially.

Thomas Sowell warned us:

> *"One of the common failings among honorable people is a failure to appreciate how thoroughly dishonorable some other people can be, and how dangerous it is to trust them."*

As did Jim Rickards:

> *"It may be too late to save the dollar, but it is not too late to preserve wealth. We live in an ersatz monetary system that has reached its end stage."*

Q: Will pensions have to be bailed out?

A: That might be something you want to research and study so you can decide that for yourself. If I had a pension, I would be worried. I am always concerned about things I do not or cannot control.

Pensions are part of GRUNCH, the Shadow Banking System, and "The Swamp" that President Trump was draining.

America Is Born

In 1913, the IRS, the Internal Revenue Service, was created when the 16ᵗʰ Amendment was passed. It's worth noting that America's real founding date was not 1619. The real America was founded in 1773, the year Americans disguised as Indians held a party dumping English Tea into the Boston Harbor. The Boston Tea party was a tax revolt. And America was born.

Marx warned:

> *"A heavy or progressive or graduated income tax is necessary for the proper development of Communism."*

Lenin warned:

> *"Taxes are the source of life for the bureaucracy, the army and the court, in short, for the whole apparatus of the executive power. Strong government and heavy taxes are identical."*

Destroying the Dollar

Money, power, and freedom... so intertwined. Whenever I look at the strength of the U.S. dollar I think of Lenin's words of warning:

"The best way to destroy the capitalist system is to debauch the currency."

In 1971, President Richard Nixon took the U.S. dollar off the gold standard. Inflation took off. In 1971, just as Lenin warned, the U.S. dollar was being debauched.

Lenin also warned:

"The way to crush the bourgeoisie is to grind them between the millstones of taxation and inflation."

Once the dollar was no longer backed by gold, the Marxists could fulfill Lenin's prophetic warning. They could now cause inflation, by printing money.

In 2020, after the economy was shut down, the Fed and Treasury began printing trillions of dollars.

Q: Is that why you flew behind enemy lines, in 1972 to buy gold?
A: Yes. It's the same reason why I began investing in Bitcoin in 2020.

In 1972, a Vietnamese woman taught me that "gold and silver are god's money." Money made by God. Bitcoin is "people's money."

Gold, silver, and Bitcoin are not controlled by a central bank... The Fed.

I am not suggesting you invest in gold, silver, and Bitcoin. That is your decision. I just state what I do.

As I written about in *Rich Dad Poor Dad* and other books in the Rich Dad series, "Saves are losers." Since 1972, I have not saved U.S. dollars. Today, when I need money, I use debt, pay as little as legally possible in taxes, and save gold, silver, and Bitcoin.

Jim Rickards warns:

> *"From its creation in 1913, the most important Fed mandate has been to maintain the purchasing power of the dollar; however, since 1913 the dollar has lost over 95 percent of its value. Put differently, it takes twenty dollars today to buy what one dollar would buy in 1913."*

Q: Is that why after September 17, 2019, the crash in the Repo Market, which did not make the news, followed by COVID-19, your senses went on Red Alert.

A: Yes. Then came the market crashes, shutting down small businesses, race riots, CRT taught in schools, impeachment of Donald Trump, fake elections, burning of cities, defunding the police, school closures due to COVID-19, mandating masks and vaccines, fake news coverage, Fed and Treasury printing trillions in fake money, fake stock market, pensions looted as baby boomers retire, the fall of Afghanistan... and the list goes on.

I suspected Lenin's warning was coming true:

> *"There are decades where nothing happens, and there are weeks where decades happen."*

My Red Alert brought together warnings from Senator Joseph McCarthy, Congressman Ron Paul, and Presidents Eisenhower and Reagan. We were warned...

Thomas Sowell, too, warned:

> *"One of the common failings among honorable people is a failure to appreciate how thoroughly dishonorable some other people can be, and how dangerous it is to trust them."*

Reparations... and Hitler's Rise to Power

In 2020, Black Lives Matter is beating the drum for reparations, for paying blacks for wages not paid during slavery. The irony is the reparations will be paid to people who were never slaves by people who never owned slaves.

Before America agrees to paying reparations, it might be timely to look at history for lessons.

Hitler rose to power after the end of World War I, and the Treaty of Versailles was signed in 1918. The Treaty of Versailles required the German people to pay reparations" to the winning nations.

The problem was, Germany was so devasted it could not produce, could not export, and could not pay reparations. To keep their agreement, the German government, the Weimar Republic, began printing trillions in Reichsmark.

That led to hyper-inflation, starvation, civil unrest, and the rise of Adolf Hitler... who was a private in World War I.

Due to reparations, the printing of money, and the failure of the Germany economy in 1933, Hitler was elected Chancellor of Germany... and we all know what happened next.

In 1933 Hitler warned:
> *"As a matter of fact, the policy of reparations could only be financed by German exports. To the same extent as Germany, for the sake of reparations, was regarded in the light of an international exporting concern, the export of the creditor nations was bound to suffer. The economic benefit accruing from the reparation payments could therefore never make good the damage which the system of reparations inflicted upon the individual economic systems.*

World War II began on September 1, 1939, with the German invasion of Poland.

Hitler was a racist. Hitler hated the Jewish community and wanted to erase them from the face of the Earth. A rough estimate points that around 11 million people died during the terror reign of Hitler, including 6 million Jews.

Q: Beyond 2021 will there be inflation or deflation?

A: Both, most likely. If the rise of Hitler is any indicator, first there will be hyperinflation followed by depression, then a crash in the economy.

Jim Rickards uses John Maynard Keynes definition of a depression:

"John Maynard Keynes's definition of depression as a "chronic condition of subnormal activity for a considerable period without any marked tendency either towards recovery or towards complete collapse".

Jim also warns:

"In the fullness of time, the 2020 lockdown of the U.S. economy will be viewed as the greatest policy blunder ever. Lost wealth and income will be measured in trillions of dollars."

In his book, *The New Great Depression*; Jim warns that COVID-19:

"Will lead to the greatest economic collapse in U.S. history".

Q: Is Jim Rickards correct?

A: I'm not sure that's the most important question. Jim, who has run currency war games for the Defense Department and CIA, knows more than most people about war games with money. The better question to ask yourself is:

"If Jim is right and the greatest economic collapse in history is coming, the 'WOKE' question is: What will you do?"

In 1972, when the tiny Vietnamese woman "woke me up" I began saving gold and silver, not dollars, and today, Bitcoin.

Again, what will you do?

Is history repeating? Hitler rose to power in 1933, after the German Weimar government, kept printing money pretending they were paying for WWI reparations.

In 2021, The Fed, Treasury, and Wall Street keep printing money, pretending the US economy is strong.

Jim Rickards warns:

> *"Gold is the world's least understood asset class. Confusion arises because gold is traded like a commodity, yet gold is not a commodity, it is money."*

> *"Central banks and finance ministries do not hold copper, aluminum, or steel supplies, yet they hold gold. The only explanation for central bank gold hoards is the obvious one - gold is money."*

Jim saves "things that last." He invests in gold, real estate and museum-quality art.

Ernest Hemingway warned:

> *"The first panacea for a mismanaged nation is inflation of the currency; the second is war. Both bring a temporary prosperity; both bring a permanent ruin. But both are the refuge of political and economic opportunists."*

Repeating Thomas Jefferson's warning:

> *"If the American people ever allow private banks to control the issue of their currency, first by inflation, then by deflation, the banks and corporations that will grow up around [the banks] will deprive the people of all property until their children wake-up homeless on the continent their fathers conquered.*

And Lenin's:

> *"The establishment of a central bank is 90% of communizing a nation."*
> *"The best way to destroy the capitalist system is to debauch the currency."*
> *"The way to crush the bourgeoise is to grind them between the millstones of taxation and inflation."*

In 2019... COVID-19 entered our lives.

Lenin warned:

> *"Medicine is the keystone of the arch of socialism."*

COVID-19 appeared in October, after the September 17, 2019 crash in the Repo market.

The economy was shutdown, people were locked down, not allowed to work, go to church, or go to school, censor ship began as rioters began burning and looting.

Marx warned:

> *"Change the economic base and you will change human beings."*

Although Trump campaigned vigorously and tirelessly, and Biden hid in his basement, Trump still lost the reelection.

Stalin warned:

> *Voters decide nothing. Vote counters decide everything!*

Trump's Wall

In 2020, why did President Biden and Vice-President Kamala Harris, stop Trumps Wall and allow millions to pour into America?

In August of 2021, 340,000 illegals crossed America's southern border.

I think of Thomas Sowell's words of warning:

> *"The more people who are dependent on government handouts, the more votes the left can depend on for an ever-expanding welfare state."*

War is always about money.

Jim Rickards writes about a war fought with money, in his book *Currency Wars*.

> *"Printing dollars at home means higher inflation in China, higher food prices in Egypt and stock bubbles in Brazil. Printing money means that U.S. debt is devalued so foreign creditors get paid back in cheaper dollars. The devaluation means higher unemployment in developing economies as their exports become more expensive for Americans. The resulting inflation*

also means higher prices for inputs needed in developing economies like copper, corn, oil and wheat. Foreign countries have begun to fight back against U.S.-caused inflation through subsidies, tariffs and capital controls; the currency war is expanding fast."

As we learned in the Marine Corps, war uses many different types of weapons. The U.S. dollar is one weapon. COVID-19 might be another one of those weapons. COVID-19 appeared around the same time the people of Hong Kong were rioting against the Chinese Communist Party. Is the timing suspect... and the target mass destruction of the U.S. economy?

CHAPTER SIXTEEN

RISE ABOVE

How do we protect ourselves from the loss of our freedoms? While it's easier said than done, it starts with each of us taking responsibility of what we can control. We can control the information we put into our heads and how we process that information. We can choose teachers — sources of all that will shape so many lives — that we trust and who want to support our freedoms, versus quash them.

Freedom Means... Rise Above
We can control our emotions and not fall victim to the rhetoric and opinions designed to fuel fury and division. We can rise above the fray... and look at the facts. From the edge of the coin, so we can see and appreciate both sides.

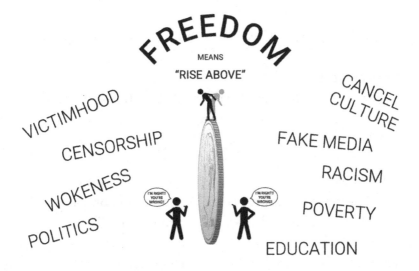

In July 2021, I was sitting in a picturesque café, having breakfast in Botswana, Africa.

All around me was an array of people, African, white, and Asian, teens, middle age, old, rich, and poor. All had cellphones. Even a beggar on the street, had a cell phone.

I, too, was on my cell phone. I was texting Marin Katusa, in Vancouver, British Columbia, Canada. We were finalizing a "Green New Deal," that would have made Socialist Alexandria Ocasio-Cortez happy. Marin Katusa is the author of *The Rise of America,* for which I wrote the Foreword. Marin and I were finalizing a Carbon Credits business, which was to be taken public in a few months.

> Q: Are you saying a socialist like Alexandria Ocasio Cortez is making you, a capitalist, rich?
> A: Yes. The irony there *is* really rich, isn't it? Socialists like AOC are pros at blaming and complaining. She does not know how to save the environment or how to make money. That is why she is a socialist. She is a "political hustler" whose money comes from campaign contributions... handouts from rich socialist liberals on the left who hate capitalists.

The good news is that her "Green New Deal" will make capitalists very rich.

Fake Environmentalists
The "environmental movement" has been called the Trojan Horse of Marxism. Marxists enter our schools, hiding in their Trojan Horse, a gift to the schools known as "educational curriculum."

In the *Aeneid* by Virgil, after a fruitless 10-year siege of the city of Troy, the Greeks, led by Odysseus, constructed a huge wooden horse and hid a select force of men inside. After the Greeks pretended to sail away, the Trojans pulled the horse into their city as a victory trophy. That night the Greek force crept out of the horse and opened the gates for the rest of the Greek army, which had sailed back under cover of night. The Greeks entered and destroyed the city of Troy, ending the war.

Marxists enter our schools in the same way. Under the cover of "saving the environment," Marxist plant their ideas into the head of students. "Black Lives Matter" and "Critical Race Theory" get into student's heads in the same way.

> Q: Are you saying Marxist ideology has enters our schools as Trojan Horses?
>
> A: It certainly is something to think about. As Thomas Sowell warned:
>
> *"Education is not merely neglected in many of our schools today... but is replaced to a great extent by ideological indoctrination."*

Emotions vs. Facts

Marxist ideology enters educational systems, as gifts to teachers — teachers already steeped in post-modernist education doctrine. Post-modernist education, Marxism, socialism, communism, and fascism are driven by emotion and opinions, not facts.

Capitalism requires facts. The reason bankers ask me for my financial statement is because bankers want to know the facts. And numbers tell the story. My financial statement is my report card that tells a banker how smart I am with money.

Money is a very emotional subject, and most people cannot handle the facts. Truth is measured in facts. For example:

1– You have $3,000 in savings earning 1.5% in interest and you have $15,000 in credit card debt at $18% interest.

2 – You have $95,000 in student loan debt and earn $35,000 a year.

3 – You earn $50,000 a year but spend $55,000.

4 – You lease a $75,000 car, then worry when gas prices go up.

Those are facts. Those are truths.

Post-modernist education will blame capitalists for causing these personal financial problems. That is why I doubt post-modernist education could ever include real financial education. To paraphrase Jack Nicholson's character, Col. Jessup, in *A Few Good Men*: "They can't handle the truth."

Excuses vs. Facts

When I was about 14 years old, rich dad had his son and me collect rent from his tenants. I'm sure I've shared this story before...
We quickly learned why most were poor. Everyone who could not pay the rent had an excuse.

When rich dad asked us what we learned, I jokingly replied:
"I now have a PhD in excuses."

I also realized that I had heard many of the same excuses from my parents.

Repeating Nicholson's warning again, in response to the attorney's demand for the truth: "*You can't handle the truth.*"

That is why financial statements are essential "capitalist tools" for entrepreneurs in the B and I quadrants.

If you want to change your life and grow richer, a person who learns how to make mistakes, learns from the mistakes you must be able to handle "the truth" and "the facts" Handling the truth often means looking in the mirror. Your personal financial statement is your mirror. Your moment of truth. Your report card in the real world once you leave school.

> Q: Is that why the *CASHFLOW* game was created? I've heard you say that the real game board is the financial statement...
> A: That's right. And that's why the "auditor" is an important component of the game and the Financial Statement. In the real world of capitalism, auditors are essential for you to know and "handle" the truth. The auditor needs to know the facts.

Q: Es and Ss do not require financial statements?

A: Correct. Bank statements and tax returns are usually all Es and Ss require.

Q: Is that why schools will never teach real financial education?

A: As you probably know, I have my opinion on that. Teachers might be able to teach financial education for Es and Ss, but not for Bs and Is. They can teach people how to get a high school or college diploma, how to get a job, balance a check book, save money, live debt-free, and invest in a government retirement program, sponsored by Wall Street, such as a 401(k). But that's probably about it.

I doubt teachers in the E and S quadrant can teach real financial education for people who want to become entrepreneurs in the B and I quadrant. I doubt most teachers, even college professors, have quarterly audited financial statements, a requirement for real capitalists.

Many schoolteachers live paycheck to paycheck, on financial opinions and emotions... not facts. And we often see 'equality of outcomes' confused with 'equality of opportunities' in discussions on inequality.

Most schoolteachers have low financial IQ, which a person's ability to solve financial problems.

Most teachers are financially illiterate, which means they do not speak the language of money.

Most teachers teach environmental issues with a socialist twist, Critical Race Theory, gender pronouns, and the everyone-gets-a-trophy philosophy. Winners are seen as oppressors.

These are all good questions for you to think about:
What's your opinion? What do you think? How financially sophisticated are most teachers? How many teachers that you know are living paycheck to paycheck like the parents of the students they teach?

Parents Become Terrorists

On October 11, 2021: U.S. Attorney General Merrick Garland opened an investigation into alleged threats of violence against school boards across the country. Garland directed the FBI and the U.S. Attorneys' Offices to carry out the investigation, which will be looking into parents who've participated in protests, demonstrations, and lively debates at school board meetings.

Q: Are you saying the FBI is now tracking down *parents* as terrorists?
A: They've been called "domestic terrorists" The FBI does not realize the terrorists are the teachers and Marxist curriculum.

Q: Why does the Attorney General of the United States do this?
A: In looking at the facts I found that Merrick Garland's daughter is married to founder of an education group that promotes Critical Race Theory.

More facts:
- Rebecca Garland married Xan Tanner, Panorama Education co-founder, in 2018.

- Xan Tanner's company partners with schools on a number of data tools including surveys that gauge students' emotional and mental well-being.
- A survey given to 12-year-olds allegedly asks them about their sexuality.
- Panorama Education has contracts with schools in NYC, San Francisco, and Dallas.
- Critics of the company's surveys say they promote Critical Race Theory.

And one more: In 2016, Merrick Garland was nominated by President Barack Obama to the Supreme Court of the United States.

Q: Is President Obama behind teaching Critical Race Theory?
A: I don't know. What do you think?

Q: So who are the real terrorists? The teachers? Parents? Garland? Obama?
A: I suggest you look at the *facts,* do more fact-finding, then form your own *opinion.*

I Am an Environmentalist

That's a fact. I agree we need to protect and save our environment. I love our oceans. Facts are, I grew up surfing and went to the academy to sail our oceans. So did Bucky Fuller, who grew up on the ocean and graduated from the U.S. Naval Academy. That is why Fuller said to our class:

"Men of the sea are different from men of the land."

Q: What did Fuller mean when he said that?
A: Men and women of the sea must be aware, live-in harmony, and respect the power of the ocean, the environment, universe, and God. Man can pretend to be God on land...but man is not God on the ocean.

I could also probably be called a "tree hugger." Facts are, I plant trees everywhere I go. Our oceans and trees are the lungs and purification systems of planet earth.

I am *not* a Marxist, socialist, or communist. A person can be an environmentalist and a capitalist.

Q: What makes you an environmentalist?
A: Facts are a good start: I invest in projects that protect the environment. I put money where my heart lies.

Q: Does Alexandria Ocasio Cortez invest in environmental businesses?
A: I don't know. What do you think? What are the facts? What is your opinion? My opinion is... I doubt AOC invests in the environment. I suspect she uses her "Green New Deal" to troll for contributions from the socialist, liberal left.

In 2021, every time President Biden got into hot water, he would "mumble" something about saving the environment. He is the worst type of environmentalist — a fake one.

The Good News
Capitalists make money solving problems. I invested in a Carbon Credits "start-up" because the business will solve massive environmental problems and offer high-paying technical jobs. As an environmentalist and a capitalist, I am likely to make a lot of money investing with Marin Katusa in his "Carbon Credits" start-up. That is freedom.

I invested with Marin because his Carbon Credits business plan calls for Carbon Rangers.

Q: What are Carbon Rangers?
A: Carbon Rangers are young people who are trained in the use of the latest technology, to go into the environment, such as the woods. A Carbon Ranger's job is to gather fact-based information on the state

of the trees, soil, water, air, insects, and animals, aka the environment. Carbon Rangers will gain hands on technical experience and a lifetime career, without the requirement of a college degree.

In alignment with the motto of Kings Point — *Acta Non Verba... Deeds not words* — put my money where my heart is.

Another saying is: *"Money talks... and BS walks."*

Fake Bankers

Q: Is that why you invested in Bitcoin? As a protest to the Fed being a Marxist enterprise?

A: In my opinion, the Fed Chairman is like the Wizard of Oz. The Fed is a joke. The Fed Chairman is a small man — like the Wizard himself was, tucked behind a curtain with a microphone to project a "great and powerful" Oz — hiding behind his PhD. In 2008, rather than fix the mistakes the Fed caused, the Fed bailed out the richest people on earth and fellow bankers.

This Wizard of Oz, aka The Fed, hands out "fake money." Fake money known as Quantitative Easing... or producing money out of thin air. This "fake money" makes the rich richer... and makes the poor and middle class poorer. Since 1980, the Fed has caused rising inflation and falling interest rates. Rising inflation and falling interest rates have destroyed workers' wages and savers' savings.

In 1983, Fuller's book, *GRUNCH of Giants* was published.

Since the 1980s the Fed has trained the Pavloff Dogs of Banking and Wall Street to say things like "The Greenspan Put," "Don't fight the Fed," and "Buy the dips."

By 2020, the gap between the rich and everyone else was an IED, an Improvised Explosive Device, a pile of straw waiting for a match to ignite it.

Are we headed for a market crash? Or another Depression? The crash already happened. And we have been in a depression since 2008.

The Crash

On September 17, 2019, the day there was a crash in the Repo Market of the Shadow Banking System the Fed began handing out billions in fake money, aka fiat currency. Rather than fix the problem, the Fed turned a bad situation into a future financial disaster.

The giant crash was in the "credit market" not the "stock market." That is why my opinion is that there is something fishy about the timing and appearance of COVID-19. I have no facts. I am not a doctor. It's just my opinion.

Repeating Lenin's warning:

"Medicine is the keystone of the arch of socialism."

Unfortunately, I see a bigger crash is coming. The crash will start in the credit markets, which will lead to the crash in the stock market, real estate market, and the global economy.

In his latest book, *The New Depression*, Jim Rickards defines the word "depression" and why the world entered the "New Depression" in 2009. The Fed saved competent and incompetent bankers. The Fed gave trillions of dollars to bad banks and crooked bankers at extremely low interest rates.

The Fed should have let bad banks fail. The Fed was like a teacher who gives trophies to everyone.

Bailing out rich and incompetent bankers weakens the economy. Bailing out rich bankers makes life more difficult for honest working people.

Printing money creates inflation in financial markets, as it blows bubbles in the stock market, bond market, and housing market. In 2021, millions of working people cannot afford a home. Many homeless people have jobs but cannot afford a place to live.

When the Fed saves incompetent bankers, the Fed contributes to the ever-widening divide between rich and poor. The gap between rich and poor creates economic instability and social unrest.

Repeating Marx's warning yet again:
"Revolutions are the locomotives of history."

It's good to remember that the Federal Reserve Bank is not Federal. The Fed is as "Federal", as Federal Express. The Fed is a private business. It is owned by a global cartel of extremely rich people. The Fed is not American in spirit. The heart of the Fed is Marxist.

Remember Lenin's warning:
"The establishment of a central bank is 90% of communizing a nation."

And Thomas Jefferson's:
"If the American people ever allow private banks to control the issue of their currency, first by inflation, then by deflation, the banks and corporations that will grow up around [the banks] will deprive the people of all property until their children wake-up homeless on the continent their fathers conquered. The issuing power should be taken from the banks and restored to the people, to whom it properly belongs."

Here's another fact: The Fed we have today is America's 3rd Central Bank. The Fed was created in 1913, the same year the Internal Revenue Service was created. An interesting coincidence... if that's all it is.

Q: Why was the Fed created in the same year as the Internal Revenue Service?

A: Because for the Fed to print fake money, the government must be able to collect taxes. One reason why the dollar has more power than Bitcoin is because all U.S taxes must be paid in U.S. dollars.

Q: So it's all connected — the Fed, the government, money, and taxes?

A: Yes. The U.S. dollar would not exist without taxes. Remember Marx's warning:

"A heavy or progressive, or graduated income tax is necessary for the proper development of communism."

A Tax-Free America

America was born as a tax revolt, the Boston Tea Party, in 1773. America was born as a "tax-free" nation. It was not born as a "slave nation" as the 1619 Project wants us to believe.

Two more facts:

One: In 1944 the U.S. dollar became the reserve currency of the world at the Bretton Woods Conference. In 1944 the United States promised to back every dollar with gold. In 1944, the U.S. dollar became, literally, "as good as gold."

And two: In 1971, President Nixon took the US dollar off the gold standard.

Lenin's words predict the future:

"The best way to destroy the capitalist system is to debauch the currency."

I believe it was Mao who said these prophetic words in 1971 after Nixon took the dollar off the gold standard: *"I can now see the end of America."*

The Fed, our money, and taxes are core of Karl Marx's dream of central government control over capitalism.

Tax the Rich

Alexandria Ocasio Cortez used her gown as a political statement at the 2021 Met Gala. What was her message... and is she a capitalist or a communist?

I say: Look at the facts. Look at the picture. Reread Marx's warning about a graduated income tax. Remember the Fed and IRS were created together. Reread Lenin's warning about "debauching the currency." Then you decide if AOC is a capitalist or communist.

Making matters more suspect, AOC wore the gown to the New York Met Gala, an event that cost $30,000 for a ticket and $275,000 for a table. Did AOC pay for her ticket? Did she buy a table? Or was she there fishing for more campaign contributions from fellow Marxists?

I want to be as free and independent from the Fed, the U.S. Treasury, and Wall Street as possible. I value my freedom from money. I use debt to buy assets and don't save money — I save gold, silver, and Bitcoin. Debt is tax free because when you borrow money you "print money."

Words of Warning

Debt is dangerous. The reason rich dad advised me to take real estate courses when I returned from Vietnam, was to learn how to use debt to create infinite returns. Infinite returns means you do not need money to make money and can pay little to no taxes.

Before you use debt as money, I strongly suggest you read Ken Mc Elroy's books on how he invests in real estate, Tom Wheelwright's book on tax-free wealth, and Garrett Sutton's books on how to use corporations to accelerate tax losses, accelerate corporate gains, and protect your assets from predators.

I encourage you to be extremely cautious in taking on debt if you have limited financial education. That said, taking the time to learn about how to use debt to your advantage can impact your taxes. Tax breaks are tax incentives for entrepreneurs who do what the government wants done. As an entrepreneur in the B quadrant, I pay less taxes because I create jobs.

Killing Jobs

When President Biden killed the Keystone Pipeline project, not only did he kill thousands of high-paying jobs, he caused the price of oil to rise, causing inflation, making life harder for the working class, making the United States more dependent on foreign oil and a weaker militarily. Add to this poor decision-making and leadership, he left billions of dollars of American weapons in the hands of enemies of the United States and Israel.

How do we achieve freedom? We rise above by utilizing another of Bucky Fuller's Generalized Principles: *"Unity is plural...at minimum two."*

This illustration of the three-sided coin puts this generalized principle into a picture...

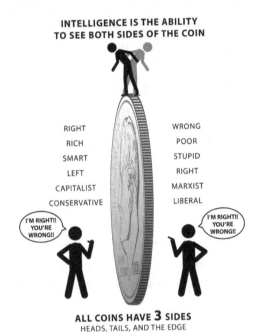

INTELLIGENCE IS THE ABILITY
TO SEE BOTH SIDES OF THE COIN

RIGHT	WRONG
RICH	POOR
SMART	STUPID
LEFT	RIGHT
CAPITALIST	MARXIST
CONSERVATIVE	LIBERAL

I'M RIGHT!! YOU'RE WRONG!!

I'M RIGHT!! YOU'RE WRONG!!

ALL COINS HAVE 3 SIDES
HEADS, TAILS, AND THE EDGE

And what do we need to rise above? All the things that can turn us into victims... versus architects of our own futures.

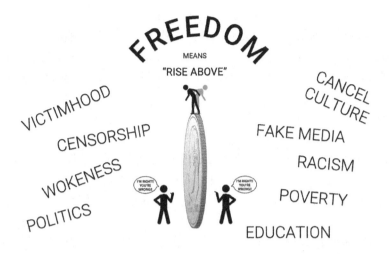

FREEDOM
MEANS
"RISE ABOVE"

VICTIMHOOD
CENSORSHIP
WOKENESS
POLITICS

CANCEL CULTURE
FAKE MEDIA
RACISM
POVERTY
EDUCATION

We Are All Equal

The Marxist liberal elite left wants us to believe capitalists are oppressors. Capitalists are not the oppressors. The academic elite liberal left wants us to believe capitalists create inequality. It is the academic elite liberal left who divide, creating inequality. Capitalists create equality.

How do capitalists create equality? There are many examples of this. One is Henry Ford. Ford was one of America's greatest capitalists. His personal mission statement was: *"Democratize the automobile."*

His mission was to make the automobile available to the masses. Other car builders were producing cars only for the rich. Henry Ford changed all that. He made his cars affordable for more people. Ford followed another of Bucky Fuller's Generalized Principles: *"The more people I serve...the more effective I become."*

In my opinion, serving as many people as possible — legally, honestly, morally, and ethically — is the best way to get rich.

Can equality be achieved? I think it can. The academic, liberal elite want to divide us. That is why they focus on inequality. They complain, bitch, moan, and blame capitalists for inequalities in the world. Rather than unite, the academic socialist elite divide us. A Divided States of America serves their agenda.

The Great Equalizers

Regardless of the color of our skin, we all bleed red. We all have 24 hours in a day, we all need food, air, water, and shelter. We all have problems, we all have emotions, we all have highs and lows... goals and dreams.

In 1873, Samuel Colt, an inventor and capitalist, invented the Colt 45 revolver. It was marketed as "The Peace Maker." It was also marketed as "The Equalizer." It was called the equalizer because it gave all men and all women a relatively "equal" chance in a physical confrontation. A person's size, strength, gender, or age no longer mattered. A small weak person with a Colt 45 could stand up to a bigger stronger person.

College drop-out and entrepreneur, Steve Jobs created another equalizer — his Apple iPhone.

Today billions of people hold access to information and facts in the palm of their hand. We no longer need an expensive college education to learn from some of the smartest people on planet earth.

Heaven or Hell

The reason I have spent so much time in the book writing on the Federal Reserve Bank, is because we have been warned. Without real financial education, it seems to me that billions of people are heading into financial hell. George Washington warned the world. Thomas Jefferson and Marx warned the world. Congressman Ron Paul has warned the world. My instructor at Kings Point warned our class.

It wasn't until I joined the Marine Corps, flying in Vietnam, that I saw it with my own eyes... Karl Marx's Communist Manifesto in real life.

It took flying behind enemy lines in 1972, looking for gold, for me to meet my best teacher. The Vietnamese woman selling gold turned my instructor's lessons at the Academy...into real life experiences.

She validated Lenin's warning:
"The best way to destroy the capitalist system is to debauch the currency.

She verified my instructor at Kings Point's lessons... his warnings. What he had taught to our class in 1965 was coming true.

School vs. Studies

In 1983, I read Fuller's *GRUNCH of Giants*, and for the first time in my life I became a student.

Another of Fuller's books, *Education Automation: Freeing the Scholar to Return to His Studies,* is about getting the student out of school and allowing him or her to study what the student's native genius draws them to and what they are interested in. As I've said, it was at that point that the pieces of my life's puzzle — my past, present, and future — fell into place.

After reading *GRUNCH,* I understood why, as a 9-year-old child, I was making nickels, dimes, and quarters out of lead toothpaste tubes I melted down. I understood why I had asked my teacher, repeatedly, when I was nine years old, "When will we learn about money?" When she informed me that money was not taught in schools, I went in search of a new teacher. That teacher was my rich dad. Rich dad taught his son and me about money playing *Monopoly.* That love of games and the power they have as teaching tools ignited the fire for education that led to creating the *CASHFLOW* game.

Although I did not know it at the time, my study was about how governments and banks play winners and losers with fake money.

Most important of all, I learned that I had to get out of school... to return to my studies.

CHAPTER SEVENTEEN

BE THE FED

I'm far from the only one supporting this battle cry:
  Don't Fight the Fed — Be the Fed

The Fake Fed
Financial experts say: "Don't fight the Fed."

I say the "Fed is Fake." So is the Fed Chairman.

Rather than "Don't fight the Fed," I prefer to "Be the Fed."

I say, "The Fed Chairman is the Wizard of Oz." I say that because, just like the wizard in *The Wizard of Oz*, the Fed has no power. I wrote about that in an article for *Jetset* magazine in 2020.

A picture is always worth 1,000 words and this illustration simplifies an extremely complex subject — the Fed, the monetary system, and the Shadow Banking System... the real banking system. The illustration on the following page supports my promise to KISS... keep it simple.

Q: Are you saying the Shadow Banking System has more power than the Fed?

A: Yes. Much more power because the Shadow Banking System is much bigger and does not have to follow the Fed's rules.

Q: Is that why crashes in the Repo Market and Reverse Repo Markets are important?

A: Yes. Remember this: In 2008, the Fed started QE, Quantitative Easing. Whenever financial experts hear those words, they believe the Fed is "printing money." The facts are that the Fed does not print money. The Fed produces "bank reserves," which are not money. You and I cannot spend "bank reserves."

Q: Is that why you called the Fed Chairman the Wizard of Oz?

A: Yes. When the Fed Chairman announces more QE everyone thinks the Fed is printing money. When people think the Fed is "printing money," people think "inflation is coming."

Q: Is inflation coming?

A: Not necessarily. But that is what the "wizard" wants you to think. It is known as *managing expectancy*. In the stock market, it is called *forward guidance*.

Q: People expect inflation?

A: Yes. In 2021, the facts are, while millions drank the Kool-aide, "Don't fight the Fed, expecting inflation, the massive shadow banking system was "deflating."

Q: Is that why you say, the Fed Chairman has no power?

A: Yes. The shadow banking system is massive. It has more power than the Fed because it is so much bigger than the Fed? In 2021, everyone was expecting "Inflation," because the Fed is reportedly "pumping billions every month into the economy."

Two major events happened in 1913:

    1 – The Fed was created.

    2 – The IRS was created.

Taxes paid to the IRS must be in U.S. dollars. The Fed issues "bank reserves" to the banks. Money is created when people borrow money from the banks. That is the money system the Fed controls. The IRS collects taxes paid in U.S. dollars.

Q: So how does a person Be the Fed?

A: The way to "Be the Fed" is to be able to "create your own assets." The FED and the IRS need Bs and Is, big-business entrepreneurs who can "create their own assets." The money system needs a lot of money. Es and Ss do not borrow enough money — via credit cards, student loans, home and auto loans, and consumer debt — to provide enough money for the economy to float.

When a B-I entrepreneur creates a "big asset," like Ken McElroy does when he acquires a 400-unit apartment building, the banks are happy to lend Ken millions in U.S. dollars. That is how money is created. The IRS, the Tax Man, is happy to offer tax incentives to B and I entrepreneurs. That is how those in the I quadrant can often pay 0% in taxes.

You can Be the Feb by creating assets and borrowing money.

By creating your own assets, and borrowing money?

When Ken McElroy borrows, let's say, $30 million dollars, using his apartment complex as collateral and paying little to nothing in taxes for the money he makes or borrows... Ken is The Fed.

Bank Reserves, issued by the Fed, back up Ken's collateral, his apartment complex. The money Ken borrows, enters the economy as U.S. dollars.

That is how you can Be the Fed.

CHAPTER EIGHTEEN

POST-MODERNISM VS. ANCIENT WISDOM

The purpose of this book, *Capitalist Manifesto*, is to counter the post-modernist Marxist education taught in our schools.

Opinions and Emotions vs. Facts

Postmodernist idea pathogens are taking root in education. Post-modernist education has all but replaced STEM — Science, Technology, Engineering, and Mathematics.

Post-modernist education is education based upon opinions and emotions — versus facts and evidence.

In words often attributed to Plato, the ancient Greek philosopher:

> *"Opinion is the lowest form of human knowledge. It requires no accountability, no understanding."*

And Thomas Sowell warned:

> *"Facts are not liberals' strong suit. Rhetoric is."*

Q: So how do you counter post-Modernist education taught in schools?
A: By teaching facts... not opinions driven by emotion.

Repeating this warning and paying close attention to the choice of words:

> *"Opinion is the lowest form of human knowledge. It requires no accountability, no understanding."*

Opinion... lowest form... human knowledge...

It follows, then, that Post-modernist, Marxist education is based upon the lowest form of human knowledge.

Two more important words: *accountability* and *understanding.* "Opinion... requires no accountability or understanding."

Those two words are the foundation of our Capitalist Manifesto, which began in 1996, with the creation of a tool, an artifact, for gaining both knowledge and understanding as well as an appreciation of the personal accountability related to personal finance and money. It was the *CASHFLOW* board game.

Kim and I created *CASHFLOW* to teach personal financial *accountability* and *understanding* of how money works. And that process starts with facts... not opinions.

As Rich dad repeatedly said to his son and me:

> *"My banker has never asked me for my report card. My banker does not care what school I went to or how many degrees I have. My banker wants to see my financial statement, because my financial statement is my report card in the real world."*

Bankers want to see your facts... not your opinions.

When Thomas Sowell was asked what led to his shift away from embracing Marxist principles, he didn't hesitate for a moment and answered with one word: "Facts."

The Highest Form of Knowledge
The complete quote, attributed to Plato, includes these words:

> "... it requires profound purpose larger than the self."

> *"The highest form of knowledge is empathy, for it requires us to suspend our egos and live in another's world. It requires profound purpose larger than the self."*

And that's where our mission comes in... "to elevate the financial well-being of humanity."

In very simple terms, Rich Dad's Capitalist Manifesto positions post-modernist education against ancient wisdom. My rich dad's position on facts and the power of a financial statement versus academia and today's willingness to trade facts for opinions.

In the 1930s, Marxists left the Frankfurt School in Germany. Frankfurt School teachers are disciples of Marx. In the 1930s, the Karl Marx's teachings metastasized into Columbia University's Teachers College.

As Lenin warned:

> *"Give me four years to teach the children and the seed I have sown will never be uprooted."*

From Columbia University, the "roots" of Marxism spread and metastasized into public education, religion, banking, government, Wall Street, media, Hollywood, Silicon Valley, and — most recently — the military.

In his book *Madness of Crowds* (2019) Douglas Murray estimates that 18 percent of all university professors today are avowed Marxists.

Murray's book examines the 21st century's most divisive issues: sexual orientation, feminism, transsexuality, technology, and race. He reveals the astonishing new culture wars playing out in our workplaces, universities, schools, and homes in the names of social justice, identity politics, and intersectionality. We are living through a postmodern era in which the grand narratives of religion and political ideology have been distorted by a sense of victimhood and political correctness.

A KISS snapshot of that: Postmodern education teaches students to be snowflakes.

Alexander the Great warned:

> *"I am not afraid of an army of lions led by a sheep; I am afraid of an army of sheep led by a lion,"*

Repeating Jordan Peterson's words:

> *"And if you think tough men are dangerous, wait until you see what weak men are capable of."*

And Maria Montessori's warning:

> *"An education capable of saving humanity is no small undertaking: it involves the spiritual development of man, the enhancement of his value as an individual, and the preparation of young people to understand the times in which they live."*

Lenin promised:

> *"Whenever the cause of the people is entrusted to professors, it is lost."*

It's hard to believe that nearly a quarter of a century has passed since we launched the *CASHFLOW* game and watched CASHFLOW Clubs popping up all over the world. Kim and I created the game so that it — not us — could teach what we had learned about the road to financial freedom. We saw, first-hand, the power of people teaching people... using the game as their roadmap. Teachers are leaders and we have seen students transform into leaders in CASHFLOW Clubs around the world.

Q: Are you saying, with a real financial education, a cell phone, and access to the greatest real teachers in the world, you can be rich?

A: I am.

Q: Are you saying, even if you live the poorest cities of America or the most remote places of the world, you can become a rich capitalist?

A: I am.

Q: Are you saying, we all have the power to rise above the insanity of the world and achieve financial freedom?

A: Yes. You do not have to get into the arguments of who is right and who is wrong. You do not have to wear a mask or not wear a mask, take the jab, or lose your job. You don't have to work harder... only to pay more in taxes. That is not freedom.

Real Freedom

Rising above all the noise — the mandates, the dogma, the blame, and the anger — is real freedom. Freedom is worth studying for... and fighting for. And, most important of all: freedom is worth living for. Real freedom requires real financial education.

Repeating this ancient wisdom from earlier in this chapter:

"The highest form of knowledge is empathy, for it requires us to suspend our egos and live in another's world. It requires profound purpose larger than the self."

CASHFLOW Clubs are not about beating the other players. They're not about who makes the most money. The purpose of the Clubs is to learn by making mistakes, help fellow players learn, have fun, be patient and kind and understanding. They are a tremendous way to develop empathy for our fellow human beings... as we all learn together. Because it's a learning environment, players can "suspend their egos" and enjoy the fact that they are all students and not experts or specialists who are expected to know all the answers.

More of Plato's wisdom related to empathy that seems especially relevant today: "Be kind. Every person you meet is fighting a difficult battle."

In 2021 there are thousands of CASHFLOW Clubs all over the world, fulfilling the Capitalist Manifesto:
"The way to counter communism taught in our schools... is by teaching capitalism in our homes."

Plato's Ancient Wisdom
CASHFLOW Clubs put Plato's ancient wisdom into practice by avoiding opinions, using numbers as facts, teaching with empathy, and that requiring all players to suspend their egos and live in another's world.

Just because someone may be slow in learning the *CASHFLOW* game, does not mean they are stupid or will always be poor. The game is designed to be played over and over again, because repetition is the best way to learn. Tiger Woods would not have become a great golfer if he had quit the first time if he missed a putt or hit a ball into the water. Talent alone is not enough. Failure leads to success. Only people who never fail are failures.

The Language of Money
Playing the *CASHFLOW* game is like learning a language. By playing the game and watching the videos, players are learning the language of money and capitalism. They learn practical lessons about how money works in our everyday lives. It's called financial literacy.

As you know, it takes time to learn a language. For example, just because I am Japanese does not mean I can learn Japanese any easier than any other person who only speaks English, or Spanish, or Chinese. Like learning a new language, a commitment to becoming financially literate takes time and perseverance.

Why Post-Modernist Education Fails Students

Apart from using opinions versus facts as its foundation, the two biggest problems I see with post-modernist education are:

1 – Students are punished for making mistakes... which teaches them that making mistakes make them stupid.

2 – Post-modernist education teaches students to be brain slaves, "specialists," who must know all the answers on their own. "Brain slave specialists" do not help a fellow student because helping another student is called "cheating" and asking for help means you're "stupid."

As Einstein warned:

"Specialization is in fact only a fancy form of slavery wherein the "expert" is fooled into accepting a slavery by making him feel that he in turn is a socially and culturally preferred-ergo, highly secure-lifelong profession."

Bucky Fuller warned:

"Everyone is born a genius...but the process of living de-geniuses them."

He also said the most important of life lessons is:

"The courage to adhere to the truth, then, the courage to face ourselves with the clear admission of all the mistakes we have made. Mistakes are only sins when not admitted."

If we give a man a fish, we feed him for a day and keep him dependent and under the control of the government and its programs. If we teach men and women and children to "fish" — learn skills so they can be self-reliant — we empower them to take control. Teaching is at the foundation of The Rich Dad Company... and using the *CASHFLOW* game, people can teach other people. They can learn together and learn from each other and have so much fun in the process that they forget that it's "education" and a life skill that is a part of their everyday lives.

The ancient wisdom of Plato, as well as that of Einstein and Fuller, can be applied to many facets of our lives: *"Opinion is the lowest form of human knowledge. It requires no accountability, no understanding."*

Who will be accountable for the future of education — not only who is teaching, but what is taught — or will we let the "opinions" of postmodernism take root and grow?

Today it seems as though we are all fighting battles... different kinds of battles, all fought in different ways. Many of those battles are for our freedoms — and one of the most precious freedoms is financial freedom.

PART FOUR

The Future of Money
and
the Future of Communism

INTRODUCTION
TO PART FOUR

BIG BROTHER IS WATCHING

'We've been warned...' is a theme of this book and weaves together past, present, and future.

In words that are often attributed to Abraham Lincoln, from a speech he gave in 1838, came this warning:

> *"America will never be destroyed from the outside. If we falter and lose our freedoms it will be because we destroyed ourselves from within"*

I know that the idea of Big Brother "watching" us isn't anything new.

I know this book, *Capitalist Manifesto*, and I will be attacked, discredited, and invalidated.

That is why Jordan Peterson warns:

> *"If you think strong men are dangerous. Wait until you get a load of weak men."*

In today's social media environment, millions of weak men and women hide in the shadows, attacking people from their cell phones, stabbing strong people in the back for standing up for their convictions, attacking via mobs of fellow cowards. They murder our freedom of speech and impose censorship by spreading the pandemic of fear.

In the real world, strong men and women prefer face-to-face dialogue, holding debates and discussions... respectful of others' rights to their beliefs and opinions even when they disagree with them. That takes courage. The Cancel Culture, BLM, Antifa, and others operate on cowardice.

Fighting Fire with Fire
In preparation for the attacks by the socialist Cancel Culture and social justice warriors, we have developed series of You Tube educational videos and animated educational cartoons to fight back, no neutralize the fear and hatred spread by weak men and women... videos that feature real people who have fought communism with courage.

These gut-wrenching educational videos are real-life accounts of what happened when communist took over their countries, and when their freedom and wealth were stolen.

Included are other educational videos from military officers who describe what it feels like to go to war, against Marxists and communists.

Their personal accounts on communism may be the best real-life education you will receive on how communists are taking over the free world, democracy, and capitalism.

All of us are already under attack. Our freedoms are being stolen by fear — the fear of speaking out, censorship, political correctness, and gender pronouns.

I expect that after *Capitalist Manifesto* is released, the attack from weak men and women will escalate.

So remember George Orwell's warning:
> *"Big brother is watching you."*

These videos were created to give you the power to fight back with stories of courage and education... not threats, bullying, or bullets.

As Oprah Winfrey encourages:
> *"Where there is no struggle, there is no strength."*

All of these people have struggled against communism and have shared their stories:

1. Yenonmi Park
2. Debbie D'Souza
3. Philip Haslam
4. General Jack Bergman
5. Barry Mitchell
6. Trina Maduro
7. Nely Galan
8. Patrick Bet-David
9. Dan Cambell
10. Brigadier General Robert Spalding

The Rich Dad Company

To learn more about The Rich Dad Company
you can visit **Rich Dad.com**
A good place to start:
The Rich Dad Brand Story

CHAPTER NINETEEN

THE DAY AFTER TOMORROW

"The future depends on what you do today."
— Mahatma Gandhi

So, in 2020 and 2021, did Marx win?

We all have our points of view on this and mine is that he did. In 2020, Marx won. Marx won when my friend and co-author Donald Trump lost his bid for reelection.

I realize this sounds like sour grapes, but hear me out. If you dislike Donald Trump, I understand. Politics is a dirty, nasty, and corrupt game. I checked out of politics in the 1970s, when my poor dad ran for Lt. Governor of the State of Hawaii as a Republican. I avoid politics as much as possible.

Donald Trump and his sons have been friends of mine for years. I know them personally

This is not about politics. If you hate my friend, that is your freedom of choice. I did not write this book to change your mind about Donald Trump. I do not care if you are Republican, Democrat, conservative, or liberal. This book is not about religion or gender. Your religious beliefs and sexual preferences are none of anyone's business.

This book is about something far more important than politics, religion, sex, or race. This book is about our freedoms. This book is about how we have been warned for years that our freedoms are being stolen.

For example, how can you, me, and the President of the United States be censored by social media? What happened to our freedom of speech? Who gives Silicon Valley the right to censor and deny our freedom of speech? I certainly didn't.

In many ways we should have seen this coming. As I've said: we were warned. And I remind myself that it's hard to expect that we'd be taught this — so we could prepare and protect ourselves — when the primary organization stealing our freedoms is our educational system.

That is why, at great personal risk, I began this book with the NEA, the National Education Association, a labor union made up with highly educated people like my poor dad.

My generation, the Baby Boomers, had our heroes: John Kennedy, Martin Luther King, and Bobby Kennedy. They were all murdered and we watched it, and the aftermath, on television. Were their murders our warning? Was it our censorship? Were the messages "Stay in your lane" and "Obey... or else"? Were those horrific 'warnings,' in the 1960s, the same as "Get vaccinated, wear a mask... or get fired" threats in 2020 and 2021?

In 2021, Jordan Peterson, himself a college professor, warned:
> *"If you think strong men are dangerous, wait until you get a load of weak men."*

The sentiments in the song *Abraham, Martin, and John* and Jordan Peterson's warning prompted me create my Iron Dome. My Iron Dome is the series of YouTube videos that I've discussed throughout this book. The videos were created to give me and my company some degree of protection from weak men and women, the Woke Cancel Culture once this book is release.

As Mahatma Gandhi warned:
> *"The future depends on what you do today."*

Books on the Future

I want to be clear that I am not blaming academics and liberals for being Marxists, socialist, fascists, and communists. Most did not have the advantage I did of studying the books of Marx, Hitler, and Mao.

And most people do not realize Marx's *Communist Manifesto* is a book about the future.

There have been many books that warned us about the future. A few are:
Bucky Fuller's book *Critical Path*
Ayn Rand's book *Atlas Shrugged*
George Orwell's book *1984*
Jeff Booth's book *The Price of Tomorrow*
Strauss and Howe's book *The Fourth Turning*

Marx's View of the Future

Marx's *Communist Manifesto* is about Stage One and Stage Two, Marx's vision of the future once capitalism ends in revolution.

As I see it, Marx's Stage One ended in 2020. Stage One ended when, in 2020, President Trump lost his bid the reelection.
As Stalin warned:
It's not the people who vote that count. It's the people who count the votes.

As Marx warned:
"Democracy is the road to socialism.

In 2020, America became a socialist nation.

How do we know that? In 2020, America is now an 'entitlement' nation... a nation of Social Security, Medicare, Medicaid, and other entitlement and subsidy programs. Few dare to speak about personal responsibility.

Unfortunately, in 2020, millions of the Baby Boom generation are much like my poor dad, totally dependent upon the government for survival. That is socialism.

I've looked for other signs that Stage One is complete. Stage One was complete when postmodernist education took control of our education system. Postmodern education runs on opinions and emotions. Capitalists must operate on facts.

Here is an excerpt from *Communist Manifesto*, published in 1848, that we studied and discussed extensively at the Academy. In 1965 and 1996 we discussed what Communism would "look like." And how a shift from capitalism to socialism to communism could happen. The focus of our discussions was on the future. Today, that "future" is here. Marx's Stage 2... is here.

These words from *Communist Manifesto*,:

> "*Thus, in 1847, Socialism was a middle-class movement, Communism a working-class movement. Socialism was, on the continent at least, "respectable"; Communism was the very opposite.*"

Repeating the Warnings

Marx warned:

> "*Education is free. Freedom of education shall be enjoyed under the condition fixed by law and under supreme control of the state.*"

Marx also warned:

> "*The education of all children, from the moment that they can get along without a mother's care, shall be in state institutions.*"

Lenin warned:

> "*Give us a child for eight years and it will be a Bolshevik forever.*"

Hitler warned:

> "*Let me control the textbooks and I will control the state.*"

This I why I began this book with the NEA, The National Education Association.

Academics Jordan Peterson, Thomas Sowell, Victor Davis Hanson, Gad Saad, and Dennis Prager have been warning that postmodernist education is indoctrinating students, via Critical Race Theory, that they are "victims" and that "white people" are "oppressors."

Fuller, another academic warned us when he said:
"We are called to be the architects of the future, not its victims."

Postmodernist is teaching students to be victims, wimpy snowflakes from Snowflake U.

In 2020 Stage One was complete. Americans were now dependent upon the government for financial survival. Postmodern education was now under the supreme control of the state.

And not only is America socialist, but we have lost our First Amendment rights. In 2020, censorship is enforced by socialist media. A President is censored by socialist media. The World Health Organization (WHO) keeps finding new mutant strains of COVID, and soon we may all be vaccinated, wearing masks, and carrying a vaccine ID card.

What Mandates Mean
Mandates mean a loss of freedoms. Mask mandates, vaccine card mandates, business shut-down mandates, travel mandated... are all similar to Hitler mandating the Jews to wear a yellow star.

Our freedoms have been stolen. And the NEA is complicit by encouraging teachers to indoctrinate students into being snowflakes, victims, and racists.

Before Stage One, Marx believed that humans went through four levels of socio-economic development. The four levels are:

1. **Tribal**
   Hunter gatherers, with no class structure. The job of men was to hunt. The job of women was to gather and raise the kids. Their social economic structure was a tribe. Almost everyone, save for the chief, was equal.

Today many native Americans, and throughout the world, humans continue to operate as tribes.

2. Primitive Communism

The union of several tribes, communes, forming a city-state. Ancient Rome was formed in this way. Today Italy is a country.

Today, Rome and the Vatican are powerful city-states

3. Feudal Estates

City states evolved into feudal estates, castles, and walled cities. Feudal estates were ruled by kings, queens, priests, war lords... over serfs, and slaves. Cultivation of land created landlords. Craftsmen became entrepreneurs, small business owners such as butchers, bakers, and candlestick makers. Peasants worked the land. A proportion of production was handed over to the aristocracy and the church. It was a tax. England and Japan are remnants of feudal estates. You can still see castles and palaces, in many parts of the world.

Today, England still has a queen and Japan has an emperor.

4. Capitalism

As commerce grew, members of feudal society began to accumulate capital, as well as debt. Inventions such as steel and gunpowder produced industrialists, which eventually led to the English Revolution of 1640 and The French Revolution of 1789, which led to capitalistic societies, structured around commodities, production, and profit.

Modern capitalism began when the agrarian age ended, and the industrial age began.

According to historians, the Industrial Age is a period of history where animals and hand tools with replaced with power-driven machines such as the power loom, the steam engine, and internal combustion engine.

Today America and even China are capitalist nations.

A Book About the Future

As I've said, Marx's *Communist Manifesto* is a book about the future.

Capitalism infuriated Marx. Marx believed the proletariat; the working class were fooled into believing he or she is free because he or she is paid for their labor... but owned nothing. Only a small percentage of the population was in control of capital. The working class, labor, employees, are alienated. As the gap between rich and poor grew, the importance of kings and queens diminished, capitalists became the new sources of wealth and power... which further infuriated Marx.

Marx believed workers were out of control of their lives. He believed external forces were driving workers into "getting a job" but someone else owns the means of production. Marx was in this category of people, an academic.

It further angered Marx that factories, farms, and businesses were private property, which are passed on to their children, but not to the proletarians, labor, employees, the paid slaves.

That is why the theme of his *Communist Manifesto* is in his words:
> *"The theory of Communism may be summed up in one sentence: Abolish all private property."*

Fueled by his anger, he wrote *Communist Manifesto* in 1848. He saw the future in to waves, Stage One and Stage Two.

Stage One has ended.
   In 2021 American education is now under state control.
   In 2021 more and more Americans are now depended upon the state for money.
   In 2021 America's First Amendment rights are muzzeled by Socialist media
   In 2021 America is now a socialist nation.

And Stage Two is beginning...

Ripe for Revolution
What will happen in Stage Two, in the future? What can we expect in 2022 and beyond?

America is ripe for revolution.

Three events I will cover in this chapter on the future include:
1. Violence will increase
2. Murders will increase
3. Government crypto will take over economy.

As Ayn Rand predicted in her book *Atlas Shrugged,* capitalists will go into hiding. Today many capitalists have second passports, second homes, and overseas bank accounts.

Violence Escalates
In Marx's Stage One, socialism replaces democracy. As Ayn Rand predicted, when socialists take over the economy falls apart. People do not work, trains do not run, and shelves are bare.

In Stage Two, Communism replaces socialism. Historically, communists murder socialists.

Marx warned:
> *"The socialist state would control the economy and means of production and suppress the bourgeoise's counter revolution and any opposition."*

We've all been a witness to parents being labeled as terrorists.

In 2021, the FBI declared: "vocal parents" are "domestic terrorists." Parents are arrested as terrorists for questioning Critical Race Theory being taught in schools.

And so it began...

On June 22, 2021 *it was reported that*
"Parents were arrested while protesting against Critical Race Theory (CRT) and a transgender policy at a Virginia school board meeting Tuesday.

"The meeting in Loudoun County, Virginia, abruptly ended after the crowd became too rowdy and was later declared an unlawful assembly, footage posted to Twitter showed.

"Two arrests were reportedly made for trespassing after some parents refused to leave.

"The Loudoun County sheriff's office declared the school board meeting an unlawful assembly. Everyone told to get out or will be trespassing.

"Parents also began singing the Star-Spangled Banner when the board abruptly ended public comment due to the eruptions from the crowd in the room."

Murders Increase
If history repeats, murders will increase as communist begin murdering socialist. That is why the "body count" increases when Stage Two begins. Case in point: the city of Chicago. The statistics are horrifying and 2021reports indicate a new record of more than 800 homicides.

Our instructor at the Academy taught our class that, historically, the transition from socialism to capitalism begins when communists begin murdering the socialists, the academic elites... the teachers.

Why kill intellectuals, teachers, and academic elite?

Because most socialist intellectuals, teachers, and academic elites are pacifists. They are peaceful people. They are "lovers not fighters." That is why postmodernist education is based on emotions and opinions. Many students today are highly emotional and opinionated... snowflakes. It is easy to round up the academic elites and kill them because they do not fight back.

Many among the academic elite are anti-guns... and I'm reminded of Lenin's words of warning:

> *"One man with a gun can control 100 without one."*

We've witnessed campaigns for gun control and seen the fallout from movements to defund the police. A pandemic of fear spreads... making the masses easier to control.

A High-Profile Murder Trial

On November 19, 2021, The *New York Post* reported:

> *"Kyle Rittenhouse was acquitted Friday on all charges in the shootings that killed two men and injured a third during last year's violence in Kenosha, Wisconsin. The 18-year-old defendant broke down in tears and collapsed in his seat as the not guilty verdict was read out in court."*

The liberal elite did everything possible, to convict Kyle of being a "racist" and "murderer," in spite of the fact the men he shot were white. They accused him of carrying a gun across state lines which is not illegal. Kyle Rittenhouse was not a wimpy snowflake. Instead, he fought back, he defended himself.

The world watched as the academic and liberal elite were willing to turn a courtroom into 'political theater.' It's all part of Marx's Stage Two.

Fear as a Weapon

In 2021, President Biden used his vaccine mandates to get people to obey. The problem is, Biden is not a dictator. He isn't frightening. Many see him and his administration as a joke... with one fumble and misstep after another. I would say Biden fits Strauss and Howe's description of a weak leader. That is why the public makes fun of him chanting: *"Let's go Brandon."*

"Let's go Brandon" has become a rallying cry for the Republican base... a kind of communications code that people use when people are censored, and "Big Brother" is watching.

Every dictator in history has used fear as a weapon, a means by which they get people to do their will. Joe Biden is not frightening. He is entertaining. He's an embarrassment, some say, who is killing the Democrats.

Here is a list of dictators who have used fear to kill people:
1. Joseph Stalin: 40 to 62 million people
2. Mao Tse Tung: 45 to 60 million people
3. Adolf Hitler: 17 million including 6 million Jews
4. King Leopold: 15 million people in the Congo
5. Vladimir Lenin: 7 to 12 million people
6. Chiang Kai-Shek: 10 million people
7. Hirohito: 6 million people
8. Hideki Tojo: 5 million people
9. Ismail Pasha: 1.8 million people
10. Kim Il Sung: 1.6 million people

Different Types of War
Marines are taught there are three different types of warfare, apart from guns and bullets. The three are the ABCs of warfare:
1. Atomic
2. Biological
3. Chemical

At the beginning of this book, I stated there was something fishy about the Repo Market crashing on September 17, 2019... then Covid appearing in October of that same year. I suspect that the crash in the Repo Market of the Shadow Banking System and the appearance of COVID-19 is Biological Warfare.

Can I prove it? No. I can't. But I do suspect Marx's Stage Two, the transition from socialism to communism, has begun. In 2020, this Stage Two is a different type of war, biological, and a different type of murder — financial 'deaths,' wiping out millions of small businesses and firing workers for not taking the vaccine. I suspect Marx's Stage Two, our financial crisis, is just beginning.

The Real Anthony Fauci is a book written by Robert Kennedy Jr., published in December 2021. The book is a warning. Kennedy's book details how Dr. Fauci, Bill Gates, and Big Pharma and friends have used their control over media outlets, scientific journals, government agencies, global intelligence agencies, influential scientists, and physicians to muzzle and ruthlessly censor dissent related to COVID-19.

In *The Real Anthony Fauci,* Kennedy courageously details how Fauci and Gates:

> *"Repeatedly violated federal laws to allow their Big Pharma partners to use impoverished and dark-skinned children as lab rats in deadly experiments with toxic AIDS and cancer chemotherapies."*

Fauci, Gates, and Big Pharma call this *research*. A Marine would call this *biological warfare*.

Fake Assets
In 2021, the Biden administration and the Federal Reserve Bank printed trillions of fake dollars to prevent the U.S. banking system from collapsing. (I'll go on record here to state that I am not blaming Biden for the coming disaster. This disaster has been coming for years, ever since Nixon took the U.S. dollar off the gold standard in 1971.) Since 1971, the trillions in fake dollars and quadrillions in fake assets have been the real problem.

As I've said, it all seemed fishy to me. Inflation in fake assets, stocks, bonds, and real estate has made millions of Americans feel rich and happy. Unfortunately, inflation has put owning a home out of reach for millions of Americans, even those with jobs.

If history is any guide, inflation in 2021 and 2022 will lead to hyper-inflation in the future. Hyperinflation will lead to a possible economic collapse, what some are calling "the Great Reset," a fake-money collapse, ending in what Jim Rickards predicts as a New Great Depression.

When will this happen? I do not know. No one knows when the final snowflake — as Jim puts it — will set off the biggest financial avalanche in world history. But I expect it's coming soon.

All the more reason, today, to heed Mahatma Gandhi's warning:
"The future depends on what you do today."

And to pay attention to another of Bucky Fuller's generalized principles:
Emergence through emergency

CHAPTER TWENTY

EMERGENCE THROUGH EMERGENCY

"Imagination is more important than knowledge."
— Albert Einstein

During the times I studied wth Fuller, he explained to our class that the root word of emergency is *emerge*.

Was he saying that out of emergencies emerge a new future? I think so. And we are at that point today.

What will cause the emergency? I think it will be a convergence of these three Ds:

1. **Demographics**
   Baby boomers who don't have the money they need to retire and millennials deep in student loan debt.

2. **Debt**
   The global debt can never be paid back. All the Central Banks of the world know to do is print more money and create more debt. They will do it again and again until the house of cards comes crashing down.

3. **Destructive Technology**
   The powerhouses of Silicon Valley, companies such as Amazon, Facebook, and Twitter, became richer than most countries in the world, due to demographics and debt, quadrillions in fake dollars.

If history is any guide, a new technology will take them down, just as Netflix wiped out Blockbuster video rental stores... and Zoom is changing how businesses use travel and office buildings, and Amazon and on-line retailers (vs bricks and mortar stores and shopping malls) are changing how we see (and do) business.

One of the best books on the future of Destructive Technology is Jeff Booth's book, *The Price of Tomorrow.*

I'm often asked what I'm most concerned about?

Again, if history is any guide, the primary reason revolutions begin is not unhappiness or income inequality. The primary reason is hunger.

That makes China, the biggest superpower in 2020, the country to watch... simply because China has over a billion mouths to feed.

It's predicted that in approximately 100 years the population on Earth will exceed 10 billion. And why Fuller warned our class, in 1981, that mass diseases, famine, environmental, money, energy challenges, and war are the real problems for my generation, the Baby-Boom generation.

In his book *Critical Path*, Fuller warned that the way to solve overpopulation and hunger was to raise the standard of living of everyone on planet. He had charts, facts, and stats supporting his position that when the standard of living rises, birth rates go down.

Q: So as long as people are struggling for survival, they have more children?

A: Yes. People in poorer countries have more children because more children die young. And parents want to have children to take care of them when they get old. In poorer countries, children and family are a form of 'social security'.

Which brings me full circle to why, in 1996, Kim and I began our Capitalist Manifesto. Our mission statement for The Rich Dad Company was
To elevate the financial well-being of humanity.

Q: By raising the standard of living of people, we solve many of the challenges facing humanity today?

A: It has long been my believe that addressing many of the challenges that humanity faces today begins with real financial education, the lessons on money that are not taught in our schools. Real financial education begins with understanding how money is created, manipulated, and corrupted.

Keep in mind that, in 2020, Marx's Stage Two was just beginning. We still have the power to change our future, save our freedoms.

In 1981, Fuller asked our class to ask ourselves this question... the question he had asked himself many times:
"What can I do, I'm just a little guy."

In 1996, Kim and I began our Capitalist Manifesto with our *CASHFLOW* board game.

Government Cryptos Take Over the Economy
Real financial education begins with understand what money actually is and what the future of money will look like.

In 1913 the Fed, a Central Bank was created. In 1913, with the 16th Amendment, the Tax Man, the IRS, was born. In 1913, the U.S. dollar became a product of both debt and taxes.

As Lenin warned:
"The way to crush the bourgeoisie is to grind them between the millstones of taxation and inflation."

In 1913, Lenin's warning came true.

As Mayer Amschel Rothschild (1744-1812) warned:

> *"Let me issue and control a nations money and I care not who writes the laws."*

Bitcoin to the Rescue

On May 8, 2021, an article in *The Economist* called Govcoins "the digital currency that will transform finance." It reported:

> "The least noticed disruption on the frontier between technology and finance may end up the most revolutionary: the creation of government digital currencies, which typically aim to let people deposit funds directly with a central bank, by passing conventional lenders.

> "These 'govcoins' are a new incarnation of money.

> "Entrepreneurs have built an experimental world of 'decentralized finance,' of which bitcoin is the most famous part and which contains a riot of tokens, databases and conduits that interact to varying degrees with tradition finance. Meanwhile financial 'platform' firms now have over 3-billion customers who use e-wallets and payment apps."

Q: Three billion people? Isn't that nearly a half of the world's population?
A: It is. Crypto serves more people than the U.S. dollar. And makes me think of another of Fuller's Generalized Principles:
  The more people I serve... the more effective I become.

Q: Does that mean traditional banks such as Bank of America, JP Morgan, and Wells Fargo will become obsolete?
A: It's possible. Commercial banks are expensive to use. *The Economist* article states:
  "As a result, govcoins could cut the operating expenses of global financial industry which amounts to over $350 a year for every person on Earth. That could make finance accessible for 1.7 billion people who lack bank accounts."

In 2021, as I observed homelessness spreading across America, I thought of Thomas Jefferson's warning:

"If the American people ever allow private banks to control the issue of their currency, first by inflation, then by deflation, the banks and corporations that will grow up around them will deprive the people of all property until their children wake up homeless on the continent their fathers conquered."

Q: Do crypto currencies such as Bitcoin worry about Central banks like the Fed or the Bank of England?

A: I'll answer that with these words from an article in *The Economist:*

"One motivation for governments and central banks is a fear of losing control."

"Government or central-bank digital currencies are the next step up, but they come with a twist, because they would centralize in the state rather than spread it through networks or give it to private monopolies. The idea behind them is simple. Instead of holding an account with a retail bank you would do so direct with a central bank, through an interface resembling apps such as Alipay or Venmo."

Q: How could government crypto put commercial banks out of business?

A: I explained in Be the Fed, earlier in this book, the commercial banks need capitalists to borrow money. When money is borrowed, money is created.

Q: So the Fed *doesn't* print money?

A: That is correct. The Fed does not print money. The Fed prints "bank reserves." The Fed ships these "bank reserves," to commercial banks via the channels of the Shadow Banking System, the Repo Market, and the Reverse Repo Markets.

It takes capitalists with strong financial statements to borrow millions to billions of dollars for fiat currency, cash, U.S. dollars to come into existence.

Q: If the Fed replaces commercial banks with a Fed-coin, the commercial banks may have a difficult time, finding money to lend?

A: Correct. As you know, banks do not want your savings, because your savings are a bank's liability. Banks pay you interest on your savings. Banks need debtors — people who borrow money. Debtors make interest payments to the banks. If savers stop saving, banks have less money to lend to debtors.

Q: If the Fed produces government crypto, a Fed coin or govcoin, is that pure communist?

A: In theory yes. Simply put, communism is a socioeconomic order based on common ownership of production and banks. In theory a Fed-coin would make the United States a communist, centrally controlled economy.

Q: If the Fed produced a Fed coin, would the Fed be in partnership with the state?

A: Yes.

Q: What can a person do?

A: Ahh... now that's the real question... isn't it?

Imagination Makes Anything Possible

So what will emerge from this global state of emergency? And how can we use what we've learned to be architects of what our future will look like?

As Einstein said:

"Imagination is more important than knowledge."

It is its network that gives Bitcoin its power. Just as a franchise network gives McDonald's power. In Network Marketing, it's the network that drives the business and fuels its growth.

I can imagine Entrepreneur Cyber-Networks as a key to the future. The primary reason I wanted my network of advisors in this book is because

Rich Dad's network is an example, a prototype, of a future cyber-network of connected entrepreneurs. In our case, Blair Singer, Ken McElroy, Tom Wheelwright, Josh and Lisa Lannon, Drs. Nichole Shrednicki and Radha Gophalan, Andy Tanner, and John MacGregor are the Rich Dad Network, joined by a unifying mission:

"to Elevate the Financial Well-being of Humanity."

Our group embodies the *"Deeds Not Words"* mantra in our support of Trina Maduro, a dear friend and community leader, with whom we have worked for 17 years. The Rich Dad Company and our advisor group are working to develop an educational system to bring the teachings of capitalism into low-income neighborhoods.

Q: Are you saying that "talk is cheap" and that "action beats inaction?" Is that why "deeds not words" is important to any cyber-network groups mission?

A: Exactly. The motto of the U.S. Merchant Marine Academy is "Acta Non Verba," *Deeds Not Words.* The mission and the motto of a military academy are more important than curriculum and grades.

Most "snowflake" postmodern universities are about indoctrination, not education.

So I'll repeat Thomas Sowell's warning:

"Education is not merely neglected in many of our schools today but is replaced to a great extent by ideological indoctrination."

And Jordan Peterson words about postmodern educators,

"They don't like the poor. They just hate the rich."

And all along they claim that their hearts are *"in the right place."*

In my view, too many "do-gooders," liberal academic groups, are all "critical talk," but no action. The problem I see with postmodern, academic liberal critics is they cyber-bully the brave, encourage the "oppressed" to "smash, grab, and loot" and encourage the "oppressed" to tear down statues of real heroes.

Rich dad often said: "No one has ever erected a statue to a critic."

Rich Dad's products — our board games, books, and educational videos from Rich Dad advisors — combined with Trina's network and network marketing experience, have the power to transform lives and lift people out of poverty.

As economist Adam Smith said:
   "The real tragedy of the poor is the poverty of their aspirations."

Q: Are you saying, architects of the future will be networks of entrepreneurs, solving problems our socialist governments cannot solve?

A: Yes. And more than that, the future is about using our imagination. I foresee networks of entrepreneurs, developing their own crypto currencies.

Q: You mean a Rich Dad crypto coin?

A: Why not? We have the global network to do that. If we follow Einstein's wisdom, and let out imagination gaze into the future, why not take decentralized finance into the future? Imagination is infinite... we can create the future and don't have to be victims of the system. Why stay stuck, tethered, and oppressed by the Marxist Federal Reserve Bank, centralized banking, investments in Wall Street's assets, and the totalitarian U.S. Treasury?

Q: In 2021, didn't Russia and India sign a pact to bypass the U.S, dollar and trade in their respective currencies?

A: They did. An Entrepreneur Cyber-Network could do the same thing.

Steve Jobs left these words for future generations to follow:

> *"The greatest people are self-managing – they don't need to be managed. Once they know what to do, they'll go figure out how to do it. What they need is a common vision. And that's what leadership is: having a vision; being able to articulate that so the people around you can understand it; and getting a consensus on a common vision."*

More words of wisdom from Steve Jobs, the consummate entrepreneur:

> *"My job is not to be easy on people. My job is to make them better."*

And:

> *"Great things in business are never done by one person; they're done by a team of people."*

And:

> *"Gather 10 smart people into a room, and one or two will be creative, two are great at solving problems, the rest are critics. Keep the creatives away from the critics."*

Q: I have so many questions. Where do I start? Is that why postmodern education is destroying capitalism and stealing our freedoms? Is postmodern education teaching students to be racists and critics? Is postmodern education teaching division, not unity? Is postmodern education teaching hate instead of love and respect? Is postmodern education teaching poverty instead of prosperity? And demanding "rights" — without acknowledging the responsibilities tied to those rights?

A: You've read this book. I will let you answer those questions for yourself. The world changed in 2020. The future will not look like the past.

A more important question to think about is this: Are you going to be an architect of your future, or a victim?

As Mahatma Gandhi warned:

> *"The future depends on what you do today."*

As I've stated earlier in this book, in 1972 I flew behind enemy lines in search of gold. When I attempted to buy gold at a discount, the savvy Vietnamese woman "schooled" me about money. It was then that I better understood what my rich dad had been telling me. It was then I realized why there is no financial education in schools. It was then I decided to get out of the Fed's grip. I no longer wanted to be a puppet dangling on a string, being manipulated, and chasing money.

In 1972, I began saving gold, not dollars. In 1974, after taking my first real estate course, I began using debt as money and working with tax strategists to use every incentive possible that the government offers to reduce my taxes.

Q: Are you saying that in 1974 you decided to become a capitalist?
A: Exactly. Today, I am an entrepreneur. I do not need a job. Instead of saving man's money I save gold and silver... god's money. There is no counter party-risk with gold and silver, because god is the counter party.

With Bitcoin and Ethereum, the counter party is blockchain technology and a network of people. That is why I call "Bitcoin and other crypto's, "People's money," out of reach of the Fed.

CHAPTER TWENTY-ONE
PREPARING FOR THE FUTURE

In 1983, I began preparing for the future.

In 1984, Kim, Blair Singer, and I left Hawaii to become entrepreneurs in education, working outside the school system. We were following Fuller's predictions and his inspiration for the future of education.

Today, I save gold, silver, Bitcoin, and Ethereum. I borrow money if I need fake dollars.

Even Fuller recognized the importance of gold. He said:
"Computers will relegate all gold to its exclusively functional uses, as a supreme electromagnetic conduction-and-reflection medium — with its supremacy amongst metals also manifest, as rated in weight and bulk per accomplished function."

Gold is a precious metal. Gold is real money, god's money.

After studying with Fuller in 1981, reading *Grunch of Giants in 1983* and learning about the giant global cash heist, I suspected his prediction, decades ago, of the coming of crypto currencies would come true.

As Fuller predicted:
"Computers make it practical to electronify wealth distribution games that accomplish the movement of goods in services in more channeled, designed structures. Not big brother though, since no central planning authority – just lots of dial-in 'games" with costs and rewards, likely to attract those with a self-interest in playing. Those are the details."

Fuller passed away on July I, 1983. The first open-source bitcoin client was released on 9 January 2009, hosted at Source Forge.

Fuller saw this coming. To those who knew him, it isn't surprising that John Denver wrote a song to Fuller, and named him the Grandfather of the Future.

Fuller predicted the end of the tyranny of education stating:
> *"I would say, then, that you are faced with a future in which education is going to be number one amongst the great world industries."*

Fuller predicted YouTube:
> *"From a distance, it looks like a planet full of professors on tenure, working hard, doing more metaphysical stuff than before."*

In February 2005, a YouTube video sharing website was created by three former PayPal employees. It was sold to Google in 2006.

Today platforms such as YouTube will teach more people than all the schools in the world...and much of the education it offers is free.

Q: What is the worst thing that could happen if the Fed produces the Fed Coin?
A: America will be one step closer to being a communist country.

Q: How many events must occur for Marx's Stage Two to be? How many steps will it take for America to become a communist nation?
A: It's possible that the next two steps in Marx's Stage Two are:
  1. Everyone must carry a COVID card.
  2. Fed coins will replace the dollar.

Q: Really? Why?
A: So Big Brother can watch you. So Big brother can control your life.

In 1972, that Vietnamese woman taught me an important lesson. If you do not want Big Brother watching you via your money, consider saving gold, silver, bitcoin, and other crypto currencies not controlled by Big Brother, the Fed, the U.S. Treasury, and the commercial banking system.

Before Stage Two gets too strong a foothold, consider getting *outside* Big Brother's monetary system. Repeating, yet again, Gandhi's words of wisdom about the future:

"The future depends on what you do today."

Today... the warnings about Big Brother are all too real...
Today what we all know to be true and the reality of today's world is shocking, sobering... surreal:

- citizens and governments supporting campaigns to defund the police
- smash-and-grab looting sprees continue, getting bigger and bolder
- COVID-19 vaccine cards are required for access to more and more places
- travel restrictions continue to be enforced around the world
- lockdowns, mandates, business closures... put more stress on an already stressed economy
- voter fraud and election corruption are still topic of contention and hotly contested...
- in December of 2021 the Wall Street Journal reported that cities, including NYC, initiate "anyone can vote" legislation giving non-

citizens the right to vote in elections. [At press time, there are legal challenges to that initiative...]

- a sitting U.S. Senator appears at an award show hosted by a political advocacy organization affiliated with the Communist Party. This was the message from the emcee of the event, Ben McManus: "We invite you to join the Communist Party in this epic time as we make good trouble to uproot systemic racism, retool the war economy, tax the rich, address climate change, secure voting rights and create a new socialist system that puts people, peace and planet before profits."
- GovCoin is "floated" and explored...

... on this path to communism, paving the way for totalitarianism — the ultimate form of communism.

Stage Two began in 2020 with Donald Trump's failed bid for reelection. And I continue to stress that this book is not about Republiicans or Democrats, Donald Trump or Joe Biden. This book is about our freedoms... freedoms under attack as communist agendas are integrated into our lives, expanded social programs breed dependency... and our Constitution is hijacked.

Remember: We Were Warned.
The message from Nikita Khrushchev... in 1959...

"You Americans are so gullible. No, you won't accept communism outright, but we'll keep feeding you small doses of socialism until you'll finally wake up and find you already have communism. We won't have to fight you. We'll so weaken your economy until you'll fall like overripe fruit into our hands."

And repeating Fuller's words of wisdom about the future yet again:
"We are called to be the architects of the future, not its victims."

When my poor dad quit his job as Superintendent of Education in 1970 and ran for Lt. Governor of Hawaii and lost, he lost more than an election. My mom died soon after and we knew that the stress, disappointment, and dirty politics affected her already weak heart. My dad could not find a job in Hawaii because the governor blocked him from working in state government. Without a job, dad found out his PhD could not prevent him from being poor.

So in1974, as I prepared to leave the Marine Corps, I asked my rich dad for fatherly advice.

In conclusion, I will pass on to you his words to me... the words that set me on the road to becoming a capitalist:

Rich dad said:
> *"Don't be a victim like your dad. Don't live for security. Live for freedom. And learn to be capitalist like me."*

And I did.

In 1996, Kim and I created the *CASHFLOW* game so that you — people around the world who want to be architects of their futures — could learn to be a capitalist. It's our Capitalist Tool... that we've shared with the world.

THE FATHERS OF OUR COUNTRY... AND FATHERS OF OUR FREEDOMS

Rather than King of America, George Washington is known as The Father of our Country.

Washington, a soldier, stateman, Founding Father of the United States, and its first President, spoke these words of warning more than two centuries ago: "If freedom of speech is taken away then dumb and silent, we may be led, like sheep to slaughter."

We haven't listened well to our father, it seems, as Americans are waking up to the reality that our freedoms, most especially our freedom of speech, are being stolen. In its place... political correctness, gender pronouns, the rewriting of history, the desecration of statues, the monitoring and censorship of social media, the barrage of angry racist rhetoric... and communism being taught in our schools.

It's a brave new world... with brave being the operative word. I've asked myself, as I wrote this book, and I ask each of you: Do we have the courage to stand up for our freedoms and our rights — and shoulder the responsibilities inherent in those rights?

My closing words are those of Mahatma Gandhi:
"The future depends on what you do today."

Thank you for reading this book.

Officially launched on the
U. S. Marine Corps Birthday
November 10, 2021 – Brays Island, South Carolina

ABOUT THE AUTHOR

ROBERT KIYOSAKI

Best known as the author of *Rich Dad Poor Dad*—the #1 personal finance book of all time—Robert Kiyosaki has challenged and changed the way tens of millions of people around the world think about money. He is an entrepreneur, educator, and investor who believes the world needs more entrepreneurs who will create jobs.

With perspectives on money and investing that often contradict conventional wisdom, Robert has earned an international reputation for straight talk, irreverence, and courage and has become a passionate and outspoken advocate for financial education.

Robert and Kim Kiyosaki, both authors, are founders of The Rich Dad Company, a financial education company, and creators of the *CASHFLOW* games.

Robert has been heralded as a visionary who has a gift for simplifying complex concepts—ideas related to money, investing, finance, and economics—and has shared his personal journey to financial freedom in ways that resonate with audiences of all ages and backgrounds. His core principles and messages—like "Your house is not an asset" and "Invest for cash flow" and "savers are losers"—have ignited a firestorm of criticism and ridicule... only to have played out on the world economic stage over the past decade in ways that were both unsettling and prophetic.

His point of view is that 'old' advice—go to college, get a good job, save money, get out of debt, invest for the long term, and diversify—has become obsolete advice in today's fast-paced Information Age. His Rich Dad philosophies and messages challenge the status quo and his teachings encourage people to take initiative to become financially educated and play an active role in investing for the future.

The author of 30 books, Robert has been a featured guest with media outlets in every corner of the world—from FOX News, CNN, the BBC, Real Vision, Yahoo! Finance, Al Jazeera, GBTV and PBS to *Larry King Live, Oprah, People's Daily, Sydney Morning Herald, The Doctors, The Straits Times, Bloomberg, NPR, USA TODAY, and hundreds of others*—and his books have topped international bestsellers lists for more than two decade. He continues to teach and inspire audiences around the world.

Robert's newest books—*Who Stole My Pension?* (co-authored with former SEC attorney and pension-fraud whistleblower Edward Siedle) and *FAKE: Fake Money, Fake Teachers, Fake Assets*—are sobering reminders of the importance and power of real financial education.

In 2021 the countdown to the 25th Anniversary of the 1997 release of *Rich Dad Poor Dad* began. That book and its messages, viewed around the world as a classic in the personal finance arena, have stood the test of time and continue to resonate with audiences of all ages around the world.

Robert has also co-authored two books with Donald Trump, prior to his successful bid for the White House and election as President of the United States.

To learn more visit RichDad.com

THE CAPITALIST MANIFESTO VIDEO SERIES
COUNTER MARXIST'S CANCEL CULTURE...

There is a war on capitalism in the United States. The problem is most people don't know the difference between socialism, communism, and capitalism. The uneducated are wooed by the promise of free education, free health care, and taxing the rich — but they don't understand at what cost.

The Capitalist Manifesto series features stories told by real people from around the world who experienced socialist or communist regimes.

In this Series you will hear true stories from...

Philip Haslam... and why Robert wrote *Capitalist Manifesto* **(Episode 01)**
Philip Haslam is an economic advisor, writer, and speaker who reveals in his book, *When Money Destroys Nations* how the collapse of the Zimbabwe dollar in 2009 after years of rampant money printing is a frightening example of what lies in store for countries that resort to printing money to pay national debts, bail out banks and oligarchs, and enrich political elites.

Debbie D'Souza   (Episode 02)
Born in Caracas Venezuela, Debbie D'Souza shares her perspective of what happens to a country when political leaders capitalize on the very poor. Debbie refers to this as the socioeconomic demonization, which she sees happening right here in the U.S. with the Democratic Party, which keeps the poor, poor.

Patrick Bet-David   (Episode 03)
During the Iranian Revolution of 1978, Patrick Bet-David's family had to escape to survive and ended up living in a refugee camp in Erlangen, Germany. After moving to California, serving in the U.S Army, and being introduced to entrepreneurship, Patrick set out to create his business empire. In this episode, Patrick describes how his family strived to achieve the American dream.

Nely Galan   (Episode 04)

Nely Galan witnessed first-hand the struggles her parents faced when they lost everything they had worked for when she and her family left communist Cuba. She describes the difficulties of having to be a translator, therapist, money-maker to her parents. In this episode, she revisits the pain of living under a communist regime and the aftermath on her family.

Barry Mitchell   (Episode 05)

Zimbabwe, formerly known as Rhodesia, was known as the breadbasket of Africa. Barry Mitchell, who grew up on his family's farm in Zimbabwe, describes what it was like to watch this once flourishing country suffer under hyperinflation. In this episode, Barry describes what it was like to experience the redistribution of wealth when the government seized his father's farm.

Yeonmi Park   (Episode 06)

Yeonmi Park is a North Korean defector and human rights activist who escaped from North Korea to China in 2007 and settled in South Korea in 2009, before moving to the United States in 2014. Yeonmi contrasts what it was like to live under the dictatorship versus the free-market capitalism of the United States.

Dan Campbell   (Episode 07)

Dan Campbell was born in California, but when he was just two years old his parents moved to South America. He lived in Colombia, Costa Rica, Argentina, Venezuela, and Ecuador. In this episode, he describes "the disastrous effect of socialism" and how affects every part of one's life, but most importantly one's liberty."

Brigadier General Robert Spalding   (Episode 08)

General Spalding was the chief architect for the Trump Administration's widely praised National Security Strategy. He describes himself as "a national security expert and patriot entrepreneur identifying threats to our security, economy, and way of life. I am committed to bringing jobs back to the USA by restoring American manufacturing and securing our most critical resource... data."

U.S. Representative Jack Bergman (Episode 09)

Congressman Bergman served in the United States Marine Corps for 40 years, as a helicopter pilot in Vietnam, and most recently as Commander of Marine Forces North/Marine Forces Reserve. He retired in 2009 at the rank of Lieutenant General. In this episode, he and Robert Kiyosaki share stories of what it means to fight for freedom, and how failed leadership opens the doors to communism.

To learn more about Capitalist Manifesto
and how to **pre-order this new Fall 2021 release**
visit **RichDad.com/capitalist-manifesto**

To learn more about how to access the
Capitalist Manifesto Series of podcasts and videos
go to:
RichDad.com/capitalist-manifesto